Laughter
the Best
Medicine®

Laughter
the Best
Medicine®

**An Exclusive Collection of America's
Funniest Jokes, Quotes, and Cartoons
from *Reader's Digest* Magazine**

The Reader's Digest Association, Inc.
New York, NY/Montreal

A READER'S DIGEST BOOK

Copyright ©2012 The Reader's Digest Association, Inc.
All rights reserved. Unauthorized reproduction, in any manner, is prohibited.
Reader's Digest and Laughter the Best Medicine are registered trademarks of
The Reader's Digest Association, Inc.

ISBN 978-1-60652-115-1

Laughter the Best Medicine comprises three books previously published by
Reader's Digest:
   Laughter the Best Medicine® @ Work (ISBN 978-1-60652-479-4)
   Laughter the Best Medicine®: Holidays (ISBN 978-1-60652-546-3)
   Laughter the Best Medicine®: Those Lovable Pets (978-1-60652-357-5)

PROJECT STAFF
   Laughter the Best Medicine® @ Work
      Project Manager and Art Director: Elizabeth Tunnicliffe
   Laughter the Best Medicine®: Holidays
      Project Editor: Barbara Booth
      Project Manager and Art Director: Elizabeth Tunnicliffe
   Laughter the Best Medicine®: Those Lovable Pets
      Project Manager and Art Director: Elizabeth Tunnicliffe

READER'S DIGEST TRADE PUBLISHING
Managing Editor: Lorraine Burton
Senior Editor: Katherine Furman
Senior Art Director: George McKeon
Associate Publisher: Rosanne McManus
President and Publisher: Harold Clarke

READER'S DIGEST ASSOCIATION, INC.
Executive Editor, North America: Courtenay Smith
Creative Director, North America: Robert Newman
Chief Content Officer, North America: Liz Vaccariello
President, North America: Dan Lagani
President and Chief Executive Officer: Robert E. Guth

Cover and spot illustrations: George McKeon
Cartoon Credits: Ian Baker; John Caldwell; Dave Carpenter; Joe di Chiarro;
Roy Delgado; Ralph Hagen; Mike Lynch; Scott Arthur Masear; Harley Schwadron;
Steve Smeltzer; Thomas Bros.; Kim Warp; WestMach

We are committed to both the quality of our products and the service we provide to
our customers. We value your comments, so please feel free to contact us.

   The Reader's Digest Association, Inc.
   Adult Trade Publishing
   44 South Broadway
   White Plains, NY 10601

For more Reader's Digest products and information, visit our website:
   www.rd.com (in the United States)
   www.readersdigest.ca (in Canada)

Printed in China

1 3 5 7 9 10 8 6 4 2

✼✼✼✼✼✼✼✼✼✼✼✼✼✼✼

Contents

Laughter the Best Medicine . . .

@ Work	7
A Note from the Editors	11
The Search	13
On the Job	53
Expert Antics	105
Last Laughs	165

Holidays — 221

A Note from the Editors	225
Giving Thanks	227
Yuletide Cheer	253
Ringing in the New Year	351
Seasonal Silliness	375

Those Lovable Pets — 411

A Note from the Editors	415
To the Dogs	417
Cunning Cats	461
Tweety Birds	499
That's a Pet?	525
Not the "Vet"	561
Dumb and Dumber	589

LAUGHTER
THE BEST MEDICINE®
@WORK

WORK DU SOLEIL

@@@@@@@@@@@@@@@@@@@@@@@@@@@@@@@

Contents

A Note from the Editors   11

The Search   13
Amusing Ads   14
Ridiculous Résumés   19
Incredible Interviews   31

On the Job   53
Corporate Miscommunications   55
Extraordinary Excuses   70
Up, Down, and Out   79
The Powers That Be   91

Expert Antics   105
Law and Order   106
What's Up, Doc?   118
Airport Hijinks   132
Sales and Service Slip-ups   137
Tech Talk   142
Divine Duties   154
That's Academic   158

Last Laughs   165
Kids' Quips   166
Dumb and Dumber   171
Just for Laughs   189

@@@@@@@@@@@@@@@@@@@@@@@@@@@@@

A Note from the Editors

Bosses usually aren't very funny—at least not when it's *your* boss standing in front of your desk with eyes and mouth ablaze. But start telling boss jokes with your friends on a casual Saturday evening, and the laughter can shake the house.

Truth is, the workplace can be absurd, goofy, ridiculous, and sometimes, really fun. After all, there are so many opportunities for crazy things to be said and done—in job applications, meetings, speeches, customer complaints, and coffee breaks.

Reader's Digest has been sharing laughs about the work world in our magazine pages for decades. Now we've gathered the funniest of the funny into one volume. In the pages ahead you'll find hundreds of our most hilarious jokes, cartoons, and real-life experiences about all things work. You may wonder if someone *really* wrote that in their résumé, or said that in a meeting, or encountered such a customer in their store. Then you'll pause and say, "Sure!" because we've *all* witnessed something just like it.

What makes laughter the best medicine is its ability to erase stress, change negative moods to positive, and put the craziness of life into a bigger, happier perspective. All this is particularly true when it comes to work. So come Monday morning, when your boss is heading your way, keep these jokes in mind and smile. Because life is too short for anything else.

The
Search

"The closest to perfection
a person ever comes
is when he fills out a
job application."

—KEN KRAFT

Amusing Ads

A recent job posting on monster.com tells it like it really is: "Each new member of our team participates in eight weeks of management training classes done in on-site classrooms during the curse of the normal workday."

—SHERI JARMAN

Job ad in the York, PA., Daily Record: "Attention: Good hours, excellent pay, fun place to work, paid training, mean boss. Oh well, four out of five isn't bad."

During a recent job search, I encountered many well-meaning human resources personnel. Often, if a position was filled, they sent letters to the other candidates informing them that someone else had been chosen. One especially empathetic human-resources manager wrote, "I'm sorry to say that we were able to find a candidate who fits our requirements."

—JOAN M. WEIS

An ad in our church bulletin read: "Receptionist needed for busy chiropractic office." I faxed my resumé and got called for an interview. After hanging up, I realized I didn't know the name or location of the business. I found two listings for chiropractors in the phone book and dialed the first number. "Are you hiring a receptionist?" I asked politely.

"Why?" countered a cold-rasped voice. "Do I sound that bad?"

—JAYNE THURBER-SMITH

An employment website boasted that it provided training, counseling, and placement services. What's more, "many services are available in Spanish, and we arrange interrupters."

—CLARA EMLEN

@@@@@@@@@@@@@@@@@@@@@@@@@@@@@@@@

Outside a California penitentiary: **"Now taking applications."**

—MALLORY PRITCHARD

Walking down the street, a dog saw a sign in an office window. "Help wanted. Must type 70 words a minute. Must be computer literate. Must be bilingual. An equal-opportunity employer."

The dog applied for the position, but was quickly rebuffed. "I can't hire a dog for the job," the office manager said. But when the dog pointed to the line that read "An equal-opportunity employer," the office manager sighed and asked, "Can you type?" Silently, the dog walked over to a typewriter and flawlessly banged out a letter. "Can you operate a computer?" the manager inquired. The dog then sat down at a terminal, wrote a program and ran it perfectly.

"Look, I still can't hire a dog for this position," said the exasperated office manager. "You have fine skills, but I need someone who's bilingual. It says so right in the ad."

The dog looked up at the manager and said, "Meow."

—LAWRENCE VAN GELDER

A job application made me do a double take. After the entry "Sex," the applicant had written, "Once in Florida."

—SUSAN WEBB

Looking over the job listings on The Home Depot website, I noticed one with a highly peculiar job description: "On rare occasions there may be a need to move or lift light articles. Examples include executive assistant, bank loan officer and accounting clerk."

—DENNIS E. BOWYER

Private school has a position open for science teacher. Must be certified or certifiable.

—VILMA COOK

@@@@@@@@@@@@@@@@@@@@@@@@@@@@@@

From The (Newark, New Jersey) Star-Ledger: "Auditions for Sly Fox, seeking nine men ages 20 to 90 and two women (one young and innocent, one not)."

—CHARLES COLLINS

I just saw an ad for a position I feel completely qualified for: "Wanted: bartenders. No exp. necessary. Must have: legal ID, phone, transportation, and teeth."

—AMY GOSS

I called a temp agency looking for work, and they asked if I had any phone skills. I said, "I called you, didn't I?"

—ZACH GALIFIANAKIS

Under "Help Wanted" in The North Missourian: "Chuck Anderson Ford-Mercury is looking for new and used salespeople."

—TYSON OTTO

The sign in the store window read: No Help Wanted. As two men passed by, one said to the other, "You should apply—you'd be great."

—E. M. UNGER

These inventive ads all appeared in a neighborhood newspaper in San Antonio, Texas.

- "Man, Honest. Will take anything."
- "Wanted: Chambermaid in rectory. Love in, $200 a month."
- "Wanted: Man to take care of cow that does not smoke or drink."
- "Tired of cleaning yourself? Let me do it."

—AUDREY POSELL

"Actually, what I need in an assistant is someone who knows how to work the cappucino machine."

On a sign in a fabric store: "Help Wanted. Must have knowledge of sewing, crafts and quitting."

Experienced cooks specializing in Italian cuisine & waitresses.

—R. BETTS

Help wanted ad in the Newport News, Va., Daily Press: "Satellite installers needed. Must have own transportation."

—WAVERLY TRAYLOR

@@@@@@@@@@@@@@@@@@@@@@@@@@@@@@

On the door of a Virginia grocery store: **"Now hiring—two part-time perishable clerks."**

—BENTON TAYLOR

Here's a company that has low standards and doesn't mind owning up. Its help-wanted ad: "Seeking laborers, equipment operators, and dumb truck drivers."

—CAROLYN CHEATHAM

"Help wanted—local pallet-maker needs hardworking employees," read the ad in the Lebanon (Missouri) Daily Record. "Please do not apply if you oversleep, have no car, have no baby-sitter everyday, experience flat tires every week, leave early for probation meeting. Must be able to work and talk at same time."

—MARTINA EDWARDS

Ridiculous Résumés

An enthusiastic young woman came into the nursing home where I work, and filled out a job application. After she left, I read her form and had to admire her honesty. To the question "Why do you want to work here?" she had responded, "To get experience for a better job."

—DEBORAH L. BLAND

In the department store where I worked, my boss had asked me to look into hiring several cashiers. Reading through job applications, I burst out laughing at one answer. Next to the question "Salary expectations," the applicant had written a single word: "Yes."

—MICHEL PAYETTE

@@@@@@@@@@@@@@@@@@@@@@@@@@@@@@

I was updating my résumé and at the same time decided to update my husband's too. When I reached the "Postsecondary studies" on Marc's, I asked, "Honey, what were your minor and major when you did your Bachelor of Arts at the University of Ottawa?"

"I don't remember," he replied.

"Why don't you check on your diploma?" I suggested.

After a few moments, I heard him laughing. "There's a problem: I got my diploma printed in Latin, and I can't read it anymore."

—LISA LEVESQUE-DESROSIERS

Reviewing an employee's file in our human-resources office, I came across the information sheet he had completed when he was first hired. In the blank for whom we should contact in an emergency, he had filled in his girlfriend's name. Next to it was a blank for "relationship." He had written: "shaky."

—DONI FRAZIER

Recently, our 18-year-old daughter started hunting for her first real job. She spent an afternoon filling out application forms, leaving them on the kitchen table to finish later. As I walked by, a section of the application on top jumped out at me. Under "Previous Employment" she wrote, "Baby Sitting."

In answer to "Reason for Leaving," she replied, "Parents came home."

—DONALD GEISER

One of the less difficult blanks to fill in on our job-agency application is "Position Wanted."

One job seeker wrote **"Sitting."**

—FLO TRAYWICK

@@@@@@@@@@@@@@@@@@@@@@@@@@@@@

One read through this man's résumé and it was no wonder he was looking for a new line of work: Under "Previous Job," he'd written, **"Stalker at Walmart."**

—CINTHIA ALBERS

I stressed to my Grade XII class the need to present them-selves positively in their letters of application for employment. One of my students took my words to heart. Instead of the cus-tomary "Yours Truly" or "Sincerely," he wrote "Eventually Yours."

—LESLIE M. WALKER

Despite years of exceeding quota in my sales career, my lack of education was an obstacle whenever I searched for work. Finally, I started listing under "education" on my résumé, "College of Hard Knocks."

I was surprised, then, to be hired as regional sales manager by a Fortune 500 company that had required a degree in its job posting. Soon after I started, my boss came by and asked me, "So what was your major at the University of Knoxville?"

—JOE BOSCH

Finding a job after prison is tough. Nevertheless, I refused to run from my past. So while filling out an application for a video wholesaler, I answered questions honestly. When it asked about previous employer, I wrote: Dept. of Corrections. Job description? Barber/inmate. Earnings? Fifty cents an hour. How long? Six years. Why did you leave? They let me. I got the job.

—PAUL DEGGES

I won't be hiring this assistant soon, even if her résumé boasts, "I'm a team player with 16 years of assassinating experience."

—CINDY DONALSON

@@@@@@@@@@@@@@@@@@@@@@@@@@@@@@

Looking for a job?

Be sure to proof your résumé and cover letters!

Dear Sir or Madam:

- "I am sure you have looked through several résumés with the same information about work experience, education, and references. I am not going to give you any of that stuff."

- "My mother delivered me without anesthesia, so I have an IQ of 146 and can therefore learn anything."

- "I enjoy working closely with customers, and my pleasant demeanor helps them feel comfortable and relaxed—not afraid."

- "I realize that my total lack of appropriate experience may concern those considering me for employment." But "I have integrity, so I will not steal office supplies and take them home."

- "In my next life, I will be a professional backup dancer or a rabbi," but for now, "I am attacking my résumé for you to review."

- "Thank you for your consideration. Hope to hear from you shorty!"

Sincerely, Hapless Job Seeker

—RESUMANIA.COM

The office where I work had received a number of résumés for a job opening. Although most of them were similar, one in particular stood out. In describing her current work responsibilities, a woman had written: "I conducted office affairs in the absence of the president."

—MARY SCHAFER

"Ah, raised by wolves on the plains of Wyoming. And where did you learn about us?"

A résumé came across my desk at our software company. It was from a man clearly eager for a new line of work. Under the category "previous work experience," he'd written, "Peasant."

—M. L. HICKERSON

@@@@@@@@@@@@@@@@@@@@@@@@@@@@@

Résumé Bombs

- Candidate listed military service dating back to before he was born.

- Candidate claimed to be a member of the Kennedy family.

- Job seeker claimed to be the CEO of a company, when he was an hourly employee.

- Job seeker included samples of work, which were actually those of the interviewer.

- Candidate specified that his availability was limited because Friday, Saturday, and Sunday was "drinking time."

- A young man, whose one-line résumé showed a stint at a fast food restaurant, filled out our employment application, which consisted of three questions: "Why do you want to work here?" "What strengths would you bring to the company?" and "What did you dislike about your previous employment?"

  Skipping the first two, he answered the last question, "Pickles and onions."

—PAIGE SANDERSON

Catherine, a registered nurse, was unhappy with her job, so she submitted her resignation. She was sure she'd have no trouble finding a new position, because of the nursing shortage in her area. She e-mailed cover letters to dozens of potential employers and attached her résumé to each one. Two weeks later, Catherine was dismayed and bewildered that she had not received even one request for an interview.

Finally she received a message from a prospective employer that explained the reason she hadn't heard from anyone else. It read: "Your résumé was not attached as stated. I do, however, want to thank you for the vegetable lasagna recipe."

—HARRIET BROWN

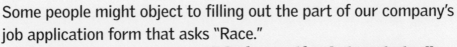

Some people might object to filling out the part of our company's job application form that asks "Race."

Not one guy. He responded, **"Only on the interstate."**

—SARAH LONG

After being laid off, I papered the town with my résumé. Days passed and I hadn't received a single phone call, so I decided to take a closer look at the copies my husband had printed at his real estate office.

I quickly realized he hadn't put blank paper in the machine. At the bottom of each copy, written in bold, was a common real estate disclaimer: "The information contained herein, while deemed to be accurate, is not guaranteed."

—MARY CHISHOLM

Business executive to job hunter: "We're looking for people who can help make this company profitable again. I'll read your résumé for $200."

—RANDY GLASBERGEN

Done with running a home business, my wife decided to look for a staff job. One day when she was out, our phone rang. A woman asked for my wife and explained she was with an investor magazine. Because of my wife's business, we had gotten many solicitation calls for such periodicals. I quickly said, "She's not really interested in your magazine."

"That's odd," replied the woman, "because she just sent us her résumé."

—STEPHEN DUFRESNE

Is there anything more likely to cause you an anxiety attack than your résumé getting stuck in the office copying maching?

—*ORBEN'S CURRENT COMEDY*

For a special season in my life, I had the pleasure of being a full-time "Mr. Mom."

During that time an acquaintance whom I hadn't seen for some time asked me what I did for a living. Sensitive to the question, I jokingly replied: "I'm the director of a residential unit, with primary responsibilities for the design and execution of life-style programs specifically targeted to a model family of four."

A week later I received a copy of his résumé in the mail.

—JAMES C. TANNER

An artist on Craigslist aimed this contest at potential employers: "Send me a week's worth of salary and benefits. I will keep and use it all. Whoever sends me the best salary package will win two days of graphic design work! Good luck.

Good luck! A college student applied for a summer job at a Welsh tourist attraction. But his e-mail address didn't help things. It was: atleastimnotwelsh.

—ANANOVA.COM

A human resources manager was going over one candidate's application. At the line saying, "Sign here," the woman had written, Pisces."

—JAMES DENT

When does a hill become a mountain?
When it fills out an application for employment.

— MARILYN VOS SAVANT

@@@@@@@@@@@@@@@@@@@@@@@@@@@@@

Our 14-year-old son brought home an application for a job at a fast-food restaurant. When he asked me to check it over, I saw that where the form said, "In case of emergency, please call _____," he had written: "911."

—ANITA K. HANSEN

If You Really Don't Want the Job ...

Robert Half International, a worldwide specialized-staffing firm, collects résumé bloopers as a cautionary exercise. Some favorites:

- "I demand a salary commiserate with my experience."
- "It's best for employers that I not work with people."
- "I have an excellent track record, although I am not a horse."
- "You will want me to be Head Honcho in no time."
- "Let's meet, so you can 'ooh' and 'aah' over my experience."
- "My goal is to be a meteorologist. But since I possess no training in meteorology, I suppose I should try stock brokerage."
- "References: None. I've left a path of destruction behind me."
- "Instrumental in ruining entire operation for a Midwest chain store."
- "Note: Please don't misconstrue my 14 jobs as 'job-hopping.' I have never quit a job."

—ANNE FISHER

I had prepared my son's résumé for a job application. I typed curriculum vitae at the top and his name underneath. He delivered the document to the company, and a week or so later, a letter came for him. The salutation read: "Dear Mr. Vitae."

—SHELAGH PRYKE

"Once they noticed your tail wagging, they stopped upping their offer."

One of the more enjoyable aspects of my teacher-librarian job is reading through letters from children applying for the prestigious job of library monitor.

I had announced that applications should be addressed to "Mrs. Slattery" but the first two I opened lost all chance of success. One read: "Dear Mrs. Slavery" and the other "Dear Mrs. Fattery."

—ANNE SLATTERY

@@@@@@@@@@@@@@@@@@@@@@@@@@@@@

Typos and grammatical errors are the most common mistakes creative professionals make on their résumés, according to a survey for *The Creative Group*. So if you're job-hunting, these examples of résumé gaffes should prove that two eyes are better than one spell-checker:

- "Languages: English and Spinach."
- "I was the company's liaison with the sock exchange."
- "I prefer a fast-paste work environment."
- "I'm attacking my résumé for you to review."
- "My work ethics are impeachable."

Having established a successful career as an architect, my uncle decided to change directions and pursue his dream of becoming a chef. After spending several years preparing elegant meals in restaurants and hotels, however, the unusual hours and low pay convinced him to return to his original profession.

He submitted résumé after résumé, and by the time he came across an ad for a Renaissance architect, his finances were running low. His cover letter obviously caught the attention of the prospective employer: "Though I don't have a wealth of experience in the area of Renaissance design, I am hoping that you will consider me for this job, because I am Baroque." He started work the following week.

—MELODY MCGRATH

A young man went to a Homosassa, Fla., hardware store looking for work but allegedly ended up stealing two hanguns and a watch. Police say he wasn't hard to find: he left his job application on the gun case.

@@@@@@@@@@@@@@@@@@@@@@@@@@@@@@

The toughest part of applying for a new job is having to explain why you're no longer at your previous one. Here are rationalizations from cover letters that did no one any good:

- "My boss thought I could do better elsewhere."
- "The company made me a scapegoat, just like my three previous employers."
- "Responsibilities make me nervous."

—CHLOE RHODES, *THE OFFICE BOOK*, READER'S DIGEST BOOKS

A friend of my son had graduated and was looking for work. One day he saw his dream job advertised. He went to send his résumé, but could not find an envelope at first. Finally he managed to find one under a pile of papers. He stuffed the letter inside and posted it.

Two weeks later he received a reply. Unfortunately, he was not being considered for the job. The company also returned a photo which had been in the envelope. Then he understood why his application had been turned down. It was a photo of him—much worse for wear, half-naked and being supported by two girls—taken at his graduation party!

—H. SCHEFFERS-VIS

Sending my résumé off in reply to a job advertisement, I thought my wealth of experience said it all. So instead of including a cover letter, I simply enclosed a note saying, "Dear Sir, I apply."

The reply was equally short: **"Dear Sir, we regret."**

—PAUL LANDSBERGER

@@@@@@@@@@@@@@@@@@@@@@@@@@@@@@@@

I stopped working for three years to care for my two daughters. When I decided to go back to work, there was a "gap" on my résumé, which was not well received by potential employers. When I interviewed for a secretarial position, I solved the problem in a special way: I added three years experience in "Management and Production." Impressed, the interviewer asked me where it was that I worked.

"I managed my home and produced two daughters," I replied. I got the job!

—ADALGISA TEIXEIRA PETUCCO

Incredible Interviews

A friend and I used to run a small temporary-staffing service. Our agency did mandatory background checks on all job candidates, even though our application form asked them if they'd ever been convicted of a crime.

One day after a round of interviews, my coworker was entering information from a young man's application into the computer. She called me over to show me that he had noted a previous conviction for second-degree manslaughter. Below that, on the line listing his skills, he had written "Good with people."

—JANA RAHRIG

When my husband was interviewing job candidates, one of his standard questions was "What are your strengths?" He received a thank-you letter from one especially nervous young man in which the fellow wrote, "There's something I'd like to mention that completely slipped my mind during the interview. One of my biggest strong points is my excellent memory."

—MITA MUKHOPADHYAY

@@@@@@@@@@@@@@@@@@@@@@@@@@@@@@@

Personnel officer to job candidate: "I notice you refer to your work history as a **'terrifying chain of events.'"**

—COTHAM IN *THE WALL STREET JOURNAL*

I was interviewing a young woman who had applied for a job in our gift shop. It turned out that her favorite sport was soccer, and she was bending my ear about her accomplishments in the neighborhood league. Trying to steer the interview back to her job qualifications, I asked, "So, tell me about your long-range goals."

After thinking a minute, she replied, "Once I kicked the ball in from midfield."

—RALPH J. STEINITZ

Interviewing a candidate for a position in a tire factory, I noticed his hobbies included playing in a pop group. The job involved operating a computer and so one of the interview panel asked the candidate if he had any keyboard experience.

"No," he answered, "but I can sing, and we have a girl who plays piano."

—PAUL CONSTERDINE

An accountant answered an advertisement for a top job with a large firm. At the end of the interview, the chairman said, "One last question—what is three times seven?"

The accountant thought for a minute and replied, "Twenty-two."

Outside he took out his calculator and saw he should have said 21. He concluded he had lost the job. Two weeks later, however, he was offered the post. After a few weeks he asked the chairman why he had been appointed when he had given the wrong answer.

"You were the closest," the chairman replied.

—S. NETTLE

CALDWELL...

"The pay is great, but the commute is ridiculous."

For her summer job, my 18-year-old daughter arranged interviews at several day-care centers. At one meeting, she sat down on one of the kiddie seats, no simple task for most people. The interview went well, and at the end, the day-care center director asked the standard question, "Can you give me one good reason we should hire you?"

"Because I fit in the chairs." She got the job.

—JUDITH L. MCKAY

@@@@@@@@@@@@@@@@@@@@@@@@@@@@@@@@

Going on a job interview?

Take pity on the poor hiring managers, who filed these reports:

- "The applicant smelled his armpits on the way to the interview room."

- "The candidate told the interviewer he was fired from his last job for beating up his boss."

- "An applicant said she was a 'people person,' not a 'numbers person,' in her interview for an accounting position."

—CAREERBUILDER.COM

Mac and Todd, two brothers, went together to an employment agency looking for work. The first brother was called for an interview. "It says here you're a pilot," said the employment counselor. Mac nodded. "Well, that's great. There's a need for experienced pilots. I have a job for you immediately." With that, Mac left for the airfield.

Todd's interview didn't go as well. When asked about his work experience, he replied, "I'm a tree cutter." The counselor said there were no openings for tree cutters. Incensed, Todd demanded: "How come you have a job for my brother and not for me?"

"Because your brother is a pilot," explained the counselor. "He has a specialized skill."

"What do you mean specialized? I cut the wood, and he piles it!"

—E. S. M.

When our daughter's boyfriend was preparing for a job interview, he balked at having to dress up. "It's a casual office," he argued. "Why should I show up in a suit and tie?"

Our daughter Heather smiled and told him, "You have to make the team before you get to wear the uniform."

—DOROTHY DAVIS

QUOTABLE QUOTES

"Never wear a backward baseball cap to an interview unless applying for the job of umpire."

—DAN ZEVIN

"When you go in for a job interview, I think a good thing to ask is if they ever press charges."

—JACK HANDY

"Oh, you hate your job? Why didn't you say so? There's a support group for that. It's called EVERYBODY, and they meet at the bar."

—DREW CAREY

"If you call failures experiments, you can put them in your résumé and claim them as achievements."

—MASON COOLEY

"Résumé: A written exaggeration of only the good things a person has done in the past, as well as a wish list of the qualities a person would like to have."

—BO BENNETT

"A lot of people quit looking for work as soon as they find a job."

—ZIG ZIGLAR

"Experience is not what happens to a man. It is what a man does with what happens to him."

—ALDOUS HUXLEY

"Beware of all enterprises that require new clothes."

—HENRY DAVID THOREAU

"Never take a job where winter winds can blow up your pants."

—GERALDO RIVERA

A job applicant was asked, "What would you consider to be your main strengths and weaknesses?"

"Well," he began, "my main weakness would definitely be my issues with reality—telling what's real from what's not."

"Okay," said the interviewer. "And what are your strengths?"

"I'm Batman."

Our friend Alex emigrated from Russia to the United States and was looking for a job in engineering. During one interview the personnel director remarked how difficult it was to pronounce typically long Russian names. "What?" Alex said. "And you think Massachusetts is easy?

—MARION H. MAIDENS

Running late for a job interview at a large men's fashion company, I grabbed a white dress shirt that I didn't have time to iron.

The interview went well—until the end. "Just a word of advice," said my interviewer. "You might want to iron your shirt before your next job interview."

I held up the back of my shirt collar, revealing the tag. On it was the name of that very clothing company and the words wrinkle free.

I got the job.

—ANDREW COHEN

@@@@@@@@@@@@@@@@@@@@@@@@@@@@@@@

I had to fill a position at our company's warehouse and decided to take a chance on a very eager—but inexperienced—applicant. Happily, Joe did well and was soon ready to be trained on the forklift. The day he started, however, I heard the scrunch of metal meeting wood, followed by the piercing sound of an alarm system. I ran over and saw that the lift's forks had been driven through the shipping bay door, severing the alarm contacts.

"Joe, what happened?" I asked, gaping at the damage.

"Well," he said sheepishly. "Did I mention that I can't drive?"

—SYLVIA SUMMERS

An electrician is interviewing for a construction job.

"Can you roll your hard hat down your arm and make it pop back on your head?" the supervisor asks.

"Sure," he replies, confused.

"Can you bounce your screwdriver off the concrete, spin in a circle and catch it in your tool pouch?"

"Yes, sir," he answers excitedly.

"And can you quick-draw your wire stripper, twirl it and slip it into your pouch like it's a holster?"

"I've been doing that for years!"

"In that case, I can't use you," the boss says. "I've got 15 guys doing that now."

—KENNETH CROUCH

"I'm tired of begging people for money," a man said to an employment counselor. "Can you help me find a job?"

"How long have you been out of work?" the counselor asked.

"Who said anything about not having a job?" the man replied. "**I work for PBS.**"

—JAMES R. WILKES

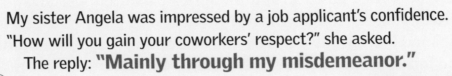

My sister Angela was impressed by a job applicant's confidence. "How will you gain your coworkers' respect?" she asked. The reply: **"Mainly through my misdemeanor."**

—GRETCHEN DUFF

So When Do I Start?

How do you get human resources to remember you? Try pulling some of these actual interview stunts.

- Balding applicant abruptly excused himself and returned a few minutes later wearing a hairpiece.

- Applicant asked to see the reviewer's résumé to see if the personnel executive was qualified to interview him.

- Applicant phoned his therapist during the interview for advice on answering specific questions.

- During the interview, an alarm clock went off in the applicant's briefcase. He apologized and said he had to leave for another interview.

- Applicant challenged the interviewer to arm-wrestle.

—GRADVIEW.COM

One applicant for a job at my print shop stood out from the rest. He was clean-cut, well-mannered and during his interview addressed me as "Sir." I discovered why when I looked over his written application.

In response to the question about military service, he had written "yes." Then he added, "It started when I was 11 and my new stepdad turned out to be an ex-Marine drill sergeant."

—PATRICK N. MCKENZIE

@@@@@@@@@@@@@@@@@@@@@@@@@@@@@@@

Our teenage grandson was eager to get his first summer job working for a bicycle rental shop. During his interview he was asked, "How are you at handling irate customers?"

"I haven't had experience with irate customers," he replied, "but I'm pretty good with irate parents."

He got the job.

—ANNE CURTIS

When we moved from Virginia to Oregon, I applied for the position of animal-control officer with the local police department. The selection process required an in-depth investigation of my past, including contacting employees at the animal shelter in Virginia where I had worked. During the final interview, the investigating officer told me that he had received some nice comments about me. Then, with a laugh, he shared a particularly memorable remark. When asked if I had any prejudices, a former colleague replied, "I don't think she likes cocker spaniels very much."

I got the job anyway.

—SUZANNE L. PILON

A man walked into a Taco Bell in Haverstraw, New York, and pulled a gun on the cashier. After grabbing the loot, he marched into the manager's office and applied for a job. He was turned down.

—LOHUD.COM

After taking early retirement, I attended an interview for the role of litter warden at the local park.

"What training do I get?" I asked the council official.

"None," he shrugged. "You just pick it up as you go along."

—KEITH HAMBER

"Our consultant recommended this temporary title until the staff gets to know you."

I had an interview for a job in a library and I asked my brother for advice.

"Just talk quietly," he said.

—CHARLOTTE JOSEPH

@@@@@@@@@@@@@@@@@@@@@@@@@@@@@@

Rajesh is at an interview for a guard's job. "Assume you see two trains speeding towards each other. What will you do?" asked a Railways official.

"Raise a red flag," Rajesh replied.

"But you haven't taken the flag with you,"said the official.

"I'll wave my red shirt at the drivers."

"You're not wearing a red shirt that day."

"Then I'll run home and bring my little sister," Rajesh smiled.

"Wow! Does she know any new technique?"

"No," said Rajesh. "But she hasn't seen two trains colliding."

"I see you were last employed by a psychiatrist," said the employer to the applicant. "Why did you leave?"

"Well," the applicant replied, "I just couldn't win. If I was late to work, I was hostile. If I was early, I had an anxiety complex, and if I was on time, I was compulsive."

—CAO XIN

Don't Call Us

Recruitment website CareerBuilder.com surveyed employers to find some of the biggest job-interview gaffes from the last year:

- Candidate who answered mobile phone and asked the interviewer to leave her own office, because it was a "private" conversation.

- Candidate who asked the interviewer for a lift home.

- Candidate who, when offered food, declined, saying he didn't want to line his stomach with grease before going out drinking.

- Candidate who flushed the toilet while talking to employer during a phone interview.

@@@@@@@@@@@@@@@@@@@@@@@@@@@@@

We'll Call You

Remember, the idea behind job interviews is to make an impression—a good one, say these hiring executives.

- "One candidate said that we should hire him because he would be a great addition to our softball team."

- "An applicant sang all her responses to interview questions."

- "One individual said we had nice benefits, which was good because he was going to need to take a lot of leave the following year."

- "A candidate told me she needed the position because she wanted to get away from dealing with people."

—ACCOUNTEMPS

A friend of mine who is manager for advertising in a fashion magazine was interviewing applicants for the job of manager of advertising sales. One of the applicants seemed ideal for the job. My friend resolved silently to hire this girl, and asked her the final question: What do you think of our magazine?"

"It's an excellent publication," answered the interviewee, "but there are too many ads in it."

—MARIA PETROVA

Bob had applied for a job in a supermarket and was attending the interview. When the interviewer asked what experience he'd had, Bob said that he'd once worked in another supermarket.

The interviewer asked why he had left.

"I was sacked for playing with the bacon slicer," Bob explained.

The interviewer was puzzled: "Surely they didn't consider that to be a serious offense?"

"They must have," replied Bob. "They sacked her too."

—ADAM CUTHBERTSON

@@@@@@@@@@@@@@@@@@@@@@@@@@@@@@

When I went for my first student-job interview at a supermarket, some friends advised me on a technique that would impress the manager. I was told to smile frequently and use the word "sir."

Unfortunately, the ploy didn't work. The more I smiled and said "sir," the grimmer my interviewer became. My interview ended when the boss suddenly stood up and showed me the door.

"Don't call us," she said coldly, smoothing down her skirt. "We'll call you."

—FRANCES WHITESTONE

Nervous during an interview for his first part-time job, my 15-year-old son tried to answer each question as honestly as he could. When he was asked to explain his strengths, he thought a moment, then offered, "Well, I can bench press 100 pounds."

—JOY GALLANT

While my wife was getting a haircut, a young man wearing jeans and a T-shirt walked in, seeking a job. After the applicant left, my wife's stylist, sporting multiple earrings, a nose ring and bright blue hair, said, "Can you believe someone would come in and ask for a job dressed like that?"

—JOHN GRATTON

A police officer was interviewing a young recruit. "If you're driving on a lonely road at night," the officer asked, "and you're being chased by a gang of criminals going 60 m.p.h., what would you do?"

The applicant replied, **"Seventy!"**

—DAVID BROOME

@@@@@@@@@@@@@@@@@@@@@@@@@@@@@@

Interviewer to job applicant: **"Can you come up with any reason you want this job other than your parents want you out of their house?"**

—MIKE SHAPIRO

Two friends go to a job interview. The first one goes in and is asked by the interviewer, "Tell me, when you look at me, what is the first thing you see?"

"Well," he answers, "that you have no ears."

"How dare you! Get out!" the interviewer demands.

He leaves and warns his friend, "Don't mention that he has no ears it apparently annoys him."

"Thank you," says the friend.

So the second interviewee is asked the same question when he enters the office: "Tell me, when you look at me, what is the first thing you see?"

"I see that you wear contact lenses," answers the second friend.

"Excellent!" exclaims the interviewer, "how did you know?"

"Simple, where would you rest your glasses if you didn't?"

—ILEANA CONTERNO

My daughter Miranda works in a lingerie shop, and one evening a young man came in and asked for a job application. After he asked a few questions, Miranda explained the rules for male employees. "You can only work behind the cash register or in the stockroom," she said. "You can't wait on customers, or go into the changing areas.

"By the way," she added, "most of our customers don't look like the models in the ads, but more like your mother."

With that, the young man tossed the application on the counter and walked out the door.

—SCOTT SWANN

A job applicant's polygraph test for the Washington State Patrol came to an abrupt end after officers discovered an interesting piece of literature on the front seat of his car. The title of the book: How to Beat a Lie Detector Test.

—KOMONEWS.COM

I'm in personnel with the government in Washington, D.C., reviewing applications for federal employment. The standard form includes the question "Why did you leave your previous employment?" One applicant, a former U.S. Congressman, responded, "The express wish of 116,000 voters."

—WILSON M. CARR III

"Obviously, we were thinking long term when we assembled this board."

I attached great importance to dressing well for job interviews. At one interview, when I noticed that the employers and other applicants were looking at me intently, I assumed they were all struck by my tidy appearance.

I got the job. However, one interviewer took me aside and said: "We chose you because you looked natural, even though you had tissue paper stuck to your forehead."

—SUPREEYA PROMTHONG

I joined a company's Human Resources department after graduating from college. In just a few years, I was promoted to be the senior officer responsible for recruiting junior and mid-level clerks. I was only 25, and most of the applicants were older than me. To impress these applicants at the interviews, I dressed and talked quite maturely.

One day, a woman in her forties applied for a clerical job. At the interview she complained that it was hard to find work since older women were discriminated against.

"That's really unfair," I tried to console her, "plus you look much younger than your age."

She smiled instantly and said politely, "Don't worry, you look very young as well."

—C. L. WONG

In an interview, a plastic surgeon was asked if he'd ever done anything shocking.

"I don't think so," he replied. **"But I've certainly raised a few eyebrows."**

—P. BACANIN

@@@@@@@@@@@@@@@@@@@@@@@@@@@@@@

To check the character of the prospective department
head, the boss says: "Let's assume you go to my
house and ring the doorbell. My wife invites you in,
but tells you that I won't be home for another two hours.
What would you do?"

The applicant hesitates, then asks,
"Could you let me see a photo of your wife?"

—LEA BERNER

As a foreman for a construction company, my friend Jim was interviewing an applicant. He asked the plasterer to bring his tools in so he could see what he could do. The fellow returned with tools slung over his shoulder and hanging from his pockets, and in one hand he was holding an unidentifiable object covered in plaster. Jim asked what it was. "My radio," the chap answered.

"All right," said Jim, "you can start tomorrow."

The applicant looked surprised. "That's it? You don't want to see what I can do?"

"Any plasterman who has a radio looking like that one," Jim said, "must have put in at least three years of work."

—JENNIFER MARCOUX

I agreed when my 17-year-old niece asked me if she could use my name as a reference on her résumé, which she planned to submit to a local fast-food restaurant. A few days later she called and asked me if I could meet her at the restaurant later that afternoon. "Yes, but why?" I asked.

"The manager wants me to come in for an interview," she explained, "and she wants me to bring my references."

—JOYCE SCHWAB

Armed with impeccable credentials, a man applied for a position with a top company. Unfortunately, he had a problem with one of his eyes—it constantly winked. "We'd love to hire you," said the company vice president, "but that winking is too distracting."

"Wait! I can make it stop by taking two aspirin," the applicant said.

"Okay, show me," the executive replied.

The job candidate reached into his pocket, pulled out a dozen condom packages and placed them on the desk before finding two aspirin. He took the tablets, and the winking stopped.

"That's fine," the VP said coolly. "But we don't condone womanizing."

"No, no. You've got me all wrong," the man replied. "Have you ever asked for aspirin at the drugstore while winking?"

—DAN GUERRA

Sales manager to an applicant: "Have you any previous sales experience?"

"Yes, sir. I sold my house, my car, the piano and almost all my wife's jewelry."

Here's a job to avoid: hiring manager.

See what you'd have to contend with?

- The candidate told the interviewer he wouldn't stay with the job long because he might get an inheritance if his uncle died—and the old man wasn't "looking too good."

- The candidate said she couldn't provide a writing sample because all her writing had been for the CIA and it was "classified."

—CAREERBUILDER.COM

@@@@@@@@@@@@@@@@@@@@@@@@@@@@@@

> The employer addressed the applicant: "We want a responsible person for this job."
>
> "Then I'm your man," announced the young man. **"No matter where I've worked, whenever anything happened, they always said I was responsible."**
>
> —JEAN BULL

All my self-confidence and poise vanished as I entered the office for a job interview. As I closed the door behind me, the woman behind the desk in the farthest corner of the room commanded, "Sit down!"

I sat in the nearest chair by the door. With a puzzled look, she stood up, her hand extended. However, before I reached her, she again barked, "Sit!".

I sat in the chair by her desk for a second before I jumped up to grasp her still-outstretched hand. Our greeting was interrupted by yet another "Sit!".

I yo-yoed, still clutching her hand, back to the chair. After I was hired, I was assured it was because of my qualifications and not because I was more obedient than her dog.

—JAN JOHNSON

Many people have been trained in interview techniques, but not my 19-year-old nephew from Amsterdam. He had applied for a job as crane operator and had an interview. He knew that, besides him, there was only one other candidate. During the interview he was asked: "Why should we employ you?"

"How should I know?" my nephew answered. "I've never met the other guy!"

—KITTY APPELMAN

@@@@@@@@@@@@@@@@@@@@@@@@@@@@@

Employer to job candidate: **"I hire only married people. They're less likely to go home early."**

—HARLEY SCHWADRON

My buddy applied for a job as an insurance salesperson. Where the form requested "prior experience," he wrote "lifeguard." That was it. Nothing else.

"We're looking for someone who can not only sell insurance, but who can sell himself," said the hiring manager. "How does working as a lifeguard pertain to salesmanship?"

"I couldn't swim," my pal replied.

He got the job.

—TEDD C. HUSTON

Interview Impact

When you're interviewing for a job, you want to make an impression. Hiring managers report that these people made one—just not the right kind:

- Applicant hugged hiring manager at the end of the interview.

- Applicant ate all the candy from the candy bowl while trying to answer questions.

- Applicant blew her nose and lined up the used tissues on the table in front of her.

- Applicant wore a hat that said "Take this job and shove it."

- Applicant talked about how an affair cost him a previous job.

- Applicant threw his beer can in the outside trashcan before coming into the reception area.

- Applicant's friend came in and asked, "How much longer?"

—CAREERBUILDER.COM

@@@@@@@@@@@@@@@@@@@@@@@@@@@@@@@@

A personnel manager was interviewing an applicant for a job with his company. "How long did you work in your previous position?"

"Fifty-five years," replied the applicant.

"And how old are you?" asked the manager, clearly shocked at the applicant's answer.

"I'm 47," said the applicant.

"I'm sorry," relied the manager, "I don't understand."

"It's simple," smiled the applicant. "Overtime."

—SHEHERYAR HAFEEZ

My husband, a tool shop manager, was in charge of interviewing applicants for a new store opening in our town. Two young brothers from the country entered his office looking for work. At the end of the interview, my husband asked them to bring him photographs for their records. Early the next day the two brothers brought in an enormous photo of the two of them, smiling and hugging each other!

—RENATA BERNARDO

In search of a new pastor, our congregation advertised for someone "able to walk on water and move mountains." We knew we had the right person when a candidate arrived for the job interview sporting a life jacket and carrying a shovel.

—MARJORIE KAUFMAN

A man saw a job advertised as 'Problem Solver' with a salary of $100,000. He applied, had an interview and was offered the job on the spot. "Do you have any questions?" asked his new employer.

"Just one," replied the man. "How can you afford to pay so much?"

"That," said the employer, "is your first problem."

—COLIN JAMES

The boss asked four job applicants the same question: "What is two and two?"

The first interviewee was a journalist. His answer was "twenty-two." The second, an engineer, calculated the answer to be between 3.999 and 4.001. The third applicant, a lawyer, cited a court case in which two and two was proved to be four.

The last candidate was an accountant. When the accountant heard the question, he leaned across the desk and said in a low voice, "How much do you want it to be?"

After many years of staying home to raise a family, my mother was nervous about her job interview for the position of librarian at our high school.

During the interview the principal asked her if she read. Since six children didn't leave her much spare time, she reluctantly admitted, "No." However, thinking this might hinder her chances, she quickly added, "But I can!" She got the job.

—ANNETTE GALLANT

On the Job

BANANACO PROFITS

"Don't stay in bed, unless you can make money in bed.

—GEORGE BURNS

"Dawson takes a lot of work home with him. But he never seems to bring it back."

@@@@@@@@@@@@@@@@@@@@@@@@@@@@@@

Corporate Miscommunications

The company where I work provides four-foot-high cubicles so each employee can have some privacy. One day a coworker had an exasperating phone conversation with one of her teenage sons. After hanging up, she heaved a sigh and said, "No one ever listens to me."

Immediately, several voices from surrounding cubicles called out, "Yes, we do."

—JO JAIMESON

At our supermarket, I noticed a woman with four boys and a baby. Her patience was wearing thin as the boys called out, "Mommy! Mommy!" while she tried to shop. Finally, she blurted out, "I don't want to hear the word mommy for at least ten minutes!"

The boys fell silent for a few seconds. Then one tugged on his mother's dress and said softly, "Excuse me, miss."

—DENNIS DOOK

One day a coworker noticed I had on a new dress. She raved about how beautiful it was and wanted to know where I bought it. I told her the name of the store and jokingly added that if she ended up buying the same dress, she'd have to tell me when she was going to wear it so we didn't show up at the office looking like twins. She replied, "Oh, I'd never wear a dress like that to work!"

—NANCY J. HIMBER

My colleagues and I recently received this e-mail from the facilities department: "Due to construction, your office may be either cooler or warmer than usual on Tuesday. Dress accordingly."

—DEBRA DONATH

@@@@@@@@@@@@@@@@@@@@@@@@@@@@@@@

Found on the bottom of an office memo:
"If you have any questions, please read again."

—STAN GLEASON

The topic in the office break room was the high price of divorce.

"I should've taken out a home improvement loan to pay for my attorney," said one disgusted woman.

"Can you do that?" I wondered.

"She got her bum husband out of the house, didn't she?" said a friend. "I'd call that a home improvement."

—MARTI MCDANIEL

The employee refrigerator at the graphic-design office where I work is notoriously messy. But I realized things were really getting out of hand when I saw an old jar of Vlasic-brand pickles that sported a new, handwritten label: Jurassic Pickles.

—HOLLY SPRINGER

The Employee/English Dictionary

- **Plutoed:** To be unceremoniously relegated to a lower position without an adequate explanation.

- **Clockroaches:** Employees who spend most of their day watching the clock instead of doing their jobs.

- **Prairie Dogging:** Occurs when workers simultaneously pop their heads up out of their cubicles to see what's going on.

- **Carbon-Based Error:** Error caused by a human, not a computer.

- **Bobbleheading:** The mass nod of agreement during a meeting to comments made by the boss.

—FROM *THE BUZZWORD DICTIONARY* BY JOHN WALSTON (MARION STREET PRESS, INC.)

A "safety message" sent out at my office warned: "Alert! The stress balls distributed at yesterday's 'How to Manage Your Stress' class are exploding all over the building. Please do not squeeze or apply pressure to the stress balls!"

—APRIL RICHEY

To be perfectly blunt, our office receptionist could be a real witch. She'd been there 20 years and lorded over the place like she owned it. One recent, freezing day, she went so far as to order a coworker to warm up her car for her. Much to my surprise, he agreed.

A few minutes later he came back holding a broom. Placing it on a heating vent, he told her, "Just give it a minute and it'll be ready to go."

—JESSICA O'NEILL

One morning at our small-town newspaper office, one of the editors was struggling to write a headline for the obituary of a woman who was noted for little besides a fondness for crossword puzzles. "What am I supposed to write," the editor whined, "'She liked puzzles'?"

Just then one of our copy editors piped up, "How about, 'Crossword fan is now six down'?"

—JAMES VLAHOS

A coworker stormed into my friend's office, yelling, "Did you tell Joan I was a witch?"

Stunned, my friend sputtered, **"No! I don't know how she found out."**

—GEORGE O'BRIEN

An executive for a phone company, my father often rode his motorcycle to the office from his suburban home. He wore coveralls over his clothing for protection, and would hang them on his clothes tree when he arrived at work. Once when he was working late, my mother called the office. His secretary answered the call. "He's not in his office," she told my mother.

"Has he left for the day?" my mother pressed.

"Oh, no," said the secretary. "He hasn't left the building—his pants are still on the clothes rack."

—WILLIAM B. MAGRUDER

I work in a small government office, and as part of the daily routine I take orders for doughnuts and pick them up on my midmorning run to the post office. A new employee looked bemused as I took orders for CCRs, GOFs and POFs—known to bakery staff as chocolate-covered raised, glazed old-fashioned and plain old-fashioned. When it was the new employee's turn to order, she laughed and said, "You know you work in a government office when even the doughnuts have acronyms."

—CINDY BEVING

Things you'll seldom hear around the office water cooler:

- "I love my boss so much I'd gladly work for free."

- "I'm going to run down to the cafeteria and ask the cook for his recipes."

- "Boy, I wish I could make coffee as good as that vending machine on the third floor."

- "I don't want the promotion if it's going to make my coworkers envious."

—*EXECUTIVE SPEECHWRITER NEWSLETTER*

My coworker is Venezuelan and has trouble understanding some English phrases. She is a top salesperson in our company and is known for being very competitive. One day she was talking with a couple of employees, complaining about her job and how she felt mistreated.

"Oh, be quiet," said a colleague. "You know you're queen bee at the office."

"Oh, really?" she replied indignantly. "And who is Queen A?"

—DENISE MADDOX

A woman and her daughter had just purchased a $1200 Persian rug at the store where I work. As they were leaving, I overheard the daughter say to her mother, "There's no way that we can tell Dad we've always had this."

—MATTHEW LARSON

"Harding is very security conscious."

Our company was conducting free body mass index checkups. When a stout colleague climbed onto the machine, it spit out a slip of paper telling him what his weight-to-height ratio was and what it ought to be.

"What does it say?" I asked.

He replied, **"I need to increase my height by six inches."**

—SOBBY KURIAN

I work for an accounting firm where it's not unusual to have an IRS agent in the office examining taxpayer records. We try to let clients know when an agent is present so they will watch what they say.

One time a coworker handed a client a note that read "There is an IRS agent in the office." The client scribbled a response and handed it back to the accountant. "I know," the client wrote. "It's my brother-in-law."

—KATHY BIGLER

As an editor of the St. Louis Globe-Democrat, I received many unwanted phone calls. My secretary was exceptionally gracious in screening callers and saving me from pests.

One day I was talking with Howard F. Baer, a distinguished civic leader and chairman of the St. Louis Zoological Commission, when my wife called on another line.

"I'm sorry, but he's talking to Mr. Baer at the zoo," my secretary said.

"Really, Florence," my wife said, "you need a better story than that."

—MARTIN LAWLER DUGGAN

During a routine companywide drug screening, a coworker was sent into the bathroom with a plastic cup, while the attendant dutifully stood guard outside.

She waited patiently for several minutes. More time went by, until finally she knocked on the door.

"Are you all right in there?"

From within, a timid voice responded, "Don't I at least get a magazine or something?"

"No," said the nurse, without blinking. "It's not that kind of test."

—MARTY GUFFIN

I work at an aviation school that specializes in five-day refresher courses for aircraft mechanics. One day, I overheard a coworker talking on the phone with a potential customer. "Actually, we don't call our classes crash courses," he said. "We like to think of them as 'keep up in the air' classes."

—RANDY G. SMITH

Who Took My Stapler?

Is your cubicle neighbor driving you nuts? You're not alone. Here are just some of the ways coworkers annoy each other, in your own words:

- "Employee eats all the good cookies."
- "Employee's body is magnetic and keeps deactivating my access card."
- "Employee's aura is wrong."
- "Employee is too suntanned."
- "Employee smells like road ramps."
- "Employee wants to check a coworker for ticks."

—CAREERBUILDER.COM

"We've been lucky. So far they've only downsized our cubicles."

A woman in my office recently divorced after years of marriage, had signed up for a refresher CPR course.

"Is it hard to learn?" someone asked.

"Not at all," my coworker replied. "Basically you're asked to breathe life into a dummy. I don't expect to have any problem. I did that for 32 years."

—PAULETTE BROOKS

At the company water cooler, I bragged about my children's world travels: one son was teaching in Bolivia, another was working in southern Italy, and my daughter was completing a yearlong research project in India. One coworker's quip, however, stopped me short. "What is it about you," he asked, "that makes your kids want to get so far away?"

—TODD W. KAISER

Following the announcement of an aggressive cost-cutting program at my company, each employee was encouraged to recommend ways to save money. A couple of days later, I stepped into an elevator where a large poster was hanging to remind workers of an upcoming blood drive. Underneath the huge words "Give Blood," someone had scribbled, "I knew it would come to this."

—CHUCK BRADFORD

The investment management firm where I worked had just moved into new offices, and the place was overflowing with gifts of large plants, mostly huge Boston ferns. Amid this jungle, I was showing off underwater photographs of sea life from a recent scuba-diving trip. Just then a senior member of the firm looked over my shoulder and asked, "Are those anemones?"

"Of course not," I replied. Then, pointing to the plants around us, I quipped, "With ferns like these, who needs anemones?"

—DAVID A. CONARY

Scene: Two coworkers conversing.

Coworker 1: My son just turned 18 months old.
Coworker 2: So, is that like a year and a half old?
Coworker 1: You really aren't sure if 18 months is a year and a half?
Coworker 2: How am I supposed to know that? I don't have kids.

—ADAM FREDERICK

One day while at work, I called home to talk to my college-student wife, forgetting momentarily that she would be at a class. After leaving a message on our answering machine, I closed with my customary "I love you." As I hung up, I was startled by a coworker who was standing in the doorway and had heard me. With a look of contempt she said, "Your wife is holding on line one."

—JASON LEIFESTER

On my rural postal route, I make deliveries only to roadside mailboxes that are accessible. For two days a woman met me at a disabled tractor that blocked her mailbox. "My husband says he'll move it as soon as he can," she said with a sigh as she accepted the mail.

On the third day the tractor was still there. I expected the woman to appear, but instead saw that the mailbox had been removed from its post. It was now strapped with black tape to the fender of the tractor—at exactly the required height for delivery.

—WILLMA WILLIS GORE

My husband works in a former supermarket that was remodeled to accommodate professional offices. One day he overheard his receptionist giving directions over the phone. "Remember the old grocery store?" she asked the caller. "You'll find us in the meat department."

—KAREN G. STOWE

Following a blowout shindig the night before, a coworker was looking the worse for wear.

"Are you feeling all right?" I asked.

"I don't know," she answered slowly. "I think I'm suffering from post-partying depression."

—MAY-LING GONZALES

Signs you don't have enough to do at work:

- You've already read the entire Dilbert page-a-day calendar for 2012.

- People come to your office only to borrow pencils from your ceiling.

- You discover that staring at your cubicle wall long enough produces images of Elvis.

- The Fourth Division of Paper Clips has overrun the Pushpin Infantry, and General Whiteout has called for reinforcements.

—LYNDELL LEATHERMAN

@@@@@@@@@@@@@@@@@@@@@@@@@@@@@

Man to coworker: "I learn more from originals left in the copier than I do from the employee newsletter."

—LITZLER IN *THE WALL STREET JOURNAL*

First thing every single morning one of the secretaries in our office opened the newspaper and read everyone's horoscope aloud.

"Gwen," said our boss finally, "you seem to be a normal, levelheaded person. Do you really believe in astrology?"

"Of course not," Gwen answered. "You know how skeptical we Capricorns are."

—DEAN MORGAN

My daughter is in the cast of a dinner-theater company, which presents mysteries in a local restaurant. While the shows are entertaining, the food leaves a lot to be desired. Near the end of the play, each member of the audience submits a form, answering the question, "Who do you think is the murderer and why?"

"It must be the cook," answered one disgruntled guest. "He tried to poison the rest of us, too."

—A. G. HARTMAN

The brave new memo about the company's revised travel policy read as follows: We were no longer allowed to buy cheap tickets via the Internet. Instead, we were required to use the more expensive company travel department.

Furthermore, to show how much money we were saving, we were asked to comparison-shop for fares—on the Internet.

I thought the typo in the last line of the memo summed it up best: "The new process is ineffective today."

—KIP HARTMAN

"QUOTABLE QUOTES

"The Brain is a wonderful organ. It starts working the moment you get up and does not stop until you get into the office."

—ROBERT FROST

"I had the most boring office job in the world—I used to clean the windows on envelopes."

—RITA RUDNER

"How to get a good raise: Request meeting with the boss. Outline accomplishments. Use words such as future and growth. Threaten to quit. Quit. Depart for higher-paying position. You did go in with another job offer, right?"

—TED ALLEN

"A cubicle is just a padded cell without a door."

—UNKNOWN

"A raise is like a martini: it elevates the spirit, but only temporarily."

—DAN SELIGMAN

"The human race is faced with a cruel choice: work or daytime television."

—DAVE BARRY

"You moon the wrong person at an office party and suddenly you're not 'professional' anymore."

—JEFF FOXWORTHY

"It's just a job. Grass grows, birds fly, waves pound the sand. I beat people up."

—MUHAMMAD ALI

"Hard work is damn near as overrated as monogamy."

—HUEY LONG

As a new employee for a discount brokerage firm, I went for a month of classroom training. Warning us about the volume of information we were required to memorize, one instructor suggested we make lots of notes on file cards.

When I completed the course, I was assigned to a team where, as suggested, I taped all the file cards, crammed with notes, onto my computer.

On my first day of trading, a veteran broker sat with me. He immediately noticed all the cards—and my apprehension—and promptly made up a new card, which he taped to my computer. It read "Breathe!"

—STEVE J. GAINES

"Anderson, we'd like to talk to you about your stand-offish attitude."

Soon after I started a new job, a coworker named Elizabeth showed me how to clear the copier when it became jammed. A few days later the machine jammed again, and I began to punch buttons and slam doors to clear it as I was shown. "What's going on?" asked a colleague.

"I'm clearing the copier like Elizabeth taught me," I replied.

"Oh, but you have to understand," the man explained. "Elizabeth has a temper."

—SHERRY MCNEAL

Even though I've worked in many state government agencies over the years, I still don't get the jargon. Here's an example of what I read every day and—worse—am expected to understand:

"Most of you will be developing subleases instead of subsubleases, so any reference to 'subsubleases' needs to be changed to 'subleases,' except for paragraph 38, which will become 'subsubleases' instead of 'subsubsubleases.' Also, there will no longer be any reference to 'Subsublessor' or 'Subsublessee,' which become 'Sublessor' and 'Sublessee,' respectively. I hope this information will get you started."

—TRUDIE MIXON

The elevator in our building malfunctioned one day, leaving several of us stranded. Seeing a sign that listed two emergency phone numbers, I dialed the first and explained our situation.

After what seemed to be a very long silence, the voice on the other end said, "I don't know what you expect me to do for you; I'm a psychologist."

"A psychologist?" I replied. "Your phone is listed here as an emergency number. Can't you help us?"

"Well," he finally responded in a measured tone. "How do you feel about being stuck in an elevator?"

—CHRISTINE QUINN

I used to work in the business office of a water-slide park where hundreds of high school and college students are employed as lifeguards, gift-shop clerks and food vendors. For many this is a first job. One day I overheard a lunchroom conversation between two teenagers. "So how do you like your job?" one asked.

"I guess it's okay," the other answered, "but it's not at all what I expected."

"What do you mean?" the first teen asked.

"Well, I thought it would be fun working here. I guess I'm more the customer type."

—KARENA SPACH

Extraordinary Excuses

One of my coworkers got a speeding ticket and was attending a defensive-driving course to have points erased from her license. The instructor, a police officer, emphasized that being on time was crucial, and that the classroom doors would be locked when each session began.

Just after one class started, someone knocked on the locked door. The officer opened it and asked, "Why are you late?"

The student replied, "I was trying not to get another ticket." The officer let him in.

—PATTY STEFFER

"Sorry I'm late, boss! I had to take my wife to the maternity ward," Konrád blurts out on arriving at his workplace.

"You don't imagine I'm going to swallow that, do you? That was your excuse last time. Your wife isn't a rabbit after all."

"No, but she's a midwife."

—ZSANETT BAHOR

"**As you both know, here at Frump, Cuttle, and Howsen, failure is not an option. So that only leaves blame.**"

Dave was late for work. "What's the big idea coming in late?" roared his boss. "The alarm clock woke up everybody but me this morning," said Dave. "What do you mean, it woke up everyone but you?" asked the boss. "You see, there are eight of us in the family, and the clock was set for seven."

— JOVELYN ALCANTARA

Found in a heap of recycled files donated to our school was this curiously labeled folder: *"Excuses I Have Used."*

—NANCY EILER

My problem is getting to work on time. One morning, driving to the office, I came across a turtle in the middle of the road. I just had to rescue the creature. It took a few minutes for me to stop the car, grab the turtle and move it off to the side. Then I rushed on to work.

When I saw my boss at the door, I said quickly, "It's not my fault, Rich. There was a turtle in the road." Before I could go any further he bellowed, "So what—you drove behind it?"

—CHRISTY STEINBRUNNER

15 percent of workers admit to getting to the office late at least once a week. And here are some of their excuses:

- "I dreamed I was fired, so I didn't bother to get out of bed."
- "I had to take my cat to the dentist."
- "I went all the way to the office and realized I was still in my pajamas and had to go home to change."
- "I saw you weren't in the office, so I went out looking for you."
- "I have transient amnesia and couldn't remember my job."
- "I was indicted for securities fraud this morning."
- "Someone stole all my daffodils."
- "I had to go audition for American Idol."
- "I was trying to get my gun back from the police."

—CAREERBUILDER.COM

@@@@@@@@@@@@@@@@@@@@@@@@@@@@@@

While working in the library at a university, I was often shocked by the excuses students would use to get out of paying their fees for overdue books.

One evening an older student returned two books that were way overdue and threw a fit over the "outrageous" $2 fee that I asked her to pay. I tried to explain how much she owed for each day, but she insisted she should be exempt.

"You don't understand," she blurted out. "I didn't even read them!"

—ALISON SATTERFIELD

A friend of mine was running late for work and in her haste to make up time was pulled over for speeding. She pleaded with the police officer, "Please, I don't have much time. I'm already late for work." Pulling out his ticket book, he said soothingly, "Don't worry, Miss. I write very quickly."

—BONA SIJABAT

A big challenge of running a small business is dealing with employees' requests for time off. One morning an employee said, "I need to leave early tomorrow." Later that same day, he followed up with, "Looks like I'll be coming in late tomorrow, but if my coming in late runs into my leaving early, then I won't be in at all."

—JENNIFER KOONTZ

"Why are you late for class every day?" the teacher asks his student. "Because every time I approach the school I see a sign that says **'School. Slow down.'**"

—BLANCA ESTELA ÁLVAREZ

One day a coworker told my husband, Cary, that she was going home early because she didn't feel well. Since Cary was just getting over something himself, he wished her well and said he hoped it wasn't something he had given her. A fellow worker piped up, "I hope not. She has morning sickness."

—BEVERLY WOOD

@@@@@@@@@@@@@@@@@@@@@@@@@@@@@@@@

The top things to say when your boss catches you sleeping at your desk:

- "They told me at the blood bank that this might happen."
- "Whew! Guess I left the top off the correction fluid."
- "This is one of the seven habits of highly effective people."
- "Why did you interrupt me? I almost had our biggest problem solved!"
- "Someone must have put decaf in the wrong pot."
- "Ah, the unique and unpredictable circadian rhythms of the workaholic."
- "Amen. Yes, may I help you?"

—SHEILA BRYAN

For the first few months of her co-op position for the state of Georgia, my sister had nothing to do, so she surfed the Web or did crossword puzzles. One day she expressed her boredom to a coworker. "I know," he complained. "Everyone thinks state workers have it easy. But there's only so much you can pretend you're doing."

—MALORY HUNTER

Uncle Jim was late for work when the red lights flashed behind him. Knowing he was busted, Jim pulled over and waited with license and registration in hand.

As the trooper wrote out the ticket, he asked Jim where he was headed.

"I'm late for an important 7:30 meeting," Jim said.

The officer checked his watch.

"If you hurry," he remarked, "you can still make it."

—BILL DAMMAN

@@@@@@@@@@@@@@@@@@@@@@@@@@@@@@

When attorney David Loudis was more than two hours late for work, he told his boss this tale of woe: He had awakened thirsty in the middle of the night and, heading for the kitchen, tripped over the cord of his clock radio. The dial began flashing 12:00, indicating that it needed to be reset. After slaking his thirst, he glanced at the kitchen microwave and noted the time—1:06. He returned to his room, reset his clock and fell asleep.

In the morning, the alarm woke him, and he went through his usual routine. Only when he turned on the TV did he discover that the early shows were over and it was 10:30 a.m. In a flash of insight, he realized that the 1:06 had signified not the hour, but the one minute and six seconds of cooking time left after he had prematurely removed some burritos from the microwave the night before.

—LAWRENCE VAN GELDER

Being the office supervisor, I had to have a word with a new employee who never arrived at work on time. I explained that her tardiness was unacceptable and that other employees had noticed that she was walking in late every day.

After listening to my complaints, she agreed that this was a problem and even offered a solution.

"Is there another door I could use?"

—BARBARA DAVIES

One of my jobs as a teacher is checking on the reasons students give for being late or absent. One mother sent a note that explained: **"Please excuse John for being. It was his father's fault."**

—CAROLYN HARRIS

@@@@@@@@@@@@@@@@@@@@@@@@@@@@

**A boss is telling off one of his staff:
"This is the fifth day in a row that you've come late!
What am I supposed to think about that?"**

"That today's Friday!"

—WWW.KULICHKI.RU

At a company staff meeting, our president asked a supervisor why his project hadn't been started. The executive sheepishly said that he was waiting for a "go" signal. With that, the president stalked out of the room and returned a few minutes later with the company flag. Standing in front of everyone, he raised the flag and, in race-car fashion, lowered it swiftly while shouting, "Go!"

—RAMON CARLOS J. ABDON

I work in human resources and often meet with employees to discuss workplace problems. During one session, a woman who was having a dispute with one of her colleagues complained that she was "sick and tired of having to argue like a child."

"Well," I offered, "why don't you initiate a meeting with your supervisor and the coworker to discuss your unhappiness?"

"Why should I have to?" she countered. "She started it!"

—ANJELICA T. NATION

My teaching career had led me to an isolated post in the North, where winter temperatures are subzero. One such morning a latecomer handed me a note from her mother, which read: "Sorry Andrea is late. The rooster froze up."

—LEONA KROPF

A note I received from my student's father: **"Please excuse Chris's absence yesterday. Due to my poor planning, my wife had a baby."**

—MARY FILICETTI

My wife worked at a country-music radio station in North Carolina where another employee was notorious for the colorful excuses he offered to back up his habitual tardiness. One summer morning when he strolled in late again, the station manager demanded an explanation. "It was so hot today," the straggler said, "that the asphalt molecules in the highway expanded, creating a greater distance between my home and the office."

—PAUL FOERMAN

A vice president of our company was notorious for insisting on punctuality. He fined anyone arriving late for a meeting a dollar. At one gathering, a latecomer asked what the executive did with the money he collected. "It's for my early-retirement fund," he quipped. Immediately, everyone else at the meeting broke out their wallets and added their dollars to the pile.

—CHARLES WOOD

Need a reason for being late to work?

Don't try these—they didn't help any of the workers who actually used them.

- "My deodorant was frozen to the windowsill."
- "My car door fell off."
- "I dreamed I was already at work."
- "I had an early-morning gig as a clown."

—KATE LORENZ

@@@@@@@@@@@@@@@@@@@@@@@@@@@@@

Smith goes to see his supervisor in the front office. "Boss," he says, "we're doing some heavy housecleaning at home tomorrow, and my wife needs me to help with the attic and the garage, moving and hauling stuff."

"We're short-handed, Smith," the boss replies. "I can't give you the day off."

"Thanks, boss," says Smith. "I knew I could count on you!"

—JAY TRACHMAN

When one of the salesmen in our office arrived two hours late for work, he sheepishly explained that he and his wife had been arguing the previous night. "If you can't speak to me nicely, you shouldn't speak at all!" he had yelled at her. Then he spent the night on the sofa.

The next morning he awoke to find the sun high, the house quiet and his wife long gone to work. A note on the coffee table beside him said, "Bryan, it's time to wake up."

—JANET FRONKO

Up, Down, and Out

A coworker had a unique scheme to meet women. He'd call numbers at random from the phone book. If a man picked up, he apologized for dialing the "wrong" number.

But when a woman answered, he'd strike up a conversation. One day, the department manager overheard him bragging how he averaged two dates a week from this ploy. Was he fired? Did he receive a reprimand? No, he was named Director of Telemarketing.

—RICHARD REYNOLDS

Anytime companies merge, employees worry about layoffs. When the company I work for was bought, I was no exception. My fears seemed justified when a photo of the newly merged staff appeared on the company's website with the following words underneath:

"Updated daily."

—DIANNE STEVENS

@@@@@@@@@@@@@@@@@@@@@@@@@@@@@@@

The clinic where I work promoted a coworker to head the payroll department, or Payment Management Systems. The title on his door now reads **PMS Director.**

—MARILYN PEARSALL

When my boss asked for a computer diskette containing certain data, I took the opportunity to lobby for a raise. The diskette was empty except for the desired information. So, adhering to the eight-character limit, I changed the file name and called it "IncMyPay."

The diskette was returned with a note approving the data, but there was no comment on the file name or the likelihood of a raise. Days later, when I needed to update the file, I noticed the name had again been changed. It was now called "FatChanc."

—LARRY ROACH

Getting fired from my first "real" job wasn't fun, but it was quick. The sports-information director at the University of Kansas summoned me to his office. Without a trace of subtlety, he asked, "Pete, not counting today, how long have you been with us?"

—PETE ENICH

One of my first jobs was with a company that installed swimming pools. My boss called me into his office after a few days to tell me he appreciated my hard work. "As a reward, I'm going to give you a new company vehicle," he said.

At first I was in shock, and then my excitement grew as he talked about the independent front-wheel suspension, air conditioning and the color—cherry red. "This baby will really haul," he said. The next morning my boss drove up and unloaded my new set of wheels—a bright-red wheelbarrow.

—BILLY BABCOCK

@@@@@@@@@@@@@@@@@@@@@@@@@@@@

Nothing makes your clothes go out of fashion faster than getting a raise.

—*LOS ANGELES TIMES SYNDICATE*

I can't say my friend was heartbroken when her clueless coworker was let go. But she was confused when she saw her at her desk the next day and the day after that.

It all made sense when the "ex" colleague was overheard saying, "So I guess in two weeks, I have to quit."

—JOANNA THOMAS

The boss called an employee into his office. "Bob," he said, "you have been with the company for a year. You started in the mail room, one week later you were promoted to a sales position, and one month after that you were promoted to district manager of the sales department. Just four short months later, you were promoted to vice president. Now it's time for me to retire, and I want to make you the new president and CEO of the corporation. What do you say to that?"

"Thanks," said the employee.

"Thanks?" the boss replied. "Is that all you can say?"

"I guess not," the employee said. "Thanks, Dad."

—RON DENTINGER

Confiding in a coworker, I told her about a problem in our office and my fear that I would lose my job. She was concerned and said she would pray for me. I know she keeps a list of the ten people she believes need her prayers the most, so I asked if she had room for me on her list.

"Oh, yes," she replied. "Three of the people have died."

—KAYE GORDON

@@@@@@@@@@@@@@@@@@@@@@@@@@@

Just a few weeks after taking a job as a security guard, my husband announced that he'd been fired.

"What happened?" I asked. He explained that he'd fallen asleep at his desk and someone broke into the building.

"But you're a light sleeper," I said. "I'm surprised the sound of the guy breaking in didn't wake you up."

"I didn't get fired for falling asleep," he confessed. "I was fired for wearing my earplugs."

—ALBERTA J. , FROM CLASSIFIEDGUYS.COM

Shortly after Dad retired, my mother asked him, "What are you going to do today?"

"Nothing," he said.

"That's what you did yesterday."

"Yeah, but I wasn't finished."

—BEVERLY SHERMAN

Retirement is the best thing that has happened to my brother-in-law.

"I never know what day of the week it is," he gloated. "All I know is, the day the big paper comes, I have to dress up and go to church."

—DONALD REICHERT

I've been fired so many times, I sleep in a pink slip.

—TAYLOR NEGRON, *FIRED!* BY ANNABELLE GURWITCH (TOUCHSTONE)

A touching tribute to a waitress, spotted outside a local restaurant: **"RIP Sandy. We will miss you. Server needed."**

—JENNINE MURPHY

At a company retirement party for Richard, one of my husband's coworkers, the soon-to-be retiree took out a thick stack of notes for his farewell speech. Groans were heard throughout the room, as Richard was known for his verbosity. Moments later, however, Richard was greeted with a standing ovation when he smiled and slowly unfolded the wad of paper into a huge sign that read, "GOOD-BYE, TENSION. HELLO, PENSION."

—LAURA HAWKINS

Steve and Dave were laid off, so they went to the unemployment office. When asked his occupation, Steve replied, "I'm an underwear stitcher. I sew the elastic onto cotton panties."

The clerk looked up "underwear stitcher" and found it classified as unskilled labor. Steve would receive $300 a week in unemployment.

Then it was Dave's turn. When asked his occupation he said, "Diesel fitter." Since diesel fitter was skilled work, Dave would get $600—per week. When Steve found out, he stormed back into the office to complain. The clerk explained that Steve was an unskilled laborer, while Dave was a skilled worker. "Skilled?" said Steve, outraged. "What skill? I sew the elastic on the panties. Then he holds them up and says, 'Yup, diesel fitter.'"

—RICHARD A. WRIGHT

On arriving late to work, an employee was called to the supervisor's office.

"Mr. Morales, you're one of the most valuable employees who have ever worked for this company and, frankly, I don't know what we would do without you."

Timidly, the employee responded: "I'm pleased to hear that you think so highly of me, sir, but why did you call me in?"

"Because tomorrow we are going to find out."

—MARCOS ARAUJO

"Sorry Marcus . . . you've been demoted."

During her retirement party from the Cook County State's Attorney's office, coworkers told stories about my less-than-worldly mother. My favorite came from her supervisor, who recalled one of the first arrest reports Mom had created. Under "Offense," she'd typed, "Possession of cannibals."

—CATHY COTTER

My mother has tried her hand at several careers, some even concurrently. Imagine the surprise of both a hospital patient and my mom when the patient awoke after surgery and, upon seeing who her nurse's aide was, yelled, "What are you doing? You're the woman who helped me pick out interior paint colors!"

—DAN SMITH

@@@@@@@@@@@@@@@@@@@@@@@@@@@@@@

Workers usually get the ax for one pretty basic reason: They're not doing the work.

But as the job-search company Simply Hired discovered, reasons for terminating employment are not always that simple.

- I was fired from my job for eating leftover pizza from another department's meeting.

- My partner and I, security guards at a courthouse, were terminated for letting a woman ride on the conveyor belt through the x-ray machine at the front entrance.

- I was fired after I sent company data to someone named Michael Finn. Turns out, I was actually told to send it to "Microfilm."

In honor of my brother's retirement from the police force, my sister-in-law decided to throw a surprise party for him. Plans made in secrecy over a two-month period included catering and entertainment decisions as well as travel accommodations for over 100 friends and relatives from around the country. At the party, my brother stood up to address his guests. As he looked around the room at everyone who had secretly gathered on his behalf, he shook his head and said, "After 25 years on the police force, I finally know why I never made detective."

—LAWRENCE WRIGHT

Our coworker went missing for a few hours, and we tore up the place looking for him. The boss finally found him fast asleep. Rather than wake him, he quietly placed a note on the man's chest. **"As long as you're asleep," it read, "you have a job. But as soon as you wake up, you're fired."**

—KENNETH A. THOMAS

@@@@@@@@@@@@@@@@@@@@@@@@@@@@@@@

For many years I worked as a receptionist and switchboard operator at a busy company. After a good annual review, my supervisor told me I was up for a raise, pending approval of the vice president.

A month later, my supervisor called me into his office and told me the VP had refused to approve the salary hike. His reason? I clearly wasn't doing my job. Every time he saw me, I was either chatting with someone in the lobby or talking on the telephone.

—J. M. DUTZ

Boss: "I've decided to use humor in the workplace. Experts say humor eases tension, which is important in times when the work force is being trimmed. Knock-knock."

Employee: "Who's there?"

Boss: "Not you anymore."

—SCOTT ADAMS

Hey, things could be worse for you at the office! You could, for example, receive feedback like these comments, purported to be taken from actual federal-employee evaluations:

- "Since my last report, this employee has reached rock bottom and has started to dig."

- "Works well under constant supervision and when cornered like a rat in a trap."

- "Sets low personal standards and consistently fails to achieve them."

- "This employee is depriving a village somewhere of an idiot."

SMELTZER

"In other words, we'd like you to start thinking outside of another company's box."

The chairman of the board of our company called me into his office to tell me the good news: I was being promoted to Vice President of Corporate Research and Planning.

Of course I was excited, but that didn't stop me from asking for my new title to be changed to Vice President of Corporate Planning and Research.

"Why?" the chairman asked.

"Because," I said, "our organizational charts list names with abbreviated job titles, and I don't want to be known as Robert E. Reuter, VP of CRAP!"

—ROBERT E. REUTER

For more than an hour a scrawny guy sat at a bar staring into his glass. Suddenly a burly truck driver sat down next to him, grabbed the guy's drink and gulped it down. The poor little fellow burst out crying. "Oh, come on, pal," the trucker said. "I was just joking. Here, I'll buy you another."

"No, that's not it," the man blubbered. "This has been the worst day of my life. I was late for work and got fired. When I left the office I found that my car had been stolen, so I walked six miles home. Then I found my wife with another man, so I grabbed my wallet and came here. And just when I'm about to end it all," the guy said, sobbing, "you show up and drink my poison."

—PLAYBOY

The top ten signs your company is planning layoffs:

10. Company softball team downsized to chess team.

9. Dr. Kevorkian hired as a "transition consultant."

8. Pretty young women in marketing suddenly start to flirt with dorky personnel manager.

7. The beer of choice at company picnics is Old Milwaukee.

6. Giant yard sale in front of corporate headquarters.

5. Company president now driving a Hyundai.

4. Annual company holiday bash moved from Sheraton banquet room to abandoned Fotomat booth.

3. Employee discount days at Ammo Attic are discontinued.

2. Company dental plan now consists of pliers and string.

1. CEO frequently heard mumbling "Eeny, meeny, miney, mo" behind closed doors.

—PETER S. LANGSTON

@@@@@@@@@@@@@@@@@@@@@@@@@@@@

I quit my job at the helium gas factory. **I refuse to be spoken to in that tone.**

—COMIC STEWART FRANCIS

Only a few months before my father's retirement, the insurance company he worked for announced it would relocate to another state. He didn't want to move so late in his career, though, and the company was retaining ownership of the office building, so my father asked if he could stay on in some capacity.

The only available job, they told him, involved watering and caring for the building's many plants. Having little choice, my father trained with a horticulturist for a few weeks and then began his new work.

We worried about how Dad would cope with such a drastic change until he came home one day with new business cards. They read: "Raymond Gustafson, Plant Manager."

—ARLENE MORVAY

There are some predictable phases you go through after you lose a job. I know—I've been through more than half a dozen companies in the last 15 years. Here's what to expect:

- Stage one: I'll make a few phone calls and be working in no time.

- Stage two: None of these jobs in the paper are good enough for me. Now that I've stopped shaving, maybe I'll just stop bathing, too.

- Stage three: Geez, I'm not qualified for any of these jobs, but the house sure is clean.

- Stage four: Maybe I'll try a whole new career. I wonder who's on "Oprah" today? I've got to put something on my unemployment claim this week.

- Stage five: The capitalist running dogs want me to fight for their filthy money? I'm going to weave hats out of palm fronds and sell them on the beach. I won't participate in this sublimation of true human needs.

- Stage six: "You'll pay how much? Well, I've always enjoyed being part of a team!"

—MIKE SPITZ

The Powers That Be

Long, unproductive meetings are often the bane of corporate life. My very funny boss at the software company where I work has come up with what just might be the perfect way to cut business conferences short before they start rambling out of control.

There comes a time when he announces, "All those opposed to my plan say, 'I resign.' " End of meeting.

—BEVIN MATTHEWS

I bought a small sign at a novelty shop that read "I'm the Boss," and taped it to my office door. When I returned from lunch, there was a yellow Post-it note stuck to the sign. "Your wife called," it said. "She wants her sign back."

—KARL ZOLLINGER

On my first day of work at a fishing-supply company, my boss showed me many different types of lures. I asked him if the louder colors actually attracted fish. "I don't know about that," he said, "but they sure do attract the fishermen."

—FRIEDA WOODS

@@@@@@@@@@@@@@@@@@@@@@@@@@@@@@

Businessman to colleague, approaching company president's office: **"Remember to stay downwind from him. He can smell fear."**

—DAVE CARPENTER IN *THE WALL STREET JOURNAL*

I broke my collarbone in a skiing accident, so I was at home when a package arrived. It was a set of golf clubs that I had won from a sales contest at work. Excited, I phoned my boss to tell him about it. "Wonderful!" he said. "We'll have to go out soon and play a few rounds."

I told him I was looking forward to it, but that I wouldn't be able to play for several months because of my injury. "No, no, not with you," said my boss. "I was talking about your new clubs."

—MICHAEL D. PROCTOR

My boss was invited to be the principal speaker at a conference. He was told that he would have plenty of time for his talk, but that he had to finish by the noon lunch break. Unfortunately, the early speakers took longer than scheduled, and he didn't take the lectern until 11:45 a.m. "Well, now I know what principal means," he told the crowd. "It's what's left after the interest is gone."

—SHERRIE H. LILGE

To celebrate his 40th birthday, my boss, who is battling middle-age spread, bought a new convertible sports car. As a finishing touch, he put on a vanity plate with the inscription "18 Again."

The wind was let out of his sails, however, when a salesman entered our office the following week. "Hey," he called out, "who owns the car with the plate 'I ate again'?"

—CINDY GILLIS

@@@@@@@@@@@@@@@@@@@@@@@@@@@@@@

Just as our son was learning to walk, my wife brought him to the office. He staggered around awhile, then dropped to his hands and knees and took off at top speed toward the office of the company president. We grabbed him at the doorway, but not before he was noticed by a coworker. "You know," said the employee, turning to my wife, "His father goes into that office the very same way."

—ROBERT N. SORENSEN

Looking for the perfect boss? You won't find one here:

- At work today, I was making a profit-and-loss spreadsheet. "Great, we're in the red!" my boss shouted when he saw it. Then I pointed out that red was bad. "Oh," he said, "I always get those mixed up."

- We were doing icebreakers at a meeting and asked what everybody's favorite Beatles song was. My boss's answer? "Satisfaction." No one corrected him.

- At work today, I spilled a little ketchup on the corner of my suit jacket. My boss then squirted some of his ketchup on the other side so that it would match.

—PHIL EDWARDS AND MATT KRAFT, *DUMBEMPLOYED* (RUNNING PRESS)

"I've got good news and bad news," announced my boss as he came in to work. "The good news: I got the senior discount at the movie theater."

"What's the bad news?" I asked.

"I'm 52."

—PATRIC MCPOLAND

Resolving to surprise her husband, an executive's wife stopped by his office. She found him with his secretary sitting on his lap. Without hesitating, he dictated, "...and in conclusion, gentlemen, shortage or no shortage, I cannot continue to operate this office with just one chair."

—PHIL HARTMAN

Boss to subordinate: "Dan, you're my most valuable employee. Your ineptitude consistently raises the self-esteem of everyone you work with."

—RANDY GLASBERGEN

@@@@@@@@@@@@@@@@@@@@@@@@@@@@@

Boss: "I can assure you that the value of the average employee will continue to increase."

Employee: "That's because there will be fewer of us doing more work, right?"

Boss: "Right. Except for the 'us' part."

—SCOTT ADAMS

I work at a tire store, and one day my boss and I went out to run some errands. While sitting at a traffic light, we saw two young guys in sports cars loudly revving their engines. When the light turned green, they took off with their tires smoking and squealing. "Listen," my boss said, "they're playing our song."

—GARY L. LARSON

I have a reputation at work for being a strict boss. One day I was in the break room with another manager. I reached into the refrigerator for my lunch, which was packed in an Ace Hardware paper bag.

My coworker stopped mid-bite and stared at me, looking a little tense. When I pulled my sandwich out of the bag, he sighed in relief.

"What's the matter?" I asked him.

"Uh, nothing," he replied, "I was beginning to think you really do eat nails for lunch."

—AVIS S. ZABOROWSKI

Boss to secretary: "Who told you that just because I tried to kiss you at last month's Christmas Party, you could neglect your work around here?"

Secretary: **"My lawyer."**

—BILL NELSON

My boss mentioned that all our business travel was wearing him down. I said, "Einstein theorizes that as a body approaches the speed of light, it ages at a slower rate. So the more time you spend on jets, the slower you'll age."

"Interesting," my boss said pensively. "But did Einstein take into account airline food?"

—ALEX NEWMAN

I'd had enough of my employees' abusing their allotted break time. In an effort to clarify my position, I posted a sign on the bulletin board: "Starting immediately, your 15-minute breaks are being cut from a half-hour to 20 minutes."

—DON SNYDER

"It's simple, really. You're a team member when *you* want something. You're an employee when *I* want something."

@@@@@@@@@@@@@@@@@@@@@@@@@@@@@@@

To make a long story short, there's nothing like having the boss walk in.

—THE LION

One day my boss showed up for work in a new shirt from her recent trip to Wyoming. It had a picture of trees, a river and the silhouette of a mountain range. "Hey, look," a customer blurted out. "She's got the Grand Tetons on her chest!"

It was the first and last time we saw the shirt.

—DASHA HAGEN

Gail, a neighbor, wanted to buy her workaholic boss a special gift. Knowing that I create handcrafted items as a hobby, she came to me. I made a few suggestions, all of which she said weren't quite right.

Frustrated, Gail asked, "What do I get for a person who has no life?"

"How about a nice urn?" I replied.

—KENNY LEE SKY

A contest was held to find the dumbest things bosses have ever said. The winning—and true!—Dilbert-like entries were:

- "As of tomorrow, employees will only be able to access the building using individual security cards. Pictures will be taken next Wednesday and employees will receive their cards in two weeks."

- "What I need is a list of specific unknown problems we will encounter."

- "This project is so important, we can't let things that are more important interfere with it."

- "Teamwork is a lot of people doing what I say."

The miniature dartboard I received as a gift was housed in a beautiful oak case. I took it to work and showed my friends. Later in the day, my boss came and asked to see it. I proudly showed him the case, but soon discovered our secretaries had a surprise for me: they'd placed a photo of the boss right on the bull's-eye.

—RANDY WEECE

A boss is telling off an employee who has arrived late:

"It's not enough that you don't do your job properly, but you even allow yourself to be two hours late. If I were you, I wouldn't have bothered coming to work at all."

"That's you," retorts the employee, "but I have a sense of duty."

—PAVEL KRUGLOV

Finally, after years of testing business software, I landed my dream job—trying out computer games. My first day at work I was listing various ideas in a spreadsheet program when my manager walked by.

He looked at my screen for a moment, then said sternly, "I'd better not catch you using spreadsheets on company time when you know you should be playing games."

—JON BACH

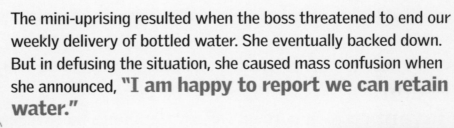

The mini-uprising resulted when the boss threatened to end our weekly delivery of bottled water. She eventually backed down. But in defusing the situation, she caused mass confusion when she announced, **"I am happy to report we can retain water."**

—ROBINETTE FLYGARE

QUOTABLE QUOTES

"No man goes before his time—unless the boss leaves early."

—GROUCHO MARX

"If you think your teacher is tough, wait until you get a boss. He doesn't have tenure."

—BILL GATES

"If you think your boss is stupid remember; you wouldn't have a job if he was smarter."

—ALBERT GRANT

"Do not underestimate your abilities. That is your boss's job."

—UNKNOWN

"I always try to go the extra mile at work, but my boss always finds me and brings me back."

—ANONYMOUS

"A boss creates fear, a leader confidence. A boss fixes blame, a leader corrects mistakes. A boss knows all, a leader asks questions. A boss makes work drudgery, a leader makes it interesting."

—RUSSELL H. EWING

"Accomplishing the impossible means only that the boss will add it to your regular duties."

—DOUG LARSON

"I don't want any yes-men around me. I want everyone to tell me the truth— even if it costs him his job."

—SAMUEL GOLDWYN

"It's for the boss. He's having a really bad day."

My wife, June, answers her boss's phone as part of her duties. One day his wife dialed his cell phone by accident. "Why didn't June pick up for you?" she asked her husband. "Be glad she didn't," June heard her boss reply. "You just dialed the phone I wear on my belt."

—DOUG MURRAY

@@@@@@@@@@@@@@@@@@@@@@@@@@@@@@

Supervisor to employee: "Don't think of me as the boss. Think of me as a coworker who's always right."

—*NEWSPAPER ENTERPRISE ASSOCIATION*

No matter how bad the situation, nothing at our school gets in the way of a day off. Case in point, this e-mail I received from our boss: "We will be out of the office Thursday and Friday," it stated. "Please hold all emergencies until Monday."

—CHRISSY CLARKE

Husband to wife: "Well, no, I didn't get the raise...but the boss pointed out a tax loophole I didn't know about!"

—DICK TURNER

As an executive vice president, my father was scheduled to meet with the board of directors of the large advertising agency where he worked. It was Thanksgiving eve, and he and my mother had exchanged numerous telephone calls all day to arrange for the arrival of family members from far away. Their plan finally set, Dad made his way to the meeting. Meanwhile, Mom had come up with a better plan. She called my dad at work, and insisted that his secretary deliver the message to him immediately. The secretary entered the boardroom and announced, "Excuse me, Mr. Harbert, but your wife just called with an urgent message. She said to tell you that she's figured out a new way to do it."

—RICHARD N. HARBERT

Did you hear about the Pepsi exec who got fired?

He tested positive for Coke.

PHILLIP REGULINSKI

When my boss returned to the office, he was told that everyone had been looking for him. That set him off on a speech about how indispensable he was to the company.

"Actually," interrupted his assistant, "you left with the key to the stationery closet."

—ALEC KAY

When my printer's type began to grow faint, I called a local repair shop where a friendly man informed me that the printer probably needed only to be cleaned. Because the store charged $50 for such cleanings, he told me, I might be better off reading the printer's manual and trying the job myself.

Pleasantly surprised by his candor, I asked, "Does your boss know that you discourage business?"

"Actually it's my boss's idea," the employee replied sheepishly. "We usually make more money on repairs if we let people try to fix things themselves first."

—MICHELLE R. ST. JAMES

Many employers motivate workers with bonuses. Some offer gym memberships. A few even supply day care for their working mothers and fathers. Our bosses go a step further. A sign posted in our break room read: "New Incentive Plan...Work or Get Fired!"

—SUSAN RHEA

My boss's tantrum climaxed with him falling out of his chair and hitting the floor. I rushed to his office, but was halted by his secretary. "If he's hurt," she said, "he'll call me in. If he isn't, he won't forgive you for finding him on the floor, and you'll be fired. If he's dead, what's your hurry?"

—BECQUET.COM

"We'll take a short break in case anyone needs to change their underwear."

@@@@@@@@@@@@@@@@@@@@@@@@@@@@@@

Management always needs to have the last word. Case in point: During a meeting at our financial consulting firm, a coworker was asked to guesstimate a realistic closing rate for the larger cases we were handling. "I'd have to say 20 percent," he answered. "No, no, no," interrupted my boss. "It's more like one in five."

—DAVID ARMSTRONG

"Do you believe in life after death?" the boss asked one of his younger employees.

"Yes, sir."

"Well, then, that makes everything just fine," the boss went on. "about an hour after you left yesterday to go to your grandfather's funeral, he stopped in to see you."

—DOROTHEA KENT

Expert Antics

BANANACO PROFITS

"Find a joy you like and you add five days to every week."

—H. JACKSON BROWN, JR.

@@@@@@@@@@@@@@@@@@@@@@@@@@@@@@@

Law and Order

I am a prosecuting attorney in a small Mississippi town and will admit to having a few extra pounds on me. Not long ago, I was questioning a witness in an armed robbery case. I asked, "Would you describe the person you saw?"

The witness replied, "He was kind of short and stout."

"You mean short and stout like me?" I asked.

"Oh, no," the witness said. "He wasn't that fat."

—WILLIAM E. GOODWIN

When I worked in the law library of the South Carolina attorney general's office, one of my duties was to handle subscriptions to various law journals. I usually printed the material carefully because I had a habit of crossing double t's so close to each other that they resembled an H.

On a particularly busy day, however, I filled out a subscription renewal form too quickly and mailed it in. A few weeks later, as I was sorting the mail, I came across the renewed publication, now addressed to "A Horney General's Office."

—RHONDA H. MCCRAY

I'm a police officer and occasionally park my cruiser in residential areas to watch for speeders. One Sunday morning I was staked out in a driveway, when I saw a large dog trot up to my car. He stopped and sat just out of arm's reach. No matter how much I tried to coax him to come for a pat on the head, he refused to budge.

After a while I decided to move to another location. I pulled out of the driveway, looked back and learned the reason for the dog's stubbornness. He quickly picked up the newspaper I had been parked on and dutifully ran back to his master.

—JEFF WALL

"But boss, when you said to apply for a *bailout,* I thought you meant for the company."

@@@@@@@@@@@@@@@@@@@@@@@@@@@@

Two lawyers walked into the office one Monday morning talking about their weekends. "I got a dog for my kids this weekend," said one.

The other attorney replied,
"Good trade."

—CHARLES M. NELMS

Our four-month-old son accompanied my wife and me to our attorney's office to sign some papers because we couldn't get a sitter. Unfortunately, it took longer to transact our business than we planned, and eventually the baby was screaming at the top of his lungs.

"Maybe we should close the door," my wife suggested, "so this noise won't bother your colleagues."

"Don't worry," our lawyer said. "They'll just think another client has received our bill."

—NARAYAN KULKARNI

My uncle testified at the trial of an organized-crime boss and then begged to be put into the witness-protection program. Instead, the FBI got him a job as a salesclerk at Kmart. It's been six months and no one's been able to find him.

—JAY TRACHMAN

I was eager to perform well in my new job as a receptionist at a law firm. One day a lawyer asked me to type up a letter that would be sent to the creditors of a man who had recently passed away. I was mortified, therefore, when soon after turning in the letter, I heard howling laughter from my boss's office. The beginning of the letter read, "To all known predators."

—JOANNA B. PARSONS

I was in juvenile court, prosecuting a teen suspected of burglary, when the judge asked everyone to stand and state his or her name and role for the court reporter.

"Leah Rauch, deputy prosecutor," I said.

"Linda Jones, probation officer."

"Sam Clark, public defender."

"John," said the teen who was on trial. "I'm the one who stole the truck."

—LEAH RAUCH

In my job as a legal secretary, I often review documents that list the allegations and responses from the defendant such as "admitted," "denied" or "have no knowledge or information to answer." One day my boss received a response from a defendant who apparently did not have the benefit of counsel. His written reply to the allegations? "Did not!"

—SHARON A. PETERSON

After making numerous calls to 911, a Lundar, Canada, man was warned that the next one would land him in jail. That prompted him to give his real reason for calling: "If you're coming to get me," he told the dispatcher, "can you bring me some smokes.

—WINNIPEG FREE PRESS

My son, a West Virginia state trooper, stopped a woman for going 15 miles over the speed limit. After he handed her a ticket, she asked him, "Don't you give out warnings?"

"Yes, ma'am," he replied. "They're all up and down the road. They say, **'Speed Limit 55.'"**

—PATRICIA GREENLEE

@@@@@@@@@@@@@@@@@@@@@@@@@@@@@

"**My car has been tipped over and rammed repeatedly. You don't know anything about this do you, Carl?**"

I'm a deputy sheriff and was parked near a motel, running radar checks, when a man approached my vehicle and asked for help. He complained that the volume on the television in the empty motel room next to his was so loud that he and his wife couldn't sleep. No one was in the motel office.

The man's wife was outside when I reached their door. That's when I got my idea. I asked her for their remote control, aimed it through the window of the empty room, and turned off the blaring TV.

—RAY ALLEN

@@@@@@@@@@@@@@@@@@@@@@@@@@@@@@

I was working the graveyard shift as a rookie police officer one night when my partner and I made a routine check at a high school that had suffered a recent rash of vandalism. Right away I noticed a window was open, so we climbed in to investigate.

We tried to be quiet as we made our way across the room in the dark, but our feet were sticking to the floor and making a squishy noise with every step. Finally when we got to the doorway, I flicked on the light. Looking back, I could easily make out our footprints on the freshly painted concrete floor. The window was open for ventilation, not vandalism.

—JEFFREY A. MOORE

As a state trooper, I drive a motor home to various weigh stations. It serves as our office on wheels while we conduct truck inspections. When the motor home is in reverse, it makes a repetitive beeping noise. One quiet morning I backed the unit out of its carport and stopped alongside my regular patrol car to retrieve something. As I walked toward the car, I heard the familiar beeping sound. My heart stopped as I turned, expecting to see the $80,000 vehicle backing itself down the driveway.

To my relief, the motor home was not moving. But at the top of a nearby tree sat a mockingbird perfectly mimicking the beep.

—JON LINDLEY

I glanced out my office window and saw that police had surrounded the motel across the road. A SWAT team had been dispatched, and people in the restaurant next door were being evacuated.

We soon learned that two armed suspects were holed up in the motel. I phoned my husband at work and described the unfolding drama. When I finished, my husband asked, "Did you call for anything special or just to chat?"

—VIVIAN J. HARTER

During an anti-harassment seminar at work, I asked, "What's the difference between harassment and good-natured teasing?" A coworker shouted, **"A million dollars."**

—MARK STEPHENSON

I picked up the phone one day in the law office where I worked, and the caller asked to speak with an attorney. I didn't recognize the voice, so I asked his name. He gave it to me, saying our office had just served him with divorce papers.

I couldn't place his name right away because this was a new case. Eager to talk, he blurted out, "I'm the despondent!"

—CAROLINE NIED

The mine operator called the nearby state prison and asked them to send over a safecracker to open his jammed safe. Soon, a convict and a prison guard showed up at the office. The inmate spun the dials, listened intently and calmly opened the safe door. "What do you figure I owe you?" asked the mine operator.

"Well," said the prisoner, "the last time I opened a safe, I got $25,000."

The sheriff's office in Alamance County, North Carolina, tried everything to stop people from using fake IDs to get a driver's license, but to no avail. Fed up, wrote the *News & Record* (Greensboro, North Carolina), one industrious sheriff's deputy concocted an ingenious plan, never before tried. He marched into the DMV waiting room and asked that everyone "with false IDs please step forward."

Six did.

—KATH YOUNG

I answered a 911 call at our emergency dispatch center from a woman who said her water broke.

"Stay calm," I advised. "Now, how far apart are your contractions?"

"No contractions," she said breathlessly. "But my basement is flooding fast."

—PAT HINTZ

When I stopped by his office, our company's security chief was laboring over a memo he was writing announcing a class about the proper use of cayenne pepper spray for personal self-defense.

"I need a good title," he said. "Something catchy that will get people's attention so they'll want to come."

I pondered for a moment and then said, "How about 'Assault and Pepper'?"

—BOB McFADDEN

My mother is on staff at the Department of Motor Vehicles, and one day a close friend of hers came in to apply for a driver's license. While entering the information into a computer, my mom noticed the woman had given 150 pounds as her weight.

Knowing she weighed considerably more, my mom commented, "You're putting down your weight as 150?"

"If a policeman pulls me over," her friend said with a grin, "that's the part of me he'll see."

—GINA BREMMER

When a Middletown, New Jersey, police officer retired, he cited low morale. But he didn't leave quietly. While walking the beat on his last day, he wrote 14 tickets for expired inspection stickers...all to police patrol cars.

—ASSOCIATED PRESS

@@@@@@@@@@@@@@@@@@@@@@@@@@@@@

Early in my career as a judge, I conducted hearings for those involuntarily committed to our state psychiatric hospital. On my first day, I asked a man at the door of the hospital, "Can you tell me where the courtroom is?"

"Why?" he asked.

"I'm the judge."

Pointing to the building, he whispered, "Don't tell them that. They'll never let you out."

—CHRISTOPHER DIETZ

My wife was raised in Sweden, yet speaks English without an accent. She does, however, sometimes confuse her idioms.

One day a man entered the law office where she works as a secretary. Using a Swedish phrase, but not quite translating it right, she asked, "May I help you take your clothes off?"

Startled by her remark, the man stepped back. Realizing what she had said and trying to put him at ease, she added, "It's okay, really. I'm Swedish."

—ROBERT E. ALEXANDER

When I worked for the security department of a large retail store, my duties included responding to fire and burglar alarms. A side door of the building was wired with a security alarm, because it was not supposed to be used by customers. Nevertheless they found the convenience of the exit tempting. Even a sign with large red letters warning "Alarm will sound if opened," failed to keep people from using it.

One day, after attending to a number of shrieking alarms, I placed a small handmade sign on the door that totally eliminated the problem: "Wet Paint."

—L. J. HINES-JOHNSON

@@@@@@@@@@@@@@@@@@@@@@@@@@@

The woman in front of me at the motor vehicles office was taking the eye test, first with her glasses on, then off. "Here's your license," the examiner said when she was done. "But there's a restriction. You need to wear glasses to drive your car."

"Honey," the woman declared, "I need them to find my car."

—NICOLE HAAKE

"Fine print doesn't work anymore— the reader can just change the font size."

@@@@@@@@@@@@@@@@@@@@@@@@@@@@@@

Executive behind desk to prospective employee: **"It's always cozy in here. We're insulated by layers of bureaucracy."**

—COTHAM IN *THE NEW YORKER*

Chris was sent to prison, and the warden made arrangements for him to learn a trade. In no time, Chris became known as one of the best carpenters in the area, and often got passes to do woodworking jobs for people in town.

When the warden started remodeling his kitchen, he called Chris into his office and asked him to build and install the cabinets and countertops. Chris refused.

"Gosh, I'd really like to help you," he said, "but counterfitting is what got me into prison in the first place."

An investment banker decides she needs in-house counsel, so she interviews a young lawyer.

"Mr. Peterson," she says. "Would you say you're honest?"

"Honest?" replies Peterson. "Let me tell you something about honesty. My father lent me $85,000 for my education, and I paid back every penny the minute I tried my first case."

"Impressive. And what sort of case was that?"

"Dad sued me for the money."

—DEE HUDSON

While working as a corrections officer at a maximum–security prison, I was assigned to the guest area one day to monitor the inmates and their visitors.

I received a call from the reception desk, and was told there was a cab out front, probably waiting for one of the visitors.

Sticking my head into the room, I announced, "Did anyone call for a cab?"

About 40 inmates immediately raised their hands.

—JANET E. HUMPHREY

@@@@@@@@@@@@@@@@@@@@@@@@@@@

The fist knocking on the door belonged to a cop. Bracing for the worst, my husband, who was working on a job site, opened up.

"Is that yours?" asked the officer, pointing to a company van that was jutting out into the narrow street.

"Uhh, yes, it is," said my husband.

"Would you mind moving it?" asked the officer. "We've set up a speed trap and the van's causing everyone to slow down."

—JUNE STILL

I am a deputy sheriff assigned to courthouse security. As part of my job, I explain court procedures to visitors. One day I was showing a group of ninth graders around. Court was in recess and only the clerk and a young man in custody wearing handcuffs were in the courtroom.

"This is where the judge sits," I began, pointing to the bench. "The lawyers sit at these tables. The court clerk sits over there. The court recorder, or stenographer, sits over here. Near the judge is the witness stand and over there is where the jury sits.

"As you can see," I finished, "there are a lot of people involved in making this system work."

At that point, the prisoner raised his cuffed hands and said, "Yeah, but I'm the one who makes it all happen."

—MICHAEL MCPHERSON

Our community still has teenage curfew laws. One night I was listening to my scanner when the police dispatcher said, "We have a report of a 14-year-old male out after curfew. The subject, wearing jeans and a gray sweatshirt, is six-foot-four and weighs 265 pounds." After a long pause, one of the patrols replied, **"As far as I'm concerned, he can go anywhere he wants."**

—JAMES VAN HORN

@@@@@@@@@@@@@@@@@@@@@@@@@@@@@

Hired by a bank as a personal trainer, I was supposed to make fitness a part of the workday routine. During one session, I told my students to lean against the bank lobby's walls and instructed them on how to stretch their hamstrings. A short time later I was shocked when several policemen stormed through the doors. A passerby had seen the people facing the wall and assumed I was robbing the bank.

—SYLVIA DOUGHART-WOOD

What's Up, Doc?

I was working as an interpreter at a hospital when I found myself in the middle of an odd conversation. The doctor warned his patient, "By drinking and smoking as much as you do, you're killing yourself slowly."

The patient just nodded. "That's OK. I'm not in any hurry."

—SALMA SAMMAKIA,

As I performed a simple medical procedure on my patient, I warned her, "After this, you can't have sex for at least three days."

"Did you hear that?" she asked her husband. "No sex for three days."

"I heard," he said. "But she was speaking to you."

—KATHLEEN HOWELL

When my daughter was home during college break, she came in for an eye exam at the optometrist's office that I manage. I gave her some paperwork to fill out, and had to laugh when I read what she had written under method of payment: **"My mom."**

—SHIRLEY KUDRNA

@@@@@@@@@@@@@@@@@@@@@@@@@@@@@@

A man walked into our medical practice complaining that he was in agony.

"Where exactly is the pain?" asked his doctor.

"Near my ovaries," he moaned.

"You don't have ovaries."

The patient looked confused. "When were they removed?"

—KELLI EAST

My nursing colleague was preparing an intravenous line for a 15-year-old male patient. The bedside phone rang, and the boy's mother reached over to pick it up.

After talking for a few minutes, the mother held the phone aside, turned to her son and said, "Your dad is asking if you've got any cute nurses."

The boy gazed at the nurse, who had the needle poised above his arm, ready for insertion.

"Tell him," he replied, "they're absolutely gorgeous."

—MATTHEW HUTCHINSON

My mother and I were at the hospital awaiting some test results when several firemen were wheeled into the emergency room on stretchers. One young man was placed in the cubicle next to us. A hospital employee began to ask him questions so she could fill out the necessary paper work. When he was asked his phone number, we had to laugh. His reply? "911."

—VICTORIA VELASCO

My 60-year-old mother-in-law, completing two years of wearing orthodontic braces, was in the office having them adjusted. As she sat in one of the waiting-room chairs, the teenager next to her looked at my mother-in-law in astonishment.

"Wow," he said. "How long have you been coming here?"

—DAVID REEVES

"Don't you hate it when there are parts left over?"

As a doctor I receive calls at all hours of the day. One night a man phoned and said, "I'm sorry to bother you so late, Doc, but I think my wife has appendicitis."

Still half asleep I reminded him that I had taken his wife's inflamed appendix out a couple of years before. "Whoever heard of a second appendix?" I asked.

"You may not have heard of a second appendix, Doc, but surely you've heard of a second wife," he replied.

—JAMES KARURI MUCHIRI

@@@@@@@@@@@@@@@@@@@@@@@@@@@@@@

I'm an obstetrics nurse at a large city hospital, where our patients are from many different countries and cultures.

One day while waiting for a new mother to be transferred to our division, I checked the chart and assumed that, because of her last name, she was of European descent. So when she was finally wheeled in, I was surprised to see that she was Asian.

As I was performing the exam, we chatted and she told me she was Chinese and her husband's ethnic heritage was Czech. After a short pause she quipped, "I guess that makes my children Chinese Czechers!"

—LISA M. EDGEHOUSE

While I sat in the reception area of my doctor's office, a woman rolled an elderly man in a wheelchair into the room. As she went to the receptionist's desk, the man sat there, alone and silent.

Just as I was thinking I should make small talk with him, a little boy slipped off his mother's lap and walked over to the wheelchair. Placing his hand on the man's, he said, "I know how you feel. My mom makes me ride in the stroller, too."

—STEVE ANDERSON

I hate the idea of going under the knife. So I was very upset when the doctor told me I needed a tonsillectomy. Later, the nurse and I were filling out an admission form. I tried to respond to the questions, but I was so nervous I couldn't speak.

The nurse put down the form, took my hands in hers, and said, "Don't worry. This medical problem can easily be fixed, and it's not a dangerous procedure."

"You're right. I'm being silly," I said, feeling relieved. "Please continue."

"Good. Now," the nurse went on, "do you have a living will?"

—EDWARD LEE GRIFFIN

@@@@@@@@@@@@@@@@@@@@@@@@@@@@@

Overheard outside my medical office—one woman complaining to another: **"My doctor says I have masculine degeneration and that I'll just have to live with it."**

—NANCY K. KNIGHT

My dentist's office was in the midst of renovation when I arrived for a checkup. As the hygienist led me to a room, I could hear the sound of hammering and sawing coming from next door. "It must really scare your patients to hear that when they're in the dentist's chair," I remarked.

"That's nothing," she said. "You should see what happens when they hear the jackhammer."

—CHUCK ROTHMAN

At the outpatient surgery center where I worked, the anesthesiologist often chatted with patients before their operations to help them relax. One day he thought he recognized a woman as a coworker at the VA hospital where he had trained. When the patient confirmed that his hunch was correct, he said, "So, tell me, is the food still as bad there as it used to be?"

"Well," she replied, "I'm still cooking it."

—SHEILA HOWARD

A man walks into a cardiologist's office.
Man: "Excuse me. Can you help me? I think I'm a moth."
Doctor: "You don't need a cardiologist. You need a psychiatrist."
Man: "Yes, I know."
Doctor: "So why'd you come in here if you need a psychiatrist?"
Man: "Well, the light was on."

—HEATHER BORSDOR

@@@@@@@@@@@@@@@@@@@@@@@@@@@@@@

On the job as a dental receptionist, I answered the phone and noticed on the caller-ID screen that the incoming call was from an auto-repair shop.

The man on the line begged to see the dentist because of a painful tooth.

"Which side of your mouth hurts?" I asked the patient.

He sighed and answered, "The passenger side."

—CHERYL PACE SATTERWHITE

I was working with a doctor as he explained to his patient and her concerned husband what would happen during and after her upcoming surgery. Then the doctor asked if there were any questions.

"I have one," said the husband. "How long before she can resume housework?"

—JONATHAN JACOB

My father is a successful cardiologist, but his busy practice and long hours left my mother with a lot of spare time. So she decided to become a substitute teacher.

At the end of her first month on the job, she bought my father a new watch. "Honey, I just spent my whole month's salary on a gift for you," she said. "It's now your turn to do the same."

—RAHUL TONGIA

The husband of one of our obstetrics patients phoned the doctor to ask if it would be okay to make love to his wife while he was taking medication for an infected foot.

"Yes, that's fine," the doctor replied. **"Just don't use your foot."**

—SABRINA HENDERSON

@@@@@@@@@@@@@@@@@@@@@@@@@@@@@@

While visiting my mother in the hospital, I stopped in the cafeteria for breakfast. I set a piece of bread on the moving toaster rack and waited for it to pass under the heated coils and return golden brown. Instead, it got stuck at the back of the toaster and I couldn't reach it. The woman next in line quickly seized a pair of tongs, reached in and fished out the piece of toast. "You must be an emergency worker," I joked.

"No," she replied with a grin. **"I'm an obstetrician."**

—BECKY LEIDNER

My husband, a doctor, received an emergency call from a patient: She had a fly in her ear. He suggested an old folk remedy. "Pour warm olive oil in your ear and lie down for a couple of minutes," he said. "When you lift your head, the fly should emerge with the liquid."

The patient thought that sounded like a good idea. But she had one question: "Which ear should I put the oil in?"

—BELINDA HIBBERT

A harried man runs into his physician's office. "Doctor! Doctor! My wife's in labor! But she keeps screaming, 'Shouldn't, couldn't, wouldn't, can't!'"

"Oh, that's okay," says the doctor. "She's just having contractions."

—DONNA WINSTON

Just because one owns a business doesn't mean it has to be all business. This sign in a dentist's office proves that point: "Be True to Your Teeth, or They Will Be False to You."

—JAMES WERTZ

@@@@@@@@@@@@@@@@@@@@@@@@@@@@@@@@@

The doctor is called late at night to a woman in labor. He goes into the room and closes the door. After a while he calls out. "Could I have some pliers, a screwdriver, and a hammer, please."

Turning deadly pale, the husband cries out, "For God's sake, what are you doing?"

"Take it easy, I'm only trying to open my bag."

—BOGNÁR JÁRFÁS

The patient who came to my radiology office for abdominal X-rays was already heavily sedated. But I still had to ask her a lot of questions, the last one being, "Ma'am, where is your pain right now?"

Through her medicated fog, she answered, "He's at work."

—JEFF DOTY

In our pediatric office, I answered the phone to hear a frantic parent say she was at a Chinese restaurant, and her son had gotten a piece of paper lodged in his nostril.

They came over, and the doctor examined the boy. When the exam-room door opened, the doctor was holding the fortune from the child's cookie. It read "You will prosper in medical research."

—KERRI PACE JACKSON

Exasperated with obnoxious patients in the clinic where she's the office manager, my aunt put up a sign that read: "If you are grouchy, irritable, or just plain mean, there will be a $10 surcharge for putting up with you."

Clearly some people took the sign to heart. That same afternoon a patient came to her window and announced, "The doctor said he would like to see me every month for the next six months, so I'm going to pay all my $60 up front."

—JUSTINE A. BACARISAS

@@@@@@@@@@@@@@@@@@@@@@@@@@@@

The doctor's office was crowded as usual, but the doctor was moving at his usual snail's pace. After waiting two hours, an old man slowly stood up and started walking toward the door.

"Where are you going?" the receptionist called out.

"Well," he said, "I figured I'd go home and die a natural death."

—SIMON BJERKE

Paying my bill at the doctor's office, I noticed one of the clerks licking and sealing a large stack of envelopes. Two coworkers were trying to persuade her to use a damp sponge instead. One woman explained that she could get a paper cut. Another suggested that the glue might make her sick. Still, the clerk insisted on doing it her own way.

As I was leaving, I mentioned to the clerk that there was a tenth of a calorie in the glue of one envelope. Then I saw her frantically rummaging around for the sponge.

—DOROTHY MCDANIEL

One afternoon a very preoccupied looking young woman got on my bus. About 15 minutes into the ride, she blurted out, "Oh, my gosh, I think I'm on the wrong bus line."

I dropped her at the next stop and gave her directions to the right bus. "I don't know where my mind is today. I must have left it at work," she apologized.

Just before she got off, I noticed she was wearing an ID card from an area hospital. "Are you a nurse?" I asked.

"Oh, no," she said. "I'm a brain surgeon."

—RACHELLE ROCK

@@@@@@@@@@@@@@@@@@@@@@@@@@@@@@

Even though it was warm outside, the heat was on full blast in my office at the hospital. So I asked our nursing unit secretary to get someone to fix it. This was a one-man job, so I could not figure out why two guys showed up—until I was handed the maintenance request form. It read: "Head nurse is hot."

—CAROLYN HOUSE

While taking a patient's medical history, I asked if anyone in her family had ever had cancer.

"Yes," she said. "My grandmother."

"Where did she have it?"

"In Kansas."

—DIXIE LEGGETT

Our crew at an ambulance company works 24-hour shifts. The sleeping quarters consist of a large room with several single beds, so we get to know one another's habits, like who snores or talks in their sleep.

While I was having my teeth examined by a dentist one day, he noticed that some of my teeth were chipped. "It looks like you clench your jaw at night," he said.

"No way," I blurted without thinking. "No one has ever said I grind my teeth, and I sleep with a lot of people!"

—KELLY WILSON

A man walks into a psychiatrist's office.

"Doc, every time I see nickels, dimes, and quarters, I have a panic attack! What can my problem be?"

"Oh, that's easy," the doctor answers. **"You're just afraid of change."**

—WAYNE BENNETT

@@@@@@@@@@@@@@@@@@@@@@@@@@@@@@

Time is a great healer. **That's why they make you wait so long in the doctor's office.**

—RON DENTINGER

Last Valentine's Day, I arrived at the doctor's office where I work as a receptionist to find a mystery man pacing up and down holding a package. As I got out of the car, he declared warmly, "I have something for you." I excitedly ripped open the bundle. It was a urine sample.

—HEATHER BOYD

Every so often I'd challenge a father visiting his newborn in the nursery, where I was a nurse, to guess his baby's weight. Few even came close, but one dad picked up his son, hefted him in his hands, and gave me the precise weight, right down to the ounces.

"That was amazing," I told him.

"Not really," he replied. "I do this all the time. I'm a butcher."

—NOLA FARIA

It was a busy day in the doctor's office where I worked, and I was on the phone trying to arrange a patient's appointment. Needing her daytime phone number, I hurriedly asked, "May I have a number between eight and five, please?"

After a moment came the timid response, "Six?"

—DEBORAH SIMONS

We were helping customers when the store optometrist walked by and smiled at a coworker. Of course, we all had to stop what we were doing to tease her. But she quickly dismissed the notion of a budding romance. "Can you imagine making out with an optometrist?" she asked. "It would always be, 'Better like this, or like this?'"

—JESS WEDLOCK

@@@@@@@@@@@@@@@@@@@@@@@@@@@@@@@@

Nothing seemed out of the ordinary when a patient's file arrived at our clerk's office in the hospital—nothing, that is, until I read the doctor's orders. He had written, "Chest pain every shift, with assistance if necessary."

—PARR YOUNG

When a patient was wheeled into our emergency room, I was the nurse on duty. "On a scale of zero to ten," I asked her, "with zero representing no pain and ten representing excruciating pain, what would you say your pain level is now?"

She shook her head. "Oh, I don't know. I'm not good with math."

—DON ANDREWS, RN

While I was on duty at a Los Angeles-area hospital as a registered nurse, a man arrived in an ambulance, accompanied by his wife and a neighbor. "I'm worried about my husband," I overheard the wife say to her friend. "Since we just moved here, I know nothing about this hospital."

"Don't worry," her neighbor replied. "The doctors and nurses here are excellent. I should know—this is where my husband died."

—MARGARET A. FRICE

Jack was depressed when he got back from the doctor's office. "What's the matter?" his wife asked.

"The doctor says I have to take one of these white pills every day for the rest of my life."

"And what's so bad about that?"

"He only gave me seven."

—ROTARY DOWN UNDER

@@@@@@@@@@@@@@@@@@@@@@@@@@@@@@

My ten-year-old son Andrew and I were waiting in a dentist's office, talking about treatments for his painful tooth. Entering the room, the dentist asked, "Well, Andrew, which one's the troublemaker?" Without hesitation Andrew replied, "My brother."

—BELINDA SMITH

One day after a heavy snowfall, this announcement appeared on the bulletin board in the nurse's lounge of my local hospital: "Student nurses will please refrain from ever again using this institution's sterile bedpans for makeshift snow sleds."

—JILL MARIE BONNIER

Employed as a dental receptionist, I was on duty when an extremely nervous patient came for root-canal surgery. He was brought into the examining room and made comfortable in the reclining dental chair. The dentist then injected a numbing agent around the patient's tooth, and left the room for a few minutes while the medication took hold.

When the dentist returned, the patient was standing next to a tray of dental equipment.

"What are you doing by the surgical instruments?" asked the surprised dentist.

Focused on his task, the patient replied, "I'm taking out the ones I don't like."

—DR. PAULA FONTAINE

One day while at the doctor's office, the receptionist called me to the desk to update my personal file. Before I had a chance to tell her that all the information she had was still correct, she asked, **"Has your birth date changed?"**

—MARGARET FREESE

@@@@@@@@@@@@@@@@@@@@@@@@@@@@@@@

Seen on a car parked outside a gynecologist's office: **PUUUSH.**

—CAROLE GROMADZKI

After practicing law for several months, I was talking with my brother, John, a doctor. "My work is so exciting," I said. "People come into my office, tell me their problems and pay me for my advice."

As older brother will, John took the upper hand. "You know," he said, "in my work, people come into my office, tell me their problems, take off all their clothes and then pay me for my advice."

—DAVID PAUL REUWER

While working as a radiologic technologist in a hospital emergency room, I took X-rays of a trauma patient. I brought the films to our radiologist, who studied the multiple fractures of the femurs and pelvis.

"What happened to this patient?" he asked in astonishment.

"He fell out of a tree," I reported.

The radiologist wanted to know what the patient was doing up a tree. "I'm not sure, but his paperwork states he works for Asplundh Tree Experts."

Gazing intently at the X-rays, the radiologist blinked and said, "Cross out 'Experts.'"

—GENIEVE MARKOVCI

It took me forever to wake up one of my nursing home patients. But after much poking, prodding, and wrangling, he finally sat up and fixed his twinkling blue eyes on my face. "

My, you're pretty!" he said. "Have I asked you to marry me yet?"

"No, you haven't," I gushed.

"Good. Because I couldn't put up with this every morning."

—DIANE WITLOX

Airport Hijinks

"**W**hat's the difference between an optimist and a pessimist?" I asked my husband. He thought for a minute before responding, "An optimist is the guy who created the airplane. A pessimist is the guy who created the parachute."

—SUZAN WIENER

@@@@@@@@@@@@@@@@@@@@@@@@@@@@@@

On a late Sunday night flight from Sydney to Brisbane, most passengers looked tired, harassed, and desperate to get off the plane. So did the cabin crew. As we were taxiing to the terminal, the steward started his spiel about remaining in your seats until the plane came to a standstill. He ended with, "Thank you for flying with us and be careful when opening the overhead toilets, which may have moved during the flight."

—GLENDA FORKNALL

After setting off the alarms at airport security, I was escorted behind a curtain. As two female officials "wanded" me, the senior officer gave instructions to the trainee on proper technique: first down the front of my body, then up the back of me, and—much to my embarrassment—up between my legs.

After she was done, her boss congratulated her. "Great job," she said. "Now do it again. But this time, try turning on the wand."

—VICTORIA RADFORD

A helicopter loses power over a remote Scottish island and makes an emergency landing. Luckily, there's a cottage nearby, so the pilot knocks on the door. "Is there a mechanic in the area?" he asks the woman who answers.

She thinks for a minute. "No, but we do have a McArdle and a McKay."

En route to Hawaii, I noticed one of my passengers in the coach section of the airplane dialing her cell phone. "Excuse me. That can't be on during the flight," I reminded her. "Besides, we're over the ocean—you won't get a signal out here."

"That's okay," she said. "I'm just calling my daughter. She's sitting up in first class."

—DAWN CALLAHAN

@@@@@@@@@@@@@@@@@@@@@@@@@@@@@

I wouldn't want to fly Virgin. **Who'd want to fly an airline that doesn't go all the way?**

—ADAM J. SMARGON

As an airline reservation agent, I took a call from a man who wanted to book a flight for two but wasn't happy with the price of $59 per ticket. "I want the $49 fare I saw advertised," he insisted, saying he would accept a flight at any time.

I managed to find two seats on a 6 a.m. flight. "I'll take it," he said, then worried that his wife might not like the early hour.

I warned there was a $25 fee per person if he changed the reservation. "Oh, that's no problem," he said dismissively. "What's fifty bucks?"

—ANNA ZOGG

When I worked in airline reservations, we had an executive desk, which did bookings for corporate clients during the day. One evening the phone rang and rang. Finally our supervisor picked it up and said in a monotone, "We are open from 8 a.m. to 5 p.m. Please call back then."

A voice on the other end asked, "Is this a recording?"

Without thinking, my boss replied, "Yes, it is."

—ANNETTE MURRAY

As a flight attendant for a commuter airline, I constantly struggle to keep people seated until the aircraft has come to a complete stop at the gate. So one day, after making the standard announcement, I added, "Those of you who would like to stay and assist me in cleaning up the cabin, please volunteer by standing up before the seat-belt sign is turned off." No one moved—and my solution has worked ever since.

—MARIE WHITEIS

@@@@@@@@@@@@@@@@@@@@@@@@@@@@@@

Working as a secretary at an international airport, my sister had an office adjacent to the room where security temporarily holds suspects.

One day, security officers were questioning a man when they were suddenly called away on another emergency. To the horror of my sister and her colleagues, the man was left alone in the unlocked room. After a few minutes, the door opened and he began to walk out. Summoning up her courage, one of the secretaries barked, "Get back in there, and don't you come out until you're told!"

The man scuttled back inside and slammed the door. When the security people returned, the women reported what had happened.

Without a word, an officer walked into the room and released one very frightened telephone repairman.

—RUSS PERMAN

Plane Ridiculous

With airlines adding fees to fees, The Week *magazine asked its readers to predict the next surcharge they'll levy for something previously free.*

- In the unlikely event of loss of cabin pressure, oxygen masks will drop down. To start the flow of oxygen, simply insert your credit card.

- $100 On-Time Departure Fee; $25 Delay-Complaint Fee

- View seating (formerly window seats), $10; Access seating (formerly aisle seats), $10

- $20 to use roll-away stairs to enter or exit the aircraft in lieu of no-charge rope-ladder alternative

- $9 fee for bumping your head on the overhead bin as you take your seat; $3 additional penalty for looking up at the bin after you bump into it

@@@@@@@@@@@@@@@@@@@@@@@@@@@@@

The flight attendant will always tell you the name of your pilot. **Like anyone goes, "Oh, he's good. I like his work."**

—DAVID SPADE

I'm a captain with a major airline, and I routinely monitor the flight attendants' announcements while taxiing to the gate. Impatient passengers often stand up and attempt to dash forward before we arrive. Once, instead of the usual terse voice reminding people to remain in their seats, I heard the attendant declare, "In the history of our airline, no passenger has ever beaten the aircraft to the gate. So, ladies and gentlemen, please remain seated."

—JOE CONFORTI

My father's colleague was on a company plane when, immediately after takeoff, a wheel fell off. The pilot did not want to land with a full fuel tank, so he circled through some heavy turbulence. When he finally touched down, he managed to tilt the plane, balancing it on only two tires until it had almost stopped.

As the pilot came out of the cabin to see if everyone was all right, the passengers noticed his name tag. It read "Bond."

—ILA COLTAS

During a business trip to Boeing's Everett, Wash., factory, I noticed several 747 and 777 airliners being assembled.

Before the engines were installed, huge weights were hung from the wings to keep the planes balanced. The solid-steel weights were bright yellow and marked "14,000 lbs."

But what I found particularly interesting was some stenciling I discovered on the side of each weight. Imprinted there was the warning: "Remove before flight."

—KEVIN N. HAW

@@@@@@@@@@@@@@@@@@@@@@@@@@@@@

My wife, a flight attendant for a major airline, watched one day as a passenger overloaded with bags tried to stuff his belongings in the overhead bin of the plane. Finally, she informed him that he would have to check the oversized luggage.

"When I fly other airlines," he said irritably, "I don't have this problem."

My wife smiled and replied, "When you fly other airlines, I don't have this problem either."

—JOE CONFORTI

Sales and Service Slip-ups

I took a part-time job as an opinion-poll sampler, calling people for their views on various issues. On my very first call, I introduced myself, "Hello, this is a telephone poll." The man replied, "Yeah, and this is a street light!"

—ANDY GOLAN

Working for a florist, I took a call from a woman who spoke to me over a very crackly cell phone. She wanted to send a wreath to a friend's funeral, but I couldn't make out what message she wanted to accompany the flowers. Finally, I just had to interrupt her. "It's a bad line," I said over the din. There was a slight pause before she said, "Well, can you think of something better to say?"

—IVOR EDWARDS

A customer who bought a book from me through amazon.com left a poor rating. The reason: "The book was dated."

The title of the book was Victorian Fancy Stitchery.

—MOIRA ALLEN

@@@@@@@@@@@@@@@@@@@@@@@@@@@@

Even though telemarketers are slightly less beloved than dentists and tax auditors, that's the job my friend took during his summer vacation. Halfway through one of his sales pitches, he heard a clicking at the other end of the line. Thinking the man may have hung up, he asked, "Are you still there?"

"Yeah, still here," said the man.

"Sorry, I heard a click and I thought you'd been disconnected."

"No," the man said, "that would sound more like this." He then proceeded to show me what it would sound like by slamming down the phone.

—TRAVIS JAMES

My wife, a real estate agent, wrote an ad for a house she was listing. The house had a second-floor suite that could be accessed using a lift chair that slid along the staircase. Quickly describing this feature, she inadvertently made it sound even more attractive: "Mother-in-law suite comes with an electric chair."

—MICHAEL KIMMIT

Two salesmen, Joe and Mike, were stranded by a winter storm and took refuge in an old farmhouse occupied by an attractive single woman. In the middle of the night, Joe heard Mike sneak out of bed and into the woman's room. Joe said nothing about it until nine months later when a registered letter arrived at his office. Clutching the letter, he walked into Mike's office. "Do you remember the night we were stranded by that snowstorm and you sneaked out of your room to be with that woman?" he asked.

"Yes," Mike replied.

"You told her you were me, didn't you?" Joe demanded.

"Yes, I did," Mike said nervously. "Why do you ask?"

"Because," Joe replied, "she just died and left me a fortune!"

—ALICE L. SMITH

My daughter and her husband were with us on vacation in Las Vegas, staying in a posh new hotel. As we were lounging by the pool, my son-in-law, whose company builds homes in the Phoenix area, used his cell phone to try to reach his salesmen.

After several unsuccessful attempts, he called his office. "Tell me something," we heard him say. "Am I the only one working today?"

—PAUL JENNINGS

@@@@@@@@@@@@@@@@@@@@@@@@@@@

Dearth of a Salesman

Corporate America lives and dies on the back of its sales force.
Based on the following stories, some companies are DOA:

- "We had a salesman who visited monthly and told me stories of his drunken escapades. After six months, I told him I was a Mormon and didn't care for them. He apologized and then joked, 'So how many wives you got?'"

- "A salesman spelled my name wrong in his presentation. It's Smith."

- "The all-male ad-agency team told my female marketing team that they understood tampons better than us."

—JIM NICHOLS

Trying to sell ads for my high school yearbook, I approached my father, who owned a house painting business with my two brothers. My father agreed to purchase an ad and said I should ask my brother Jack to write it.

"We're too busy now!" Jack protested. "If we run an ad, we'll just get more work."

"Jack," I replied, "Dad said you have to write the ad."

The next morning, Jack handed me his copy. It read, "John J. Pitlyk & Sons, Painting Contractors. For easy work, call the sons. If it's hard, call Pop."

—JOAN PITLYK

The restaurant we had lunch in is one business that knows how to handle dissatisfied customers. On the wall was an open bear trap and this sign: **"To Register Complaint, Push Button."**

—MARK VELEZ

@@@@@@@@@@@@@@@@@@@@@@@@@@@@@

Seen in a John Deere sales office: **"The only machine we don't stand behind is our manure spreader."**

—NORMAN HAUGLID

A sales representative stops at a small manufacturing plant in the Midwest. He presents a box of cigars to the manager as a gift. "No, thanks," says the plant manager. "I tried smoking a cigar once and I didn't like it."

The sales rep shows his display case and then, hoping to clinch a sale, offers to take the manager out for martinis. "No, thanks," the plant manager replies. "I tried alcohol once, but didn't like it."

Then the salesman glances out the office window and sees a golf course. "I suppose you play golf," says the salesman. "I'd like to invite you to be a guest at my club."

"No, thanks," the manager says. "I played golf once, but I didn't like it." Just then a young man enters the office. "Let me introduce my son, Bill," says the plant manager.

"Let me guess," the salesman replies. "An only child?"

My father is a skilled CPA who is not great at self-promotion. So when an advertising salesman offered to put my father's business placard in the shopping carts of a supermarket, my dad jumped at the chance. Fully a year went by before we got a call that could be traced to those placards.

"Richard Larson, CPA?" the caller asked.

"That's right," my father answered. "May I help you?"

"Yes," the voice said. "One of your shopping carts is in my yard and I want you to come and get it."

—MATTHEW LARSON

@@@@@@@@@@@@@@@@@@@@@@@@@@@

Tech Talk

The company I work for boasts a high-tech check-in system that enables our staff to monitor who is, and isn't, in the office. Recently I asked a secretary if a particular supervisor was in. She agreed to find out, and left the room. When she returned a few moments later, I asked her if she had been using the new system to see if he was clocked in.

"No," she replied. "I was looking out the window to see if his car is here."

—BILL WILLIAMS

Now that my mother's office has a fax machine, I fax my correspondence to her instead of using the post office. Although I've told her many times that it's a faster and less expensive way to communicate, she continued to mail me weekly letters.

On my last birthday, however, she showed that she now has a full grasp of technology. She faxed me a $100 bill with the note: "Happy Birthday. You're right—it is cheaper to fax than mail. Love, Mom."

—SUSAN REILLY

In the office where I work, there is a constant battle between our technical-support director and customer-service personnel over the room temperature, which is usually too low.

The frustrated director, trying to get us to understand his position, announced one afternoon, "We need to keep the temperature below seventy-five degrees or the computers will overheat."

Thinking that this was just another excuse, one of my shivering colleagues retorted, "Yeah, right. So how did they keep the computers from overheating before there was air conditioning?"

—HEIDI DYSARD

> **"It's not personal, Carlyle. I just downloaded a new phone app that will replace you."**

During a lecture on the influence of media on teens, a typo in the PowerPoint presentation revealed the professor's true opinion. The title read: "Three Reasons Teens Are Vulnerable Toads."

—MICHAEL DOBLER

@@@@@@@@@@@@@@@@@@@@@@@@@@@@@

After a lengthy course on improving computer skills, a teacher finally seemed to get the hang of it. In fact, he admitted in his self-evaluation, **"Computers have simplified and shortened my life."**

—BART ALTENBERND

One night, a few coworkers at the computer data center where I work stayed late, and we all started to get hungry. We decided to order in food by phone, but our boss thought that, since we work with computers, it would be more appropriate to order by Internet. After we contacted the fast food chain's Web site and spent a long time registering as new customers for the delivery service, a message appeared on the screen: "Thank you for your business. You will be able to order food in three days."

—THANTHIP RIOTHAMMARAT

Before retiring from my 30-year marketing career at IBM, I attended a seminar where a young salesman presented the latest PC. Impressed with the presentation, I remarked, "When I joined the company, we intended to make the computer as easy to use as the telephone. It looks like we made it."

"We have," the speaker replied. "We've made the phone a lot more complicated."

—LYNN A. SMITH

The new computer system at work allowed us to e-mail messages to one another. Soon after it was installed, my boss saw me at lunch and asked me for some reports, adding, "I left a message on your computer."

I had to laugh when I got back to my desk. There I saw his message—taped to the computer screen.

—JEANNE WASHBURN

@@@@@@@@@@@@@@@@@@@@@@@@@@@@@@

A technology fanatic, my boss is adamant about creating a paperless office. Away on a business trip, he had left instructions on my voice mail: "Fax the contract revisions to your PC, then forward the fax to my e-mail box. When the transmission is complete, send a message to my digital-display pager. Then I will call you from my cellular phone with further instructions."

Just after I finished listening to his message, though, my boss called back. He had forgotten his modem and now wanted me to send the documents to him by overnight mail.

—RENEE EAREGOOD

Learning new computer skills can be a challenge. An office manager in my software training class, taking nothing for granted, jotted down every word.

During a recent session, I peeked over his shoulder and read what he'd written: "New Computer Training—password is first name...Mine is Bob."

—TIMOTHY FOUBERT

"HTML code is automatically generated by Fireworks when you export, copy, or update HTML," stated our highly technical computer manual. But in case technophobes should begin to panic, it went on to explain, "You do not need to understand it to use it."

—KATE LINDON

During a break at the plant where I'm employed, I walked by a friend who works with computers. He was sitting at his desk with his feet propped up, staring straight ahead as if in a trance. When he didn't stir as I passed, I asked, "Are you all right?"

He blinked, smiled and said, **"I'm on screensaver."**

—ALBERT F. BECKER

@@@@@@@@@@@@@@@@@@@@@@@@@@@@

My husband and I are both in an Internet business, but he's the one who truly lives, eats, and breathes computers.

I finally realized how bad it had gotten when I was scratching his back one day.

"No, not there," he directed. **"Scroll down."**

—CHRISTINE AYMAN

The computer in my high school classroom recently started acting up. After watching me struggle with it, one of my students took over. "Your hard drive crashed," he said.

I called the computer services office and explained, "My computer is down. The hard drive crashed."

"We can't just send people down on your say-so. How do you know that's the problem?"

"A student told me," I answered.

"We'll send someone over right away."

—ROLF EKLUND

I was looking over some computer hardware at an electronics store when I overheard a customer tell the salesclerk, "I'd like a mouse pad, please."

"We have loads to choose from, sir," answered the clerk.

"Great," said the customer. "Will they all be compatible with my computer?"

—SNEHAL SHAH

"Pardon me," said the young man. I looked up from behind my desk at the library. "How do I get on the computer?"

"Just tell us your name and wait," I answered.

"Okay, it's John," he said, "125 pounds."

—LORI RICHARDSON

@@@@@@@@@@@@@@@@@@@@@@@@@@@@

At the radio station where I worked, the manager called me into his office to preview a new sound-effects package we were considering purchasing. He closed the door so we wouldn't bother people in the outer office. After listening to a few routine sound effects, we started playing around with low moans, maniacal screams, hysterical laughter, pleading, and gunshots. When I finally opened the door and passed the manager's secretary, she looked up and inquired, "Asking for a raise again?"

—NANCY ERVIN

In an attempt to complete its fiscal year figures on time, our company's finance department one day posted this sign outside its offices: "Year-end in progress. Please be quiet."

Our network specialist, whose office is right next door, put up this notice in response: "Shhh...quiet please. Information Technology works all year."

—LINDA MCGRAW

As a new federal employee, I felt a combination of excitement and anxiety about meeting the strict standards of discretion and respect that our government imposes on its workers. Fearful of making a costly mistake, I decided to read up on procedures and standards on the federal Office of Personnel Management web page. I'm not sure if I was relieved or worried when I clicked on one page and found: "Ethics: Coming Soon!"

—JAMES RESTIVO

After being on the phone forever with a customer who had been having difficulties with a computer program, a support technician at my mother's company turned in his report: "The problem resides between the keyboard and the chair."

—NICOLE MILLIGAN

"I don't understand it, sir, the computers have only been down for an hour."

I had always considered myself a with-it communicator of the '90s. But I had no clue what my friend was saying recently when he pointed out a "Double Beamer."

"What do you mean by 'Double Beamer'?" I asked.

With a grin he replied, "An IBM employee driving a BMW."

—KAY L. CAMPBELL

@@@@@@@@@@@@@@@@@@@@@@@@@@@@@@

My husband, Brian, is a computer systems administrator. He is dedicated to his job and works long hours, rarely taking time off for meals.

One afternoon, Brian was overwhelmed with solving a computer network problem, so I decided to deliver a meal for him to eat at his workstation.

When I was getting ready to leave, I said good-bye and reminded him to eat his burger and fries while they were still warm.

Staring at his monitor, he waved me away. "Don't worry," he said, obviously distracted, "I'll delete them in a few minutes."

—MICHELLE HILL

Manning the computer help desk for the local school district was my first job. And though I was just an intern, I took the job very seriously. But not every caller took me seriously.

"Can I talk to a real person?" a caller asked.

"I am real," I said.

"Oh, I'm sorry," the caller said. "That was rude of me. What I meant to say was, could I talk to someone who actually knows something?"

—SHARRON JONES

As I was cleaning my computer keyboard with a can of air duster (compressed chemicals), I noticed a slew of warnings: "Do not breathe fumes!" "Use only in well-ventilated areas!" "Avoid contact with skin and eyes!" And in BIG, impossible-to-miss letters: "INTENTIONAL MISUSE BY DELIBERATELY INHALING CONTENTS CAN BE FATAL!"

Then, I turned over the can. There, I found a symbol with a tree in it. Surrounding it were the words "Environmentally Friendly."

—SHARON BACON

@@@@@@@@@@@@@@@@@@@@@@@@@@@@@

My techie husband and I were walking in the high desert when he stopped to photograph one stunning vista after another. Overcome by the sheer beauty, he paid it his ultimate compliment:
"Everywhere I look is a screen saver!"

—LAURIE EYNON

My husband, Jeff, and I incurred several problems while assembling our new computer system, so we called the help desk. The man on the phone started to talk to Jeff in computer jargon, which confused us even more. "Sir," my husband politely said, "please explain what I should do as if I were a four-year-old."

"Okay," the computer technician replied. "Son, could you please put your mommy on the phone?"

—LENA WORTH

Driving on the interstate, I saw a vehicle with the license: ALT F7. I checked my computer at home, and as I suspected it was a Word-Perfect command. The truck had to belong to a plumber. Who else would choose the command: "Flush Right"?

—RUTHANN NICHOLS

Over the years I have heard my share of strange questions and silly comments from people who call the computer software company where I work as a tech support telephone operator. But one day I realized how absurd things can sound on the other end of the line when I heard myself say to one caller, "Yes, sir, you must first upgrade your download software in order to download our upgrade software."

—CARLOS MEJIA

@@@@@@@@@@@@@@@@@@@@@@@@@@@@@

On my way to deliver a computer to a customer, I saw a handwritten sign at the entrance of an alley. It read: "Blocked! Do not pass! Difficult to turn back." I continued anyway, only to discover that the alley was indeed blocked by a fallen tree.

As predicted, it took a while to turn the truck around. When I finally got back to the entrance, I noticed a second sign. It read: "Told you so!"

—IRWAN WIJAYA

I couldn't have been happier the day I figured out how to play my favorite CDs on my computer at the office while simultaneously doing my work. One day I was enjoying Beethoven when an administrative assistant delivered a stack of papers. Hearing classical music fill the air, she shook her head and said, "Don't you hate it when they put you on hold?"

—BENNY J. WURZ

No doubt about it, the new temp hadn't a clue about computers. Since part of her job was directing calls to our technical support department, I gave her simple instructions: "When people call with computer problems, always ask which operating system they're using—Windows, Macintosh or UNIX."

Later, she handed a technician this phone message. "Call immediately," she'd written. "Customer has problem with eunuchs.

—SUSAN CROFT

Powering up his office computer one morning, my colleague saw a unique error message: "Keyboard undetected."

Then he saw how he was supposed to clear the error: **"Press any key to continue."**

—DAVID BAUER

@@@@@@@@@@@@@@@@@@@@@@@@@@@@@

A computer company had a seemingly impossible problem with a very expensive machine. Staff engineers tried everything they could think of, but they couldn't fix it. Desperate, they contacted a retired engineer with a reputation for repairing all things technical. The engineer spent a day studying the huge machine. With a piece of chalk he marked the trouble spot with an X. The part was replaced, and the machine worked perfectly again. But when the company's accountants received the engineer's bill for $50,000, they demanded an itemized tally of his charges.

The engineer responded: One chalk mark, $1. Knowing where to put it, $49,999.

A coworker asked if I knew what to do about a computer problem that was preventing her from getting e-mail. After calling the help desk, I told my colleague that e-mail was being delayed to check for a computer virus.

"It's a variant of the I Love You virus, only worse," I said.

"What could be worse?" my single coworker asked wryly. "The Let's Just Be Friends virus?"

—ARTHUR J. ORCHEL

With five kids at home and one more on the way, I wasn't quite sure what to think when I was assigned the following password for my computer at work: "iud4u."

—CAROLYN THOMAS

I work in a busy office where a computer going down causes quite an inconvenience. Recently one of our computers not only crashed, it made a noise that sounded like a heart monitor. "This computer has flat-lined," a coworker called out with mock horror. **"Does anyone here know how to do mouse-to-mouse?"**

—MARY BOSS

@@@@@@@@@@@@@@@@@@@@@@@@@@@

The latest term being bandied about our IT office is PICNIC: **"Problem In Chair, Not In Computer."**

—ARLIN JOHNSON

The chef of the upscale restaurant I manage collided with a waiter one day and spilled coffee all over our computer. The liquid poured into the processing unit, and resulted in some dramatic crackling and popping sounds.

After sopping up the mess, we gathered around the terminal as the computer was turned back on.

"Please let it work," pleaded the guilt-ridden waiter.

A waitress replied, "Should be faster than ever. That was a double espresso."

—BRIAN A. KOHLER

I was a computer-savvy student, so the high school librarian called me to her office complaining of a computer crash. While booting up the computer, I asked her what she had done immediately prior to the crash. "I just erased some files that were taking up memory space," she replied matter-of-factly. "There was one big one that the Spanish teacher, Señorita Dobias, must have put on there. I think it was called DOS."

—BRANDIE LITTLETON

At work, my dad noticed that the name of an employee was the same as that of an old friend. So he found the man's e-mail address and sent him a message. When Dad received a reply, he was insulted. So he fired back another e-mail: "I have put on some weight, but I didn't realize it was that noticeable!"

His friend's hastily typed message, with an apparent typo, had read, "Hi, Ron. I didn't know you worked here, but I did see a gut that looked like you in the cafeteria."

—BRAD CARBIENER

Divine Duties

The pastor of my church hates to plead for money. But when the coffers were running low, he had no choice. "There's good news and there's bad news," he told the congregation "The good news is that we have more than enough money for all the current and future needs of the parish. The bad news is, it's still in your pockets."

—GILES V. SCHMITT

"What's the difference between a Catholic priest and a minister?" our daughter Sarah asked.

My husband, a pastor, answered, "Well, one big difference is that a priest can't marry. That's because he's expected to devote his life to God. A pastor also dedicates his life to God, but he can marry. It's like having your cake and eating it too."

Sarah's next question: "Priests can't eat cake?"

—JO-ANNE TWINEM

During our priest's sermon, a large plant fell over right behind the pulpit, crashing to the ground. Acknowledging his reputation for long-windedness, he smiled sheepishly and said, "Well, that's the first time I actually put a plant to sleep."

—DAVID BERGER

A Catholic priest I once knew went to the hospital to visit patients. Stopping at the nurses' station, he carefully looked over the patient roster and jotted down the room number of everyone who had "Cath" written boldly next to his name.

That, he told me, was a big mistake. When I asked why, he replied, "It was only after I had made the rounds that I learned they were all patients with catheters."

—DENNIS SMYTH

@@@@@@@@@@@@@@@@@@@@@@@@@@@@@

"But wasn't God the Father, Son, and Holy Spirit the ultimate multi-Tasker?"

As church treasurer, he had two computer files labeled "St. Mary's Income" and "St. Mary's Expenditure." While copying them from a Macintosh to a PC, he had no idea the PC would automatically truncate the file names to ten characters, eliminate spaces and replace apostrophes with periods.

Now the church's income is stored in "StMary.sin" and expenses in "StMary.sex."

—CHRISTINE THIEN

@@@@@@@@@@@@@@@@@@@@@@@@@@@@@@

One Sunday, while serving as a guest minister to a local church, I noticed in the program an order of worship with which I was unfamiliar. Since the service had already begun, I was unable to ask anybody about it. So when we reached that particular moment, I swallowed my pride and asked from the pulpit, "What do I do now?"

Someone in the congregation shouted back, "You say something and we respond."

Embarrassed, I admitted, "For the first time in my life, I'm speechless."

And the congregation responded, "Thanks be to God."

—BEN POWELL

While I was preaching in a church in Mississippi, the pastor announced that their prison quartet would be singing the following evening. I wasn't aware there was a prison in the vicinity and I looked forward to hearing them. The next evening, I was puzzled when four members of the church approached the stage. Then the pastor introduced them. "This is our prison quartet," he said, "behind a few bars and always looking for the key."

—RAYMOND McALISTER

My appointment as pastor coincided with the church's appeal for aid for victims of a hurricane.

Unfortunately, on my first Sunday in the parish, the center page of the church bulletin was accidentally omitted. So members of the congregation read from the bottom of the second page to the top of the last page: "Welcome to the Rev. Andrew Jensen and his family...the worst disaster to hit the area in this century. The full extent of the tragedy is not yet known."

—ANDREW JENSEN

@@@@@@@@@@@@@@@@@@@@@@@@@@@

When our minister and his wife visited our neighbor, her four-year-old daughter answered the door. "Mom!" she yelled toward the living room. "God's here, and he brought his girlfriend."

—KRISTEN KIMBALL

When a nun collapsed in the sales representative's office at our time-share resort, the rep ran to the front-desk manager.

"Two nuns walked into the sales office, and one of them fainted!" she yelled breathlessly.

Unfazed, the manager just looked at her.

"Well," said the rep, "aren't you going to do anything?"

He replied, "I'm waiting for the punch line."

—DONNA CAPLAN

Having grown up just outside New York City, I barely knew a cow from an ear of corn. Until, that is, I married a small-town Ohio girl. While I was in seminary school, I had a temporary assignment at a church in a rural community. The day of my first sermon, I tried very hard to fit in. Maybe too hard. With my wife sitting in the first pew, I began my discourse: "I never saw a cow until I met my wife."

—THE REV. LOUIS LISI, JR.

My friend opened a ministry, using a snippet from the Bible as the name. But he soon regretted his decision to order office supplies over the phone. When his stationery arrived, it bore the letterhead: "That Nun Should Perish."

—TOM HARRISON

@@@@@@@@@@@@@@@@@@@@@@@@@@@@@@

That's Academic

When I was 28, I was teaching English to high school freshmen in a school where occasionally the faculty and staff were allowed to dress down.

One of those days I donned a sweatshirt and slacks. A student came in and his eyes widened.

"Wow!" he exclaimed. "You should wear clothes like that every day. You look twenty, maybe even thirty years younger!"

—MARY NICHOLS

At a cross-curricular workshop for teachers, several of us from the English department found ourselves assigned to a math presentation. In the middle of the lesson, I leaned over to a colleague and whispered, "Are you getting any of this?"

He shook his head. "Math and I broke up in the '80s, and now it's really awkward whenever we get together."

—BECKY POPE

At a planning meeting at my college, I congratulated a colleague on producing some superb student-guidance notes explaining how to combat plagiarism.

"How long did it take you to write them?" I asked.

"Not long," he said. "I copied them from another university's website."

—BOB WHEELER

While I was an office worker at the local high school, a student stopped by to turn in a lost purse. I gave it to the principal so he could look inside for some type of identification. Moments later his concerned voice could be heard over the intercom: "Liz Claiborne, please come to the office. We have found your purse."

—KATY HYCHE

@@@@@@@@@@@@@@@@@@@@@@@@@@@@@

When my niece's coworker, Eula, began a job as an elementary-school counselor, she was eager to help. One day during recess she noticed a girl standing by herself on one side of a playing field while the rest of the kids enjoyed a game of soccer at the other. Eula approached and asked if she was all right. The girl said she was.

A little while later, however, Eula noticed the girl was in the same spot, still by herself. Approaching again, Eula offered, "Would you like me to be your friend?"

The girl hesitated, then said, "Okay." Feeling she was making progress, Eula then asked, "Why are you standing here all alone?"

"Because," the little girl said with great exasperation, "I'm the goalie."

—BOBBYE J. DAVIS

One of my students could not take my college seminar final exam because of a funeral. No problem, I told him. Make it up the following week. That week came, and again he couldn't take the test due to another funeral.

"You'll have to take the test early next week," I insisted. "I can't keep postponing it."

"I'll take the test next week if no one dies," he told me.

By now I was suspicious. "How can you have so many people you know pass away in three weeks?"

"I don't know any of these people," he said. "I'm the only gravedigger in town."

—SRINIVAS NIPPANI

Discovered: why our nation's education system is in trouble. When a friend delivered 20 new math books to a teacher's classroom, the teacher exclaimed, "Oh, shoot! I was hoping it was something I could use."

—ANGELA TIMPSON

@@@@@@@@@@@@@@@@@@@@@@@@@@@@@

"You need to be careful when writing comments," our principal told the faculty. He held a report card for a Susan Crabbe. A colleague had written, **"Susan is beginning to come out of her shell."**

—MARGARET WHARF

A linguistics professor was lecturing his class. "In English," he explained, "a double negative forms a positive. In some languages, such as Russian, a double negative is still a negative.

"However," the professor continued, "there is no language in which a double positive can form a negative."

A voice from the back of the room piped up, "Yeah, right."

—E. T. THOMPSON

When our students began raising donations for Child Abuse Prevention Week, the school administration did its part by setting up a collection box outside the principal's office and displaying a banner by the front door of the lobby. It read "Please give $1 to help stop child abuse in the front office."

—ANGELA LONG

After lunch at a restaurant with five other teachers, my friend Shirley realized they'd forgotten to ask for separate checks. To figure out how much each owed, the tab was passed around the table. The group laughed and chattered through the whole ordeal.

When they finally rose to leave, the man in the next booth grinned at Shirley. "You ladies sure are having a great time," he remarked. "What business are you in?"

"All teachers," she said proudly.

"Ah," he replied. "I knew you weren't accountants."

—WILLMA WILLIS GORE

@@@@@@@@@@@@@@@@@@@@@@@@@@@@@@

During the college speech course I taught, I spoke about a Chinese student who, after moving to the United States, decided she wanted an English name to honor her new home.

"She chose the name Patience," I told the class, "because she wanted to be reminded to be patient. Every time someone called her name, the message was reinforced."

I asked the students what names they would select for themselves. After considering the question, one young man raised his hand and said, "Rich."

—JOAN WALDEN

"Ms. Henson, you're going in for Ms. Simms."

@@@@@@@@@@@@@@@@@@@@@@@@@@@@@@

As a band instructor at an elementary school, I require my students to turn in practice sheets signed by their parents so I can be sure they are putting in enough time. I had to laugh, however, when one parent wrote on her child's sheet, **"Practiced 17 minutes, but it seemed like hours."**

—MEGAN E. TUTTLE

Our school had just installed a new air conditioning system, and a representative from the company wanted to make sure it was running smoothly. Poking his head into an empty classroom, he asked the teacher, "Any little problems here?"

"No," she said, smiling. "All our little problems have gone home."

—ROSALIND POPOV

My wife and I were watching the gorillas at the zoo when several of them charged at the enclosure fence, scattering the crowd, except for one elderly man. Later, my wife asked him how he had kept his composure.

"I used to drive a school bus," he explained.

—MARVYN SAUNDERS

Our architectural school had been without a department chairperson for two years, and students were growing frustrated at the lengthy process of choosing a new candidate. Finally a group of students sent a message to the dean. He arrived at school one morning to find 50 seats stacked up in front of his office. A sign said "Pick a chair!"

—SANDRA HEISER

@@@@@@@@@@@@@@@@@@@@@@@@@@@@@@@@

I'm a high school geometry teacher and I started one lesson on triangles by reading a theorem. "If an angle is an exterior angle of a triangle, then its measure is greater than the measure of either of its corresponding remote interior angles."

I noticed that one student wasn't taking notes and asked him why.

"Well," he replied sincerely, "I'm waiting until you start speaking English."

—PATRICIA STRICKLAND

After applying their lipstick in the school bathroom, a number of girls would press their lips to the mirror, leaving dozens of little lip prints. The principal decided that something had to be done. So she called all the girls to the bathroom and explained that the lip prints were causing a major problem for the custodian. To demonstrate how difficult it was, she asked the maintenance man to clean one of the mirrors. He took out a long-handled squeegee, dipped it in the toilet and swabbed the glass.

Since then, there have been no lip prints.

—PHIL PROCTOR IN *PLANET PROCTOR*

I was working as a school psychologist in a major city when I was reassigned to a different school. I arrived at my new location early and started to get acquainted with the staff.

The secretary checked for the correct spelling of my name so she could place it on the directory posted near the school entrance.

Later in the day I happened to walk past the directory and saw that she had completed the job, though not in the format I would have expected. There, in front of my name, was the word psycho.

—RICHARD E. BUSEY, JR.

Rushing to work, I was driving too fast and as a result was pulled over by the highway patrol. The state trooper noticed that my shirt had the name of a local high school on it. "I teach math there," I explained. The trooper smiled, and said, "Okay, here's a problem. A teacher is speeding down the highway at 16 m.p.h. over the limit. At $12 for every mile, plus $40 court costs, plus the rise in her insurance, what's her total cost?" I replied, "Taking that total, subtracting the low salary I receive, multiplying by the number of kids who hate math, then adding to that the fact that none of us would be anywhere without teachers, I'd say zero." He handed me back my license. "Math was never my favorite subject," he admitted. "Please slow down."

—MEGAN STRICKLAND

I'm a teacher and high school basketball coach. During one season, things went from bad to worse when we lost to our local rivals by more than 30 points.

The next day in class, when one of my students asked about the game, I answered, "Let me put it this way. If this were the NBA, I would have been fired today."

"That's not true, Coach," the student said. "If this were the NBA, you would have been fired a long time ago."

—LLOYD ALDRICH

I had been teaching my seventh-graders about World War II, and a test question was, "What was the largest amphibious assault of all time?"

Expecting to see "the D-Day invasion" as the answer, I found instead on one paper, "Moses and the plague of frogs."

—STEVEN CALLAHAN

Last Laughs

BANANACO PROFITS

"Hard work never killed anybody, but why take a chance?"

—EDGAR BERGEN

Kids' Quips

As a security officer for a defense contractor, I have to make sure all visitors sign in. One day I was in the lobby and noticed an employee's college-age daughter writing in the visitors' log. When I checked the log at the end of the day, I noticed her signature. Next to "Purpose of visit" she had written, "To get money from Dad."

—JOSEPH HOFFLER

I have my office in my home. When family matters occupy my day, I often find myself working into the night to complete business assignments. After one particularly late session, I stood in front of my mirror the next morning applying cover-stick to camouflage the dark circles under my eyes.

"Mom must have been working late last night," I overheard my son telling his siblings. "She's using Wite-Out."

—MARY J. MILLS

On Take Your Daughter to Work Day, I brought my niece to the office with me so she could experience many aspects of being a social worker. While driving her home, I asked if she had learned anything. "Yes," she answered. "I learned that I don't want to do your job."

—KIM RIDER

Trying to explain to our five-year-old daughter how much computers had changed, my husband pointed to our brand-new personal computer and told her that when he was in college, a computer with the same amount of power would have been the size of a house.

Wide-eyed, our daughter asked, "How big was the mouse?"

—CYNDY HINDS

Stopping to pick up my daughter at kindergarten, I found out that the topic of show-and-tell that day had been parents' occupations. The teacher pulled me aside. Whispering, she advised, "You might want to explain a little bit more to your daughter what you do for a living."

I work as a training consultant and often conduct my seminars in motel conference rooms.

When I asked why, the teacher explained, "Your daughter told the class she wasn't sure what you did, but said you got dressed real pretty and went to work at motels."

—MARY BETH NELSEN

My coworker's sweet six-year-old came into the office to sell Girl Scout cookies. A first-year Brownie, she carefully approached each of us and described the various types of cookies. One woman who was struggling with a weight problem asked, "Do you have anything that is not fattening?"

"Yes, ma'am!" the girl brightly answered. "We have Thin Mints!"

—JULIE SANDERS

When shopping online, it's easy to forget that you may not be dealing with a large corporation.

I recently e-mailed a website asking why my purchases hadn't arrived a week after I'd paid for them. Later the phone rang. "Sorry for the delay," said a teenager. "I'll check and get back to you. I can't get on my computer right now because my mother's vacuuming and this room only has one socket."

—TERESA HEWITT

One of my duties as a bookstore supervisor is to handle customer returns. As I helped one young woman, I noticed the book she brought back was on the subject of dating. It's the bookstore's policy to ask the reason for the return, so I did. "My mother bought it for me," she said. "She doesn't like my boyfriend."

—KELLEY MITCHELL

I stole a couple of minutes from work to give my wife a call. She put my two-year-old son on, and we chatted a while before he ended it with an enthusiastic "I love you!"

"I love you too," I said, with a dopey grin plastered on my face. I was about to hang up when I heard him ask sweetly, "Mommy, who was that?"

—MATTHEW TERRY

My aunt, a kindergarten teacher, has to interview every new student. During an interview, she asked a little girl what her mother did. The girl proudly replied, "She is a businesswoman."

"What does you father do?" my aunt asked.

After thinking for a moment, the girl said, "He does what my mom tells him to do."

—APA RATTAPITAK

As an optometrist, I had a second-grader in for his first eye exam. He insisted his eyesight was good, but when I asked him to read a line from my vision chart, with the letters APEOTF, he couldn't do it. I asked him about a line with the letters FZBDE, in larger print. Still he couldn't read the chart.

"You mean you can't read those lines," I said, puzzled, "and yet you don't think you need glasses?"

"No," he replied. "I just haven't learned those words yet."

—SEAN CONNOLLY, OD

A student tore into our school office. "My iPod was stolen!" she cried. I handed her a form, and she filled it out, answering everything, even those questions intended for the principal. Under "Disposition," she wrote, "I'm really ticked off."

—DEBORAH MILES

Before my son could start going on job interviews, he needed to dress the part. That, he decided, required a $500 suit.

"What!?" I answered, gagging at the price tag. "I've bought cars for $500!"

"That's why I want the $500 suit," he said. **"So I don't have to drive $500 cars."**

—JOE KULAKOWSKI

At our base post office, my four-year-old could not take his eyes off the Most Wanted posters. Finally, he asked, "Dad, why didn't they just capture those guys when they took their pictures?"

—RAY OSBURN

Carrying mail, I walk the same route every day. One morning a girl was playing outside her house and called out, "Hi, Bill!" Though that isn't my name, I cheerily replied, "Hi!" This went on for several weeks, until I saw the girl's mother and asked, "Why does she call me Bill?"

The mother turned red. "Because whenever I see you coming," she explained, "I tell her, 'Here come the bills.'"

—LINCOLN REHAK

I had signed up to be a school volunteer and was helping a first-grader with her homework. But it turned out I was the one in need of help. The assignment required coloring, and I'm color-blind—can't tell blue from red. As we finished our lesson, I told the little girl, "Next week you can read to me."

Looking confused, she said, "Can't you read, either?"

—HOWARD SIEPLINGA

When my neighbor's teenage son was interviewed for a job at the local discount store, he was asked, "How would you treat an irate customer?"

The boy thought for a moment. "I'd treat him the same as the customer before and the one after."

He was hired on the spot. Later, his mother asked about the interview.

"I guess it went well because I got the job," the son replied. "By the way, Mom, what does 'irate' mean?"

ANN MARIE ROWLANDS

The college football player knew his way around the locker room better than he did the library. So when my husband's coworker saw the gridiron star roaming the stacks looking confused, she asked how she could help.

"I have to read a play by Shakespeare," he said.

"Which one?" she asked.

He scanned the shelves and answered, "William."

—SANDRA J. YARBROUGH

My 17-year-old niece was looking for a job, so her mother scoured the want ads with her. "Here's one. A couple are looking for someone to watch their two kids and do light housekeeping."

"Hellooo!" said my niece, rolling her eyes. "I can't take that job. I don't know anything about lighthouses."

—KIM WILSON

A first-grader came to the ophthalmology office where I work to have his vision checked. He sat down and I turned off the lights. Then I switched on a projector that flashed the letters F, Z and B on a screen. I asked the boy what he saw. Without hesitation he replied, "Consonants."

—STEPHEN DOWNING

Dumb and Dumber

Before setting off on a business trip to Tulsa, I called the hotel where I'd be staying to see if they had a gym. The hotel operator's sigh had a tinge of exasperation in it. "We have over 300 guests at this facility," she said. "Does this 'Gym' have a last name?"

—TARA CAPPADONA

"These are very disturbing figures. So I made all the zeros little smiley faces."

In the deli where I worked, an employee was asked to post a sign advertising our latest meat special. After she put up the sign, however, our manager pointed out that she had listed only the price and needed to put the item on the placard too. Later he was shocked to see a slice of ham taped to the sign.

—SUSAN DYCUS

@@@@@@@@@@@@@@@@@@@@@@@@@@@@

An elevator in our office building is frequently out of order. The last time, maintenance posted a sign that summed up the situation: **Elevator Closed for Temporary Repairs.**

—TERRI CRUDUP

Our colleague, a frequenter of pubs, applied for a vanity license plate that would cement his reputation as the "bar king." A week later he arrived to work with his new plates: BARKING.

—NANCY SEND

I needed a passport and I needed it quickly. Luckily, a sign in the passport office told me exactly how long I could expect to wait: "Allow 10 minutes for regular processing and 15 minutes for expedited processing."

—PETER VOGEN

Just as she was celebrating her 80th birthday, our friend received a jury-duty notice. She called to remind the people at the clerk's office that she was exempt because of her age. "You need to come in and fill out the exemption forms," they said.

"I've already done that," replied my friend. "I did it last year."

"You have to do it every year," she was told.

"Why?" came the response. "Do you think I'm going to get younger?"

—JONNIE SIVLEY

It's often a challenge to explain to strangers exactly what I do in the aerospace industry. At one gathering, I didn't even try. I just said, "I'm a defense contractor."

One of the guys was intrigued. "So, what do you put up mainly? Chain-link?"

—JOHN MCGEORGE

A tree in our front yard was weeping sap, so I visited the office of the U.S. Forest Service for advice. When I explained my problem to a staff member, he stepped to the back of the office and called out, "Anyone here know anything about trees?"

—JIM BRADLEY

The stoplight on the corner buzzes when it's safe to cross the street. I was walking with a coworker of mine, when she asked if I knew what the buzzer was for.

"It signals to blind people when the light is red," I said.

Unhappy with my explanation, she shot back, "What on earth are blind people doing driving?"

—RINKWORKS.COM

In my job with a delivery company, I was getting directions to a customer's home. The woman very specifically said, "From the main road in the center of town go two lights. Look for the bank. Turn right onto the next avenue. Go 1.2 miles. Drive past a yellow hydrant and then take the next left. Go 200 yards. My driveway is the third on the right, and the number is on the mailbox."

As I entered the information into the computer, I asked, "What color is your house?"

The woman paused a second, then said, "Hold on. I'll go check."

—MELISSA A. DOOLEN

A customer called our airline's reservation office to pay for his ticket with a credit card. My coworker asked him, "Would you please spell the name as it appears on the card, sir?"

The customer replied, **"V-I-S-A."**

—CATHY MOSELEY

A customer at the post office called to complain that she hadn't received a package. "Can I have your name and address?" I asked.

"All of that is on the package," she snapped.

"Yes, I know," I replied, "but—"

"Just call me when you find it."

"Can I have your phone number then?"

"I can't remember. But I'm listed," she said, and hung up.

—CHESTER D. STANHOPE

A customer walked into our insurance office looking for a quote. But first I had to lead her through a litany of questions, including: "Marital status?"

"Well," she began, "I guess you could say we're happy—as happy as most other couples nowadays."

—SHIRLEY WALKER

Meeting with my new pastor, I asked if I could have a church service when I eventually die. "Of course," he said, grabbing his date book. "What day do you want?"

—EDITH KRZYWICKI

I was waiting tables in a noisy lobster restaurant in Maine when a vacationing Southerner stumped me with a drink order. I approached the bartender. "Have you ever heard of a drink called 'Seven Young Blondes'?" I asked.

He admitted he'd never heard of it, and grabbed a drink guidebook to look it up. Unable to find the recipe, he then asked me to go back and tell the patron that he'd be happy to make the drink if he could list the ingredients for him. "Sir," I asked the customer, "can you tell me what's in that drink?"

He looked at me like I was crazy. "It's wine," he said, pronouncing his words carefully, "Sauvignon blanc."

—CHRISTIE ECKELS

@@@@@@@@@@@@@@@@@@@@@@@@@@@@

I was going out to a business lunch with two other people, one of whom volunteered to drive. After the driver unlocked the passenger door, I decided to hop in the back to avoid one of those awkward scenes where you hem and haw over who sits where. But I had trouble getting the seat back to fold forward. I pulled the lever under the seat to slide it forward, but it only moved a few inches.

Not easily discouraged, I hiked up my skirt, and was about to dive into the back when the third member of our party intervened. "Wouldn't it be easier," she said, "just to use the back door?"

—JENNIFER DUFFIN

Working from home as I do, I need a professional-sounding voice-mail greeting so everyone will know I'm hard at work. While I was recording a new message one morning, my wife was across the hall from my office, folding clothes with my six-year-old daughter, who had just emerged from the shower. My message ended up sounding like this:

Male voice: "Hi, this is Jeff Hill with IBM."
Female voice: "Look at you! You have no clothes on!"
Male voice: "I'm not available right now..."

—SUE SHELLENBARGER

When my husband ran for local public office, I was asked if I could do some research on the cost of getting his campaign literature printed up. So I visited a large printing chain to gather pricing information on copying costs. The clerk read off the various prices for color copies, color paper, one-sided printing, two-sided, multiple-color ink, etc.

Since I could not write as fast as the clerk could read, I requested a pricing list. "Sorry, Ma'am," she said. "This is my only copy."

—KAREN ENDRES

"Weston's been watching *Mad Men* again."

At the nature park where I worked in Hawaii, cliff divers often filled in as lifeguards at the falls. On chilly days, however, they wore sweatshirts that covered the lifeguard badges on their swimsuits, so it wasn't apparent that they were safety officers. One day three preteen daredevils ignored my coworker Nancy when she told them not to dive in the pond's shallow edge. Challenging her authority, one boy said in defiance, "Who says?"

"THIS says!" Nancy replied, lifting her sweatshirt to display her lifeguard badge. Seeing their wide-eyed stares and feeling cool air, Nancy only needed a second to remember that she had already removed her wet swimsuit earlier in the day.

—SHIRLEY GERUM

@@@@@@@@@@@@@@@@@@@@@@@@@@@@@@

Employee of the Month is a good example of when a person can be a winner and a loser at the same time.

—DEMETRI MARTIN

An absent-minded coworker and I went on a business trip. True to form, he left a book on the plane, arrived at the hotel with someone else's luggage, then lost his camera in a restaurant.

Returning home a week later, we headed to the airport parking lot to get his car, only to discover that he had no keys; he had left them in the trunk lock the week before. Fortunately, someone had turned them in to an attendant. My colleague was driving me home when I noticed the gas tank was empty, so we stopped at a service station. After paying for the gas, he hopped back in the car and drove off. "Promise me that you won't tell anyone at work that I left those keys in the trunk lock," he pleaded. "Okay," I agreed, "as long as I can tell them that you paid for gas and left without pumping it."

—MICHELLE A. BETZEL

Our intern was not very swift. One day, he turned to a secretary. "I'm almost out of typing paper. What do I do?"

"Just use copy-machine paper," she said to him.

With that, the intern took his last remaining piece of blank typing paper, put it in the photocopier and proceeded to make five blank copies.

As a salesperson, I do a lot of business over the phone. One man who called to place an order had a nice voice, so when he asked if I wanted his number, I took the opportunity to offer mine as well.

"Um," he stammered, "I was talking about my purchase-order number."

—IRIS MADDEROM

As a personal-injury attorney, I often get clients who have unsuccessfully attempted to settle their claims themselves. During a phone interview one woman told me that having lived on both coasts, she was more than capable of handling her claim, but the insurance company was giving her trouble. "Where did the accident occur?" I asked.

When she answered "Washington," I inquired, "Washington State or Washington, D.C.?"

There was a slight pause. "Hold on," she said. "I'll check the police report."

—CHRISTOPHER J. CARNEY

My daughter attends Oregon State University and works part time at a grocery store. With the holidays approaching, she worried about having enough time to study for finals, so she penned a memo to her manager. "It is absolutely imperative that I receive four days off," she wrote. "Otherwise I will not have time to study."

The next day her request was tacked to the employee bulletin board along with a note from her boss. "If I allow these days off," read the reply, "it is absolutely imperative that I know who you are."

—JANEY POWERS

When a client died, her daughter told our agency that she would cancel the home policy the following week, once her mother's belongings were removed.

Simple, right? Here's the note that was placed in the client's file: **"Deceased will call next week to cancel moving her things out."**

—KARLA WYNDER

Working as a server at a sushi bar, I saw a customer trying to get my attention. "What's up, babe?" he asked in a strong foreign accent. "Everything is fine, sir," I replied. After a while the patron hailed me again, asking "What's up, babe?" Puzzled and annoyed, I gave the same reply. Observing this was my supervisor, who called me over. "What did that customer ask?" he inquired. When I told him, he smiled. "He doesn't want to know how you're doing," my boss said with a laugh. "He's asking for wasabi!"

—VIJAY KRISHAN

"I don't dare leave my desk, dear. Ferguson's waiting to pounce on my job."

While auditing one of our departments, an assistant asked me what I was doing. "Listing your assets," I told her.

"Oh," she said. "Well, I have a good sense of humor and I make great lasagna."

—ALEC KAY

I was on the phone at the end of the day when my boss walked in and pressed a sticky note onto a nearby filing cabinet. I had already put away my glasses and was in a rush to leave, so I quickly scanned the slip of paper and called after him, "I have feelings for you, too!"

He looked back at me quizzically and was gone. Then I took a closer look at the note. It read, "I have filing for you."

—MELODY DELZELL

Tourists say some odd things when they charter my boat in Key West. "How many sunset sails do you have at night?" asked one. Another wondered, "Does the water go around the island?"

But the most interesting came when I asked a customer why she'd brought along a dozen empty jars. She answered, "I want to take home a sample of each color of water that we'll be going in."

—DENISE JACKSON

As an amusement-park employee, I am often asked for directions to specific attractions. Although detailed maps are given to each customer who enters the park, some people need more help. One exasperated guest approached me after she'd gotten lost using the map. "How come these maps don't have an arrow telling you where you are?" she asked.

—J. B. HAIGHT

Here's an ad for a job that should be filled quickly:
"Animal Hospital is seeking an Assistant.
Must be flexible, reliable, and irresponsible."

—MARGERY JOHNSON

A blonde was settling into a first-class seat for a flight to Los Angeles when the flight attendant asked to see her ticket. "Ma'am, you can't sit here," the attendant explained. "You have a coach ticket."

"I'm blond, I'm beautiful, and I'm going to Los Angeles first-class," the blond passenger declared.

So the flight attendant went to get her supervisor, who explained, "I'm sorry, but you'll have to move to coach because you don't have a first-class ticket."

"I'm blond, I'm beautiful, and I'm going to Los Angeles first-class," repeated the gorgeous young blonde.

The two attendants went to the cockpit and told the captain. He came back and whispered something to the blonde. She jumped up and quickly took a seat in the coach section. Astounded, the flight attendants asked the captain what he had said. "I told her that first class wasn't going to Los Angeles," he replied.

—CORY CAMPBELL

A friend stopped at a convenience store, but the automatic doors wouldn't open. Thinking there was an electronic eye, he began to wave his arms. An employee inside the store waved back. My friend then wedged his fingers between the sliding glass doors and created an opening wide enough to enter. "Your doors are out of order!" he hollered to a clerk. "Why didn't you help me?"

"Sir," he replied, "we're closed!"

—KEVIN J. SHANNON

At the funeral home where my husband works, the funeral director asked a recent widower, "Did your wife's illness come out of the blue?"

"No, she'd been sick before," he said. "But never this bad."

—JACKIE WISSMUELLER

While working in a clothing store, I noticed that people had no shame about returning items that obviously had been worn. One rainy morning I walked in and found a discolored blazer hanging on the rack with other returns. "People return the most filthy, nasty things," I commented to my supervisor who was standing nearby.

Eyebrow raised, she said, "That's my jacket."

—JOYCE A. WATTS

A fellow nurse at my hospital received a call from an anxious woman. "I'm diabetic and I'm afraid I've had too much sugar today," she said.

"Are you lightheaded?" my colleague asked.

"No, I'm a brunette."

—PAM FORST

Plate-glass windows cover the front of the office where I work. One day a military plane on maneuvers caused a sonic boom that cracked one of the windows. My boss called the local air base to file a claim and was finally transferred to a woman who handled such matters. After she carefully asked him the pertinent details of the incident, she had one final question: **"Did you get the ID number off the plane?"**

—MICHELLE BURTON

A customer called our service line demanding help with her TV set, which wouldn't come on.

"I'm sorry, but we can't send a technician out today due to the blizzard," I told her.

Unsatisfied, she barked, "I need my TV fixed today! What else am I supposed to do while the power is out?!"

—ARIELLE MOBLEY

Our new assistant, Christy, 16, was in her first office job. Coworkers were giving her basic instructions as the boss stepped out of his office and the telephone rang. Christy answered professionally, but then burst out with, "He's in the restroom now."

"Oh, no," one employee whispered to her. "Say he's with a customer."

"He's in the restroom with a customer," Christy told the caller.

—JIM OTTS

As I was waiting for my wife at the reception desk at a spa, a flustered woman entered. She apologized to the receptionist for being late. "I walked up and down both sides of the street for 15 minutes trying to find the entrance to the spa," she said. When she finished her explanation, the receptionist's first question was, "Have you ever been here before?"

—ED SWARTZACK

During a conference, I was pleasantly surprised to be seated next to a very handsome man. We flirted casually through dinner, then grew restless as the dignitaries gave speeches. During one particularly long-winded lecture, my new friend drew a # sign on a cocktail napkin. Elated, I wrote down my phone number. Looking startled for a moment, he drew another # sign, this time adding an *X* to the upperleft-hand corner.

—KARI MOORE

"The plan is to re-establish confidence in my leadership abilities."

Following the birth of my second child, I called our insurance company to inquire about my short-term disability policy.

"I just had a baby," I proudly announced to the representative who picked up the phone.

"Congratulations! I'll get all of your information and activate your policy," she assured me. After taking down basic facts like my name and address, she asked, "Was this a work-related incident?"

—HEIDI TOURSIE

My colleague used to work as a receptionist at an upscale salon. After greeting clients, she would ask them to change into a protective gown.

One afternoon a serious-looking businessman entered the salon, and was directed to the changing room and told the gowns were hanging on the hooks inside. Minutes later he emerged.

"I'm ready," he called out. My friend gasped. Instead of a gown, the man was wearing something another client had left hanging in the room—a floral blouse with shoulder pads.

—SHERRIE GRAHAM

Standing in line in a hardware store, I noted a woman looking at a rack full of signs priced at $1.79 each. She took one out and put it back a couple of times. Suddenly she held up the sign that read "Help Wanted," and asked the clerk, "Is there a discount on the sign if it's just going over the kitchen sink?"

—NANCY M. BAUMANN

An art lover stopped by my booth at a crafts fair to admire one of my paintings.

"Is that a self-portrait?" he asked.

"Yes, it is," I said.

"Who did it?"

—FLORENCE KAUFMAN

The secret to why librarians spend their days shushing people. Here are actual questions asked of librarians:

- "Can you tell me why so many Civil War battles were fought in national parks?"

- "Do you have any books with photos of dinosaurs?"

- "I need to find out Ibid's first name for my bibliography."

@@@@@@@@@@@@@@@@@@@@@@@@@@@@@@@

A sign outside a nursery: **"It's spring! We're so excited, we wet our plants!"**

—BECKY ADAIR

Applying for my first passport, I took all the relevant papers to the passport desk at the post office. The clerk checked over my application form, photos, marriage license, and other identification. All seemed in order until she came to my birth certificate. She handed it back to me and said, "This isn't any good. It's in your maiden name."

—JACQUELYN S. CAIN

A woman called the county office where I work and asked me to look up a "Mark Smith."

"Is that 'Mark' with a 'C' or 'K'?" I asked.

"That's 'Mark' with an 'M,'" she corrected.

—ANN KEKAHUNA

When a body was brought to her funeral home, my friend contacted the next of kin. Per previous instructions, the deceased would be cremated, she told him, so he needed to come in to identify the body.

Considering the task at hand, the relative asked, "Does this need to be done before or after the cremation?"

—JANICE PIERSON

When a water main broke, a customer called my friend at the utility office with this question: **"The water in my toilet is brown. Do you think it's safe to drink?"**

—DAVID KEGLEY

"Hargett is still adjusting from working at home."

Every couple of months I do a bulk mailing for my company, which requires a special form from the U.S. Postal Service. I had a faxed copy of the form that was illegible, so I phoned the post office and asked the postal employee to mail me a new form. "I can fax you the form but I can't mail it to you," she replied. "We no longer send mail from this post office."

—CHRISTY ADAMS

@@@@@@@@@@@@@@@@@@@@@@@@@@@@

Just for Laughs

"**A** recession," claimed the stockbroker, "is when your neighbor loses his job. A depression is when you lose your job. And panic is when your wife loses her job."

—WINSTON K. PENDLETON

In my role as a human resources officer, I was visited by a staff member who wanted to make a formal complaint about his line manager. The boss had described him as "indecisive", which he felt was grossly unfair.

As I was helping him prepare his case, I noticed that the appraisal was almost a year old.

"Why has it taken so long for you to come and see me?" I asked.

"Well," he said. "I couldn't make up my mind if it was the right thing to do or not."

—ALEC KAY

My musical director wasn't happy with the performance of one of our percussionists. Repeated attempts to get the drummer to improve failed. Finally, in front of the orchestra, the director said in frustration, "When a musician just can't handle his instrument, they take it away, give him two sticks and make him a drummer!"

A stage whisper was heard from the percussion section: "And if he can't handle that, they take away one of his sticks and make him a conductor."

—QUINN WONG

My nephew gave up his lucrative job to become a writer. "Have you sold anything yet?" I asked him one day.

"Yes," he said. "My car and my television."

—PATRICK DICKINSON

After earning my degree in broadcast journalism, I was fortunate to land a job as a disc jockey at a top-rated local radio station. One day before work, I stopped by my parents' house, where my mother was chatting with some friends. She introduced me to everyone and proudly mentioned that I had my own radio show. "How is it having a son who's a popular radio personality?" asked one friend. "It's wonderful!" Mom replied with glee. "For the first time in his life, I can turn him off whenever I please."

—TERRY ERHARDT

Near St. Vincent's Hospital in New York City I noticed two firefighters standing at the door of their ambulance. The window was partly down, and they were talking to a small child inside, instructing her how to open the latch. Nearby, a young mother looked on patiently.

Assuming they had invited the curious girl into the ambulance to check it out and she'd locked the doors by mistake, I said, "She locked herself in, eh?"

"No, we locked ourselves out," one of the men said. "We borrowed her from her mom because she fit through the back window."

—GILBERT ROGIN IN *THE NEW YORK TIMES*

A friend's daughter worked part-time in his office while she attended graduate school. One morning, a call came in for her. "She's not in yet," my friend said. "Can I take a message?"

"I'll call back later," the woman answered.

At 11 o'clock, she tried again, and he reported that his daughter had gone to lunch.

The last call came at 3:30. "Sorry, she's left for the day. Anything I can help you with?"

"Yes," the caller replied. "How can I get a job with you?"

—JOSH PATE

@@@@@@@@@@@@@@@@@@@@@@@@@@@@

If your name is on the building, you're rich; if your name is on your desk, you're middle-class; if your name is on your shirt, you're poor.

—RICH HALL

A small display at the fish hatchery where I work describes a now-extinct fish called the Michigan grayling. Last summer, I had the following conversation with a tourist:

Tourist: Is the grayling still extinct?
Me: Yes, sir. It no longer exists.
Tourist: Any thoughts of bringing it back?
Me: I don't think that's possible.
Tourist: Why not?
Me: Because it's extinct.
Tourist: Still?

—RINKWORKS.COM

Every time my construction crew began pouring a concrete foundation, our foreman would repeatedly warn us not to drop any tools into the mixture because we'd never get them out. During one particularly hard job, a coworker asked the foreman how many more minutes it would be until our break. "I really don't know," he replied sheepishly, looking down at the foundation we had just poured. "I dropped my watch in there over an hour ago."

—BRAD VICTOR

I'd just lobbied a Congressman in his Washington, D.C., office when I stopped to use the rest room. After washing my hands, I stepped up to the hand dryer and noticed a note pasted to it. The note said **"Push button for message from Congress."**

—MICHAEL BROKOVICH

Light bulb jokes are an innocent way to poke fun—or so I thought. Working as a sound technician, I asked an electrician, who was also the local union steward: "Hey, Mike. How many Teamsters does it take to change a light bulb?" (I expected the classic answer: "Twelve. You got a problem with that?") But Mike replied in all seriousness, "None. Teamsters shouldn't be touching light bulbs."

—TODD PILON

While my fellow "financial services representatives" and I were making phone calls one day, I noticed a colleague bristle at something the business owner at the other end of the line had said. Later, when I asked him what had happened, he frowned. "She called me an insurance agent," he said, obviously taking offense at the negative stereotypes that go along with that title.

"Don't kid yourself," I told him. "You are an insurance agent."

"No I'm not!" he replied hotly. "I'm a telemarketer!"

—URI ONDRAS

As a writer for one of the less glamorous sections of a newspaper, I also do entertainment features on rare occasions. Once, I was assigned to review a play that hadn't opened yet. After the rehearsal, I was chatting with the cast and mentioned what I usually do at the paper.

One thespian, shaking his head, remarked, "Oh, great. The play hasn't even opened yet, and they send in the obituary writer."

—ERIKA ENIGK

When he blew a wad of money at my blackjack table in the casino, a customer stood up and yelled, "How do you lose $200 at a $2 table?!"

Before I could speak, another customer replied, "Patience."

—ROBERT GENTRY

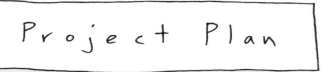

The large fire department where I work sometimes runs out of the official forms we use for inspecting equipment. Headquarters will then allow us to create our own forms on the station's computer.

Once, after composing a replacement document, we sent copies to other fire stations in need of them.

Afterward, we noticed that under the signature line, someone had mistakenly typed "Singed."

—ALBERT LEGGS

Our supervisor recently made a casual comment about my shaggy mane. He then went on to extol the virtues of a good haircut, which, he insisted, makes an elderly man look younger, and a younger man seem more mature.

"How would a haircut make a middle-aged man like me appear?" I asked, trying to stump him.

"Still employed," he answered.

—BRIAN CHEN

A bar in our neighborhood got lots of interesting traffic. Cars swerved into the parking lot, and the drivers would run inside only to reappear minutes later looking confused. One reason might have been the sign outside: "Free Beer, Topless Bartenders, and False Advertising."

—MARKIE REICHERT

A young man hired by a supermarket reported for his first day of work. The manager greeted him with a warm handshake and a smile, gave him a broom and said, "Your first job will be to sweep out the store."

"But I'm a college graduate," the young man replied indignantly.

"Oh, I'm sorry. I didn't know that," said the manager. "Here, give me the broom—I'll show you how."

—RICHARD L. WEAVER II

I returned home from my ninth business trip of the year with a severe bout of jet lag–induced foot-in-mouth disease. As we prepared to go to sleep that night, I wrapped my arms around my better half, gave her a kiss, and announced, **"It's good to be in my own bed, with my own wife!"**

—MARIO NASTASI

@@@@@@@@@@@@@@@@@@@@@@@@@@@@@@@

Cashier: And what form of payment will you be using today?
Customer: Money.

—OVERHEADINTHEOFFICE.COM

Expenses were out of control at our data supply company, and our bosses weren't happy. "When you travel," the vice president said in a meeting with his sales force, "lunch can't be expensed. Lunch is a normal employee cost. And while we're on the topic, your dinner expenses have been way too high." A rep shouted, "That's because we don't eat lunch."

—CHARLES FENDER

At the Social Security office, I eavesdropped on an interview between a staffer and someone who was applying for benefits.
Staffer: Married or single?
Applicant: Single.
Staffer: Previous marriages?
Applicant: Two.
Staffer: Did either of them end in death?
Applicant: No. Both times I got out alive.

—JOHN K. COLE

I received a letter saying I would not be given the American Express credit card I'd requested because my income wasn't substantial enough. Oddly enough, I work for American Express.

"Do you want to insure this?" asked the clerk at the post office when I handed her my package.
"Nope," I answered. "The contents aren't breakable."
The clerk wasn't so sure. "Ma'am, we are professionals. We can break anything."

—CYNTHIA FRANKLIN

The day before our office's new computer was to arrive, we got a call: the machine wouldn't be ready until the following week. Delays continued. Finally, more than a month later a computer arrived—the wrong model. Office management, however, decided to accept it.

Weeks later, a package came with a letter from the computer dealer, apologizing for the inconvenience. To show that they valued our business, they asked us to accept the enclosed VCR. It was a CD player.

—LYNDON OLFERT

"This performance evaluation is getting weird, sir."

While I was handling the reception desk at a women's magazine, the children of several employees sat in the adjoining conference room watching an action video. Trucks screeched, horns honked, people shouted, dogs barked, and cars collided. Just then, a bike messenger arrived to drop off a package. He listened to the cacophony emanating from the conference room, and sighed, "Ah, the soundtrack to my life."

—CHRISTINE ROBERTS IN *THE NEW YORK TIMES*

After I took a job at a small publishing house, the first books I was assigned to edit were all on the topic of dieting. "Isn't the market flooded with these types of books?" I asked another editor. "How do we expect to turn a profit?"

"Don't worry," he assured me. "These books appeal to a wider audience than most."

—WILL STEVENS

The pressure of a workday can bring out the weirdness in people. Possibilities for stupidity are endless. Just check out these chats from overheardintheoffice.com:

Boss: You make too many mistakes! You're not very consistent.

Cube Dweller: Well, you can't be consistent all the time.

—OVERHEADINTHEOFFICE.COM

I work for a mortgage company where I verify financial information about home buyers. One day I was processing a loan for a psychic reader and needed to confirm his income. In response to my request, I received the following letter from his employer: "He is a subcontractor for our psychic readers group. He is not a salaried employee. We therefore cannot predict his future earnings."

—VINCENT A. PATTI

When I drove up to the front of our small post office, I was surprised to see plywood covering the area where the plate-glass window used to be. Pasted on the plywood was a sign: "Please leave your car outside."

—AMY DIETZ

While getting dressed one morning, I decided I'd been spending too much time on my computer: I caught myself checking the lower right corner of my makeup mirror to see what time it was.

—DARLENE JACOBS

Corporations' lunch time seminars tend to run long. At one particular company, employees need a supervisor's okay to attend. This led to an interesting memo: "Next Lunch and Learn topic: Who's Controlling Your Life? (Get your manager's permission before attending.)"

—LUKE SECOR

A friend of mine plays piano in a local restaurant. One night, I listened to him play "Send in the Clowns," one of my favorite songs. As he finished, a woman approached him.

"Can you play "Send in the Clowns?" she asked.

My friend shook his head sadly and replied, "Apparently not."

—ERIC LANE BARNES

My husband and I attended a bridal fair trying to drum up work for his fledgling wedding photography business. One vendor assumed we were engaged and asked when the big day was.

"Oh, we've been married ten years," I said.

"Really?" she asked. "But you look so happy."

—IONA DORSEY

"QUOTABLE QUOTES

"Nothing bad can happen if you haven't hit the Send key."

—DAVID SHIPLEY AND WILL SCHWALBE IN *SEND*

"I always arrive late at the office, but I make up for it by leaving early."

—CHARLES LAMB

Dennis Miller defines body piercing: "A powerful, compelling visual statement that says 'Gee, in today's competitive job market, what can I do to make myself even less employable?'"

—DENNIS MILLER

"His insomnia was so bad, he couldn't sleep during office hours."

—ARTHUR BAER

"Every day I get up and look through the Forbes list of the richest people in America. If I'm not there, I go to work."

—ROBERT ORBEN

"A raise is like a martini: it elevates the spirit, but only temporarily."

—DAN SELIGMAN

"Eighty percent of success is showing up."

—WOODY ALLEN

"I used to work at the unemployment office. I hated it because when they fired me, I had to show up at work anyway."

—WALLY WANG

"You go to your TV to turn your brain off. You go to the computer when you want to turn your brain on."

—STEVE JOBS

"I do not like work, even when somebody else is doing it."

—MARK TWAIN

One night, I stopped my city bus and picked up a drunk woman and her male companion. While the guy sat down in the back near two other men, she regaled me with stories about the great birthday party she'd just had. Finally, she went to take a seat but came back seconds later.

"Umm ..." she whispered. "Do you remember which guy I got on the bus with?"

—RICHARD SAWCHIN

Back when I was employed by the state of Michigan, I took a call from an angry worker.

Caller: "Do you know there are no doors on the toilets at our office?"

Me: "How long has this been going on?"

Caller: "At least three months."

Me: "I can see your problem."

Caller: "So can everybody else."

—JAYNIE WELLS

The receptionist for the company where I'm employed found some cash in the office, apparently mislaid by a coworker.

She sent the following e-mail: "If anybody can say where they lost $66, please let me know and it will be returned to you."

Within minutes one employee replied, "Kentucky Derby, 1986."

—MILLIE STEELE

Recently a young woman came into my father's insurance office with her newborn twins.

Dad asked her if she ever had any trouble telling them apart.

She gave him a funny look before responding, "No, I haven't had any problem. This is Benjamin and this is Elizabeth."

—BARB MICHEL

"Mitchell, it's not the fact you found religion that bothers me..."

At our busy stock brokerage, it's hard to find time for small talk. So I was caught off guard when a coworker leaned over to me and asked, "What's up, John?" Welcoming a brief break, I told him about my hectic weekend and the trouble I was having with my car. He seemed a little distracted, however. After our conversation ended, I saw him lean over to another colleague. "Hey, Robert," he said. "What's the ticker symbol for 'Upjohn' pharmaceuticals?"

—JOHN F. HUNT

After someone stole my brown-bag lunch at work,
I complained about it to my wife, who offered to make me
something wonderful the next day. But as I pulled into
the plant's parking lot, I noticed a guy clearly down
on his luck, so I gave him my lunch. I didn't know
there was a note from my wife in the bag:

"I know who you are, and I know where you live!"

—FRANKLIN BENNETT

Rushing from the parking lot into my office in Los Angeles, I was approached by a homeless man.

"Excuse me, can you spare some change?" he asked.

In a hurry but not wanting to be rude, I pretended I didn't understand him. "No hablo inglés," I replied.

"Oh, that's just great," the guy muttered, as he turned to walk away. "Now you even have to be bilingual to beg."

—ANA TURNER

I was vacationing in the South Carolina mountains with a friend who's a freelance journalist for a couple of small-town newspapers. When she got a call about a car running off a curve and going off the side of the mountain, we hurried to the site. Thankfully no one was hurt. After a quick scan of the spectators, my friend sought out one local man to interview. "Have you lived in this area long?" she asked him. He told her that he had lived here all his life.

Then she asked, "How often do cars go over the side of the mountains?"

"Only once, ma'am," he replied.

—SHARON MCNEIL

@@@@@@@@@@@@@@@@@@@@@@@@@@@@@@

When our U.S. corporation was acquired by a European company, I was asked to work with a team of overseas consultants who would determine the future of our business. I was thrilled by the assignment, thinking it was a great opportunity to be noticed by the new corporate management team. For weeks I was at their beck and call, taking pains to provide them with all the data they needed.

One morning while I was working feverishly, the head consultant stepped into my office. "I understand that you are the key expert here," he said as he shook my hand.

Flattered by such recognition, I thanked him and launched into a description of all the effort I had expended.

"You don't understand," he interrupted, holding up a key. "I can't unlock my office door."

—DAVID BAHR

Some of my coworkers and I decided to remove the small, wooden suggestion box from our office because it had received so few entries. We stuck the box on top of a seven-foot-high metal storage cabinet and then promptly forgot about it.

Months later, when the box was moved during remodeling, we found a single slip of paper inside. The suggestion read "Lower the box!"

—FRANK J. MONACO

A coworker in our California office flew to Chicago during a blizzard. He spent hours driving to make his appointment at a suburban office complex. The parking lot was empty, so he pulled up next to the main entrance. As he was signing in, the receptionist looked outside and asked, **"Before your meeting, could you move your car off the front lawn?"**

—RUSSELL G. GRAHAM

**"A book on male sensitivity?
Try the Fiction Section, aisle two."**

During my first trip to Japan, I was taken to a local restaurant. I had been counseled to try everything on my plate so as not to insult my Japanese hosts. They, in turn, were told to be patient with my American mannerisms. Therefore they said nothing as I crunched my way through a tasteless wafer served with my meal. Later I realized we had all taken the advice too far: I had eaten a coaster.

—LAURA PUCHER

I've been hauling trash for years, so when the sign "Garbage" appeared on a trash can, I replaced it with my own note: "After 20 years on the job, I know garbage when I see it!" I emptied the can and left.

The next week, a new note appeared on the same can: "Dear Professor Trash, the garbage can is the garbage!"

—STAN GORSKI

Scene: A phone conversation between a client and me—an art director.

Me: Hi. I was wondering if you received the invoice I sent?

Client: Yes, I received it, but I am not going to pay you yet.

Me: Why not? Was something wrong?

Client: No, I don't need to use your design yet, so I will pay you when I use it.

Me: Well, I still need to get paid now. If a plumber fixes your toilet, you don't tell him you will pay him as soon as you need to go to the bathroom, do you?

Client: That's disgusting! My bathroom habits are none of your business, and as soon as I use what you sent me, you will get paid!

—FROM CLIENTSFROMHELL.NET

It was Halloween night when a driver called our road-service dispatch office complaining that he was locked out of his car. I forwarded the information to a locksmith, along with one more detail: The car was parked at a nudist colony.

Of course, the locksmith arrived in record time. But when he called in later, he wasn't amused.

"Figures," he said. "I finally get to go to a nudist colony, and they're having a costume party!"

—NEIL KLEIN

A Rochester, N.Y., firm posted a notice announcing it would pay $100 to anyone who came up with an idea that could save the company money immediately. The first winner was an employee who suggested that the award be cut to $50.

—*EXECUTIVE SPEECHWRITER NEWSLETTER*

The day I started my construction job, I was in the office filling out an employee form when I came to the section that asked: Single____, Married____, Divorced____.

I marked single. Glancing at the man next to me, who was also filling out his form, I noticed he hadn't marked any of the blanks. Instead he'd written, "Yes, in that order."

—*BECQUET.COM*

The company I work for recently purchased a building that had once been a hospital. Management asked for volunteers to help with some light renovation. I joined up, and my first task was to take signs down in the parking lot.

One read, "Reserved for Physician." I said to a coworker that I should keep the sign and post it on my sister's garage door. My friend asked, "Is your sister a doctor?"

"No," I replied. "She's single."

—JOHN ALLEN

While driving through South Carolina, I kept on having to slow down for road repair crews.

To keep the workers safe, the highway department posted a series of signs that read, "Let 'em work. Let 'em live."

On one of the signs an exasperated motorist had added, **"Let 'em finish!"**

—JOYCE BURDETT

I arrived at the office early one morning and noticed someone had left the lid to the copy machine open. I closed the lid and settled in for the workday. Over the next few weeks I found someone was continually leaving the lid up. Finally I caught the guilty party, surprised I hadn't figured out who it was long before. The culprit was Richard—the only male on our staff.

—TRUDY M. GALLMAN

My friend, a grocery store manager, chased a shoplifter through dry goods and frozen foods before catching the perp with a leaping tackle in cleaning supplies. That's when my friend noticed that all of the customers in line at the cash registers were staring.

"Everything's fine, folks," he assured them. "This guy just tried to go through the express lane with more than ten items."

—PAT PATEL

A famous scientist was on his way to yet another lecture when his chauffeur offered an idea. "Hey, boss, I've heard your speech so many times, I bet I could deliver it and give you the night off."

"Sounds great," the scientist said.

When they got to the auditorium, the scientist put on the chauffeur's hat and settled into the back row. The chauffeur walked to the lectern and delivered the speech. Afterward he asked if there were any questions.

"Yes," said one professor. Then he launched into a highly technical question.

The chauffeur was panic-stricken for a moment but quickly recovered. "That's an easy one," he replied. "So easy, I'm going to let my chauffeur answer it."

—KUMIKO YOSHIDA

When flooding closed the pressroom at a U.S. government office last spring, a spokeswoman remarked, "This is the first time that a leak has stopped the press from writing."

—RONALD G. SHAFER IN *THE WALL STREET JOURNAL*

I'm a mechanic who was called to help a stranded motorist. When I arrived, the woman was telling her car, "C'mon" as she tried to start it. She said that the car belonged to one of her children, and that she didn't know what was wrong with it. I suspected the engine was flooded, so I waited a few minutes before trying the ignition again. Then I, too, said "C'mon" as I turned the key. The vehicle started immediately.

"Great," said the woman. "Not only don't my kids listen to me, but they've trained their cars not to listen to me either."

—JOHN PUSHKO

At the bank where I was employed as a teller we were not allowed to eat while working. But one day, five months pregnant, I was ravenous. I opened a bag of potato chips and started to devour them.

Just then I spotted one of our best customers and his wife heading my way. Quickly, I wiped my mouth and greeted them. As I processed their transaction, I noticed they were looking at me oddly.

On their way out, the man said, "I don't understand these young people."

"Dear, that's a fashion statement," his wife explained. "It's a new type of brooch."

I looked down to see what could have caused such controversy. To my horror, a large potato chip was resting neatly on my left shoulder.

—JOANN MANNIX

Conductor Sir Neville Marriner was leading the Boston Symphony at Tanglewood, in Massachusetts. During the final chords of the program many concert-goers would leave their seats so they could beat the traffic. When asked if he was irritated, Marriner reacted with English aplomb. No, he said, he preferred to think that he was being rewarded with "a standing evacuation."

—MICHAEL RYAN

As personnel assistant for a printing company, I had to update the job descriptions and asked various managers for their input. When the controller, the owner's son, returned a form I had distributed, the section entitled "job qualifications" was left blank. I sent it back and asked that he complete the form. He did, adding this reply: "Must be related to the boss and have an accounting degree from Notre Dame."

—JANET PETZNICK

"That's two 'ayes', two 'nays' and one 'whatever.'"

Late for work already, I was annoyed to find a strange car in my reserved parking space again. After locating a spot far away, I stormed into my office determined to have the car towed. As the morning wore on, however, my anger mellowed and I decided to give the driver another chance.

During lunchtime, I went outside and left this note on the driver's windshield: "Please don't take my parking space. If you do, and your car disappears, don't say I never towed you!"

—LARRY HOUPT

Scanning the phone book for a garbage collection service, I came across one that clearly wasn't afraid to tackle any job. Their ad read: "Residential hauling. All types of junk removed. No load too large or too small. Garages, basements, addicts."

—MARY BETH CARROLL

At the hardware store where I work, our manager was writing out a bill when he turned to me and asked, "Hey, what are these nuts worth?"

A new clerk looked up and said, "I thought we were getting seven bucks an hour."

—DENNIS SCARROW

The new city hall in Chandler, Arizona, is eco-friendly and uses recycled gray water in the toilets. Just to be safe, a sign went up in the bathrooms warning employees not to drink out of the toilets. "I'm glad I saw that sign because I was very thirsty," deadpanned the mayor.

—AZCENTRAL.COM

Getting into my car one night, I turned the key and was dismayed to discover that the battery was dead. I took out my cell phone and dialed the automobile club. Just as the dispatcher answered, there was a loud fender bender on the highway nearby.

"Wow," the dispatcher said, hearing the crunch of metal on metal. **"Most people wait until after the accident to call."**

—TIM O'BRIEN

The large office building that I work in is showing signs of its advanced age. Structural and cosmetic renovations began well over two years ago, and no end is in sight. The chronic chaos moves unpredictably from floor to floor.

The tenants apparently are feeling the stress. Posted in the elevator one morning was a hand-lettered warning sign left by the workmen: "Watch your step—floors 3, 4, and 5." By lunchtime, someone had added, "have been removed."

—CAROLE M. SAMPECK

Ernest, my husband, was playing golf with our town's fire chief when he hit a ball into the rough. As Ernest headed for the brush to find his ball, the chief warned, "Be careful, the rattlesnakes are out."

The chief explained that calls had been coming in all week requesting assistance with removing the snakes.

"You've got to be kidding," Ernest replied in astonishment. "People actually call you to help them with rattlesnakes? What do you say to them?"

"Well," said the chief, "the first thing I ask is, 'Is it on fire?'"

—LAURA PETERSON

"It's $50 for fixing the sink, and $300 for babysitting your husband."

I owned a taxi service with my husband, William. While sitting in a cab waiting for a fare, William saw that a downpour had left puddles stretching to the curb. Then he heard someone open the back door and get in. When he turned around to ask the destination, William saw the would-be passenger exiting the other door. "Thanks," said the passenger. "I just wanted to get over the water."

—MARY SPROULE

Being in the bee removal business, I'm used to frantic phone calls, like the one from the woman whose home was infested with bees.

"You don't understand," she said, explaining why she was so upset. "I have two small children here."

"I do understand," I reassured her. "I have six children of my own."

"Oh," she said, now calmer. "I guess you don't have the 'birds' part down yet."

—KAY JONES

My budget-minded mother is always clipping coupons and keeps detailed records of how much money she saves. One day while running the cash register at the drugstore where she works, she had a self-conscious young man approach the counter to buy some condoms. My mother noticed a dollar-off coupon on the box and asked him if he'd like to use it, adding that she and her husband had saved over $400 redeeming coupons last year.

The stunned young man replied, "On these?"

—ELAINE EHRCKE STARNES

On my first day at the gas station, I watched a coworker measure the level of gasoline in the underground tanks by lowering a giant measuring stick down into them.

"What would happen if I threw a lit match into the hole?" I joked.

"It would go out," he answered very matter-of-factly.

"Really?" I asked, surprised to hear that. "Is there a safety device that would extinguish it before the fumes are ignited?"

"No," my coworker replied. "The force from the explosion would blow the match out."

—DAN WALTER

At the large bookstore where my son works, the clerks tend to watch out for one another, trading shifts and covering for each other in emergencies. Recently, though, a disagreement between two clerks escalated into a fistfight. One of them ended up going to the hospital, leaving my son to cover for him.

The store manager, who had missed the whole episode, later came looking for the injured clerk. "Where's Jack?" the man asked.

My son didn't miss a beat. "Oh," he said, "he punched out early."

—ELLEN KAHN

I'm a counselor who helps coordinate support groups for visually impaired adults. Many participants have a condition known as macular degeneration, which makes it difficult for them to distinguish facial features.

I had just been assigned to a new group and was introducing myself.

Knowing that many in the group would not be able to see me very well, I jokingly said, "For those of you who can't see me, I've been told that I look like a cross between Paul Newman and Robert Redford."

Immediately one woman called out, "We're not that blind!"

—BOB SHANKLAND

Neither snow, nor rain, nor heat, nor gloom of night will stop my fellow mail carriers and me from delivering junk mail.

One day, I delivered an envelope full of coupons to a home that was addressed: "To the Smart Shopper at ..."

The next day, the envelope was returned with this note scrawled on it: **"Not at This Address."**

—VANESSA PEEBLES

Bill Gates and the president of General Motors were having lunch. Gates puffed out his chest and boasted of the innovations his company had made. "If GM had kept up with technology the way Microsoft has, we'd all be driving $25 cars that get 1,000 m.p.g."

"I suppose that's true," the GM exec agreed. "But would you really want your car to crash twice a day?"

We bank tellers receive a lot of sweets as gifts from our customers around the holidays. One morning at breakfast, I was telling my husband that the bank employees had the potential to gain weight on the job. "Yeah," my husband said slyly, "you're all going to turn into 'teller tubbies.'"

—STEPHANIE BURTON

Pulling into my service station 45 minutes late one morning, I shouted to the customers, "I'll turn the pumps on right away!" What I didn't know was that the night crew had left them on all night. By the time I got to the office, most of the cars had filled up and driven off. Only one customer stayed to pay. My heart sank.

Then the customer pulled a wad of cash from his pocket and handed it to me. "We kept passing the money to the last guy," he said. "We figured you'd get here sooner or later."

—JIM NOVAK

My son, Earl, is a construction foreman. One day he tumbled from a scaffold, managing to break his fall by grabbing on to parts of the scaffold on the way down. He received only minor scratches.

Embarrassed by the fall, he climbed back up to continue working. Then he noticed his coworkers holding up hastily made signs reading 9.6, 9.8, and 9.4.

—JANICE A. CRABB

@@@@@@@@@@@@@@@@@@@@@@@@@@@@@

As a trail guide in a national park, I ate with the rest of the seasonal staff in a rustic dining hall, where the food left something to be desired. When we were finished with meals, we scraped the remains into a garbage pail and stacked our plates for the dishwasher. One worker, apparently not too happy after his first week on the job, was ahead of me in line. As he slopped an uneaten plate of food into the garbage, I heard him mutter, "Now stay there this time."

—IAN A. WORLEY

My boss at the warehouse told the new guy not to stack boxes more than head-high. "If the inspector shows up," he said, "we'd get in trouble. So, questions?"

"Yeah," said the new guy. "How tall is the inspector?"

—CYNTHIA FRANKLIN

On the door of the post office in rural Esperance, N.Y.:
PULL
If that doesn't work, PUSH.
If that doesn't work, we're closed.
Come again.

—VERA KASSON

While on a business trip, I traveled via commuter train to my various appointments. Before each stop, a petite, fragile-looking conductor entered the car. In a surprisingly booming voice, she clearly and authoritatively announced the destination.

One passenger complimented the conductor on her powerful voice, asking, "How do you manage to speak so forcefully?"

"It's easy," she replied. "I just visualize my kids sitting in the back of the train, doing something they shouldn't."

—JOSEPH FRANCAVILLA

"No, *you* roll over!"

The photo in our local paper showed a cubicle that had been destroyed by a fire. The accompanying article said it happened in a state office building and the blaze started when something fell onto a toaster, accidentally switching it on and igniting some paper.

I was about to turn the page when my husband asked, "Did you notice where it happened?"

"No," I said. "Where?"

"At the Bureau of Occupational and Industrial Safety."

—STEFANIE SWEGER

@@@@@@@@@@@@@@@@@@@@@@@@@@@@

If the people who make motivational posters are so motivated, why are they still working in a poster factory?

—JODY ROHLENA

The woman needed encouragement to keep peddling the exercise bike in her gym. So my friend, the gym manager, said, "Close your eyes and imagine you're riding along Broadway in New York City. It will be more interesting."

Inspired, the woman cycled on, but after a minute she stopped.

"What's wrong?" asked my friend.

"The traffic light's red," she replied.

—JULIA ADIE

My husband took an evening job at a large mortuary. He would arrive at 5 p.m., as most of the staff was leaving, and worked until 10 p.m. greeting visitors. On his second night I decided to call and see how he was doing. A secretary who was working late answered the phone.

"Is Mr. Sloan there?" I asked. I heard papers being shuffled. "I'm sorry," she finally replied. "Mr. Sloan is not ready for viewing yet."

—WILODEAN SLOAN

A farmer called my veterinary office and asked me to make a house call. Because the road was closed, he parked his ancient pickup in a field for me to drive the rest of the way. But once behind the wheel, I realized the brakes didn't work. The truck sped toward the stable, across the farmyard, into the barn, and embedded itself in a gigantic haystack.

Sweating, I climbed out and apologized. "Don't worry," the farmer said to me. "That's how I stop the car, too."

—JOSEPH HOLMES

Working at a major satellite company, I was expecting two technicians from the phone company who were coming by to do repairs. When they arrived, I was surprised to see that both were women. Wanting to appear equally emancipated, I called the only woman in our information-technology department to be their guide.

As we waited for Ellen, I thought about the strides women have made over the years.

When Ellen showed up, she smiled and nodded to the two women. Then she turned to me and said, "So, what happened to the guys from the phone company?"

—VICTORIA TOLINS

Recently, I went to use the ladies' room in the office building where I work. I beat a hasty retreat, however, after seeing this sign inside: "Toilet out of order—please use floor below."

—CLAIRE ROSKIND

World's worst jobs:

- Nuclear Warhead Sensitivity Technician
- Vice President, Screen Door Sales, Reykjavík, Iceland, Division
- Sperm Bank Security Guard
- Road Kill Removal Crew
- Russian Cartographer
- Prison Glee Club President
- Assistant to the Boss's Nephew

—CLUBFUNNY.COM

LAUGHTER
THE BEST MEDICINE®
HOLIDAYS

Contents

A Note from the Editors — 225

Giving Thanks — 227
Fowl Humor — 229
Thanks, I Guess — 241
Turkey Day Classics — 246

Yuletide Cheer — 253
'Tis the Season — 254
The Big Man — 288
Oh, Christmas Tree! — 300
Deck the Halls with Office Follies — 306
The Art of Gifting — 312
The Very Merry Things Kids Say — 329

Ringing in the New Year — 351
The Big Night — 353
Starting on the Wrong Foot — 360
Hard-Working Holidays — 366
Punts, Passes . . . — 368
. . . and Promises — 370

Seasonal Silliness — 375
That's Snow Funny! — 376
Festive Follies — 382
Jokes Around the Table — 396

A Note from the Editors

If you rely on television commercials, you'd think the winter holidays are a time of loving perfection: clean homes, well-behaved children, meticulously wrapped gifts, perfect cuisine, distinguished guests, and perpetual, shiny white smiles.

Then there are the holidays as they actually happen in most households. Visits from strange relatives. Food disasters. Awkward parties with coworkers who ignore you the other 364 days of the year. Tangled strands of lights. Pine needles everywhere. Shopping, cleaning, cooking—repeated in an endless cycle for what feels like months on end. Over-sugared children bouncing off the walls in anticipation. Going to bed at 1:00 a.m., exhausted, yet with so much more to do the next day. Oh, joyous season!

If ever there was a time of year in which we need a sense of humor, it's the holidays in America. We're here to help. The stories, one-liners, cartoons, quotes, and jokes in the pages that follow capture the zaniness of the holiday season in all its glory. What makes these jokes so funny is *recognition,* the sense that we've all been there. And you know what? We wouldn't want it any other way. Because holiday joy isn't found in perfection; it's really right there in the shared madness!

Giving
Thanks

"One of the great unsolved mysteries of life is how you can get 24 pounds of leftovers from an 18-pound turkey."

—ROBERT ORBEN

**"Everyone who disappeared was plump....
I'm just sayin'."**

Fowl Humor

Around noon on Thanksgiving Day, I saw our young newlywed neighbors, Pam and Chuck, emerging from their house. They were dressed up, and I assumed that they were on their way to Thanksgiving dinner with one or the other set of parents, both of whom lived in the area. Later that afternoon, I saw them again—dressed in sweat suits as they jogged by with a cheery wave. Still later I heard them exchanging hellos with my husband. They were again dressed up and going somewhere.

The next day, Pam explained: "We didn't want to offend either my parents or Chuck's. They both have big traditional Thanksgiving dinners. So we ate one huge dinner with his family in the afternoon, came home to jog it off, then ate another huge dinner with my family in the evening."

—SONIA E. MASELLO

Last Thanksgiving morning, knowing that my sister had invited some of her husband's relatives to dinner, I dropped in to see how she was coming along. The house was in a shambles, and her four little daughters were squabbling among themselves. When she came out of the kitchen to greet me, her hair was a mess, she had turkey dressing all over her hands, and flour on her face. Before I could say anything, she looked at me and muttered, "Those damn pilgrims!"

—MRS. NED C. CARLSON

While our son was in training at Fort Knox, we joined him for Thanksgiving Day dinner at the base. On leaving the mess hall, we passed the kitchen, and I asked him if they had electric dishwashers. "Sure, Mom," he replied. "We just take a new recruit and plug him in."

—MRS. FRED PFEIFFER

A three-year-old's report on Thanksgiving: **"I didn't like the turkey, but I liked the bread he ate."**

—ART LINKLETTER

As I was basting the beautiful turkey we were having for Thanksgiving and calculating that we might have enough left over for Sunday dinner, too, my nephew came into the kitchen to watch me.

"How many stoppers are we going to have today?" he asked.

"Stoppers?" I asked. "What do you mean?"

"You know, all those courses you have first, to stop people from eating so much turkey."

—ELSIE CHASE

As the only vegetarian in my family, I often get tired of defending my food choices to other family members, especially at the large dinner gatherings we have on special occasions. I didn't realize how often the subject is actually discussed until one day around Thanksgiving, when I picked up my six-year-old son, Jordan, from school. His class had made Thanksgiving turkey crafts using potatoes and paper feathers.

Jordan proudly presented his to me, announcing excitedly, "Mom, this year we'll finally have the kind of turkey even you can eat!"

—CHARLOTTE REARDON

Many of us Kiowas have married "palefaces," but we remain proud of our Indian heritage. When my cousin invited her out-of-state in-laws for Thanksgiving dinner, a Kiowa relative asked who her guests were.

"Oh," she replied, "the pilgrims came to eat with us today."

—ALLEN C. QUETONE

Setting the table for Thanksgiving dinner, our kids weren't sure where to place some of the special dishes. After moving one dish, they noticed that juice from the cranberry sauce had spilled, leaving a large red stain on the tablecloth. "Well," quipped ten-year-old Emily, "at least now we'll know where to put the cranberry sauce next year."

—JULIE EMOND

I worked on a toll road, answering the phone, collecting money, and issuing toll tickets. One Thanksgiving Day a woman called to ask about road conditions on the turnpike. After I said everything was A-OK, she told me a friend was coming for dinner. Then came the stumper: "If my friend just left from exit twelve," she asked, "what time should I put the turkey in?"

—SANDRA SHIELDS

When an English business associate was visiting in our home one Thanksgiving, our young son asked him whether the English celebrated Thanksgiving.

"Oh, yes, indeed," replied our friend. "But we celebrate it on the Fourth of July!"

—DONALD W. DAVIS

The host was carving the turkey and taking requests. "White meat? Dark? Some of both?"
One guest asked, "Is that white good?"
The host looked at him for a moment, then said solemnly, **"Nothing but the breast."**

—JOHN A. CHARTERS

Thanksgiving is when one species ceases to gobble and another begins.

—R. E. MARINO

The manager of the cafeteria in a large eastern plant decided that his order of 350 turkeys for Thanksgiving dinner was more than would be needed. He called the purchasing department and asked them to tell the supplier to cut the order in half.

Four days before Thanksgiving, the order was received at the cafeteria loading platform. Sure enough: 350 turkeys, all neatly cut in half.

—ELISE TYNAN

I was amazed, when I returned home from school for Thanksgiving Day, to find a lavishly prepared dinner. You see, my mother is not what one might term a proficient cook. For a woman who, six months before, could have destroyed a can of vegetable soup, the preparation of such a handsome turkey with full trimmings seemed impossible.

Then my father said the blessing, and I understood. "Our Father," he began, "we thank thee for this fine day. We thank thee for our fine son. And most of all, we thank thee for Harry's Delicatessen, which made this dinner possible."

—MICHAEL WALKER

A teacher displayed pictures her second-graders had drawn after hearing about the pilgrims' voyage and the first Thanksgiving. One drawing, by an army child, a veteran of many army moves, caught our attention. There, among the pilgrims, Indians, and turkeys, was a moving van with the name "Mayflower" written on it.

—MRS. H. R. TODD

The pro football team had just finished practice when a turkey strutted onto the field.

"I want to try out," the turkey told the coach.

Stunned, the players stared as the bird caught pass after pass and ran right through the defensive line.

After 30 minutes the coach had seen enough. "You're excellent," he said. "Sign with us, and you'll get a huge bonus."

"Forget the bonus," the turkey said. "All I want to know is, does the season go past Thanksgiving?"

—UNKNOWN

After years of cooking meals for four strapping sons, I found it hard to adjust to cooking for just myself. One Thanksgiving when the boys couldn't make it home, I decided to have roast turkey anyway.

At the local poultry market, I took my time checking the birds, but they were all too large. Finally I asked the patient clerk if he had anything smaller.

"Indeed we do, ma'am," he said. "We call them eggs."

—JOAN THOMPSON

At a family meeting to decide where to celebrate the holidays, my newest son-in-law turned to my daughter and said, "Well, we have to have Thanksgiving and Christmas with either your mom or your sister."

Touched that he loved his new family so much, I started to hug him as my eyes misted over. Then he added, **"They have satellite dishes!"**

—FRANCES BRADLEY

For our first Thanksgiving, my wife's parents came over
for dinner. My bride roasted a beautiful turkey,
which she brought to the table on a silver tray.
With a very sharp knife, I carved it into lovely piles
of thinly sliced white and dark meat. I smiled at my
father-in-law, a well-known surgeon, and said,
"How was that for a stunning bit of surgery?"
He laughed and replied,

"Not bad.
Now let's see you put it back together."

—CARL ROSS

My sister Donnelly is a whiz in the kitchen, while my other
sister and I are culinary klutzes. So she was understandably
hesitant when Maureen and I insisted on making Thanksgiving
dinner on a visit to her house. After Donnelly left for work on the
day of our big meal, we studied the oven manual, set the timer,
and left to go skiing, feeling quite proud of our accomplishment.

The feeling lasted until six hours later, when we returned—
to a nice hot oven and a raw turkey sitting on the kitchen counter.

—NANCY MARLATT

A friend's college roommate was enjoying Thanksgiving
dinner at home when he accidentally overturned his cup of tea.
Forgetting that he was in the presence of his family, he released a
flood of profanity. His grandmother, visibly shocked, said to him,
"You eat with that mouth?"

—D. D.

"No, I haven't seen the cat since I put the turkey out to thaw."

Thanksgiving menu: roast turkey, candied yams, and pickled relatives.

—ARNOLD H. GLASOW

After Thanksgiving dinner, the adults gathered in the living room to exchange reminiscences, while the children went into the family room to play. Suddenly our hostess noticed that an elderly relative was missing. "Where's Aunt Florence?" she asked. From across the room came a masculine drawl, "Oh, she's with the kids, bridging the generation gap."

—FLORENCE M. MORTIMER

I was stuffing the Thanksgiving turkey when my 2½-year-old son, Joshua, zoomed into the kitchen and saw what I was doing.

With his eyes popping, he came to a quick stop and asked, "Why are you stuffing sandwiches into the turkey's pockets?"

—DEIRDRE CASKENETTE

On Thanksgiving weekend, when my father was recuperating from surgery, his friendly and efficient nurse stopped by. Dad asked her if his doctor would be in to see him that day. "No," she replied, "he's home cooking turkey for his family."

Surprised, Dad asked how she knew so much about his affairs. "I'm his wife," she said.

—CAREN SHUTTLEWORTH

What did the turkey say upon receiving an invitation to Thanksgiving dinner?

"No, thanks. I'm stuffed."

— JAYNELLE ST. JEAN

For 30 years, frantic chefs have called the Butterball Turkey Talk-Line for tips on how to save their Thanksgiving dinner. Here are some of the less appetizing calls.

A disappointed woman phoned in, wondering why her turkey had no breast meat. After a conversation with a Talk-Line operator, it became apparent that the woman's turkey was upside-down.

A gentleman called to tell the operator he cut his turkey in half with a chain saw and wanted to know if the oil from the chain would adversely affect the turkey.

One caller told the operator she had always cut the legs off the turkey before putting it in the oven, thinking that was the method everyone used. She later learned that her mother had been doing that because it was the only way to get the bird in their small oven.

—BUTTERBALL TURKEY TALK-LINE

The nun who was the principal at my granddaughter's school called an assembly to announce the results of a fund-raising drive. After a prayer of Thanksgiving by the priest, sister arose and announced the gratifying total. Oohs and aahs were heard as the students clapped with enthusiasm.

"Yes, indeed," sister continued, **"we could hardly believe it ourselves. Why, Father and I were pinching each other—"**

—HAYDEN ROGERS

QUOTABLE QUOTES

"Stress cannot exist in the presence of a pie."

—DAVID MAMET

"We're having something a little different this year for Thanksgiving. Instead of a turkey, we're having a swan. You get more stuffing."

—GEORGE CARLIN

"Thanksgiving is the one occasion each year when gluttony becomes a patriotic duty."

—MICHAEL DRESSER

"I celebrated Thanksgiving in an old-fashioned way. I invited everyone in my neighborhood to my house, we had an enormous feast, and then I killed them and took their land."

—JON STEWART

"Thanksgiving dinners take eighteen hours to prepare. They are consumed in twelve minutes. Half-times take twelve minutes. This is not coincidence."

—ERMA BOMBECK

"Thanksgiving, man. Not a good day to be my pants."

—KEVIN JAMES

"A lot of Thanksgiving days have been ruined by not carving the turkey in the kitchen."

—KIM HUBBARD

"Thanksgiving is an emotional holiday. People travel thousands of miles to be with people they only see once a year. And then discover once a year is way too often."

—JOHNNY CARSON

"You can tell you ate too much for Thanksgiving when you have to let your bathrobe out."

—JAY LENO

"I asked my mother-in-law to bring a vegetable."

Thanks, I Guess

Before we sat down to our Thanksgiving dinner, my wife spoke of our many blessings. First on her list came our six healthy children. An hour later, when we were at the table, all was pandemonium. Noticing that my wife's eyes were closed, I asked her what was the matter. "Nothing," she said. "I am just praying for patience to endure my blessings."

—E. C. STEVENSON

After sitting down to a grand Thanksgiving spread at my mother-in-law's home, she announced, "Before we get started, I think we ought to give thanks to the Lord." Without skipping a beat, her sister grumbled,

"I think we better taste the meal first."

—STEVE WISE

The oven on my almost-new stove hadn't worked in weeks, and frequent calls to the serviceman produced no results. As Thanksgiving approached, I told my husband that this year we would be having boiled turkey.

"I'll have that oven fixed in time for Thanksgiving," he promised.

The week before the holiday, the serviceman at last arrived. I asked what magic words my spouse had used. "Oh," replied the serviceman, "your husband just said that if the oven wasn't fixed by Thanksgiving, you were inviting yourselves to my house for dinner. My wife didn't like that idea at all."

—MARGARET HILLER

Some neighbors of my grandparents' gave them a pumpkin pie as a holiday gift. As lovely as the gesture was, it was clear from the first bite that the pie tasted bad. It was so inedible that my grandmother had to throw it away.

Ever gracious and tactful, she still felt obliged to send the neighbors a note. It read, **"Thank you very much for the pumpkin pie. Something like that doesn't last very long in our house."**

—KRISTA ROSE

My uncle, an Anglican archbishop, was presiding over our family's Thanksgiving dinner. My two daughters, eight and five, had been practicing saying a special grace for the occasion. When my uncle asked if one of them would like to recite it, the youngest quickly volunteered. We all bowed our heads and waited expectantly.

"Dear . . ." she began. There was a prolonged silence, then finally a loud stage whisper to her sister. "Psst! What's His name?"

—K. CURTIS

My grandfather always had the knack of saying the right thing. One Thanksgiving we explained to my younger brother the custom of breaking the turkey wishbone. Eager to have his wish come true, little Philip was bitterly disappointed when he saw that he held the small end of the bone, while his grandfather had the larger part.

"That's all right, my boy," said his smiling grandfather. "My wish was that you would get yours."

—LINDAANN LOSCHIAVO

Bless, oh Lord, these delectable vittles. **May they add to thy glory and not to our middles.**

—YVONNE WRIGHT

Last Thanksgiving my niece came home with her school project: a beautiful autumnal leaf with the words "I am thankful for my mommy" printed on it.

Her eyes tearing, my sister said, "This means so much to me."

Her daughter nodded. "I wanted to put 'Hannah Montana,' but my teacher wouldn't let me."

—KERRIANNE WOLFE

The checkout clerk at the supermarket was unusually cheerful even though it was near closing time. "You must have picked up a ton of groceries today," a customer said to the checker. "How can you stay so pleasant?"

"We can all count our blessings," the clerk replied. "The hardest part of this job is the turkeys and the watermelons. I just thank God that Thanksgiving doesn't come in July."

—L. PROCTOR

We were visiting our son, his wife, and our three grand-children for Thanksgiving. As is our custom, before the meal, we each said what we were thankful for. Our grandson Jordi, who is 10, was the last to speak.

"I'm thankful for my family," he said, "and that we could all be together today. I'm thankful for this great meal Mom and Dad cooked.

"But most of all, I'm really thankful I'm not that turkey in the middle of the table!"

—MARILYN FANCEY

For a Thanksgiving assignment, my cousin's daughter, who is in first grade, was to draw something she was thankful for. When the teacher collected the drawings, she saw that Rachel's paper was blank. When asked why, Rachel replied, "I wanted to draw a picture of God, but He was too big to fit on the page."

—KATHY HAMM

Our nephew brought a guest to our family's festive Thanksgiving dinner, a stylish young woman who sported a sparkling green stud in her lower lip, a gold stud on her tongue, and an assortment of earrings trailing up her ear. She was introduced to 87-year-old Grandma, who beamed at her and said, "Oh, my, you're already decorated for Christmas."

—MARY ANNA BARKER

The sentence in the Thanksgiving edition of my church bulletin intended to say: "Thank you, Lord, for the many miracles we are too blind to see." But in what might have been a classic Freudian slip, the sentence read: "Thank you, Lord, for the many miracles we are too blond to see."

—ANITA DAUGHERTY

Last Thanksgiving at the height of the hunting season, a couple who live in a beautiful woodland area of New York State asked their four-year-old son to say grace before the holiday dinner. Folding his hands and bowing his head, he prayed:
"Dear Lord, please take care of all the deer and let the hunters shoot each other."

—MARY S. KILBURN

Turkey Day Classics

When a music student brought his French horn to my shop for repair, he complained that the instrument "felt stuffy" and he couldn't blow air through it. It's not unusual to find partial blockages in brass instruments if small items get lodged in the tubing, but when I tested the instrument, the horn was completely blocked.

After much probing and prodding, a small tangerine dropped out of the bell. "Oh," said the musician when I handed him the fruit. Seeing the bewildered look on my face, he explained, "My mom used the horn for a cornucopia in a Thanksgiving centerpiece."

—MARK L. MADDEN

At a U.S. Army–base school, I was presenting the story of the first Thanksgiving to my first-grade class. After talking about why the pilgrims were going to America, we got them on the *Mayflower* and were almost to Plymouth Rock.

Then, using the technique of getting children to imagine themselves in the place of others, I asked, "What would you do if you were about to land in a strange country?" There was a brief, contemplative pause. Then one youngster piped up, "Fasten my seat belt."

—EDNA KNIGHTEN

We had spent most of Thanksgiving Day watching football games on television. As we sat down Friday night to a dinner of leftover turkey, yams, and cold stuffing, our college-age son asked, **"What's this, the instant replay?"**

—BETH OPENSHAW

❋ ❋ ❋ ❋ ❋ ❋ ❋ ❋ ❋ ❋ ❋ ❋

"What a wonderful meal!" wrote a German friend after spending Thanksgiving at our home last year. **"I left your house all fed up."**

—ESTHER TISSING

A young housewife with two children is struggling to earn her college degree. Since her final exams are scheduled for mid-December, she must spend a lot of time studying. But she also devotes herself as much as possible to her children and husband. Around Thanksgiving she confided to me, "I asked Jim not to look under the bed until Christmas. He thinks it's presents, but it's only dust."

—S. S.

To keep the guests occupied before Thanksgiving dinner, my aunt popped a Batman video into the VCR. Almost two hours later everyone was hungry and had had enough of the flick.

"This movie sure is dragging on," my uncle moaned. "Just how long is it?"

"Dad," his son said, "why do you think they call it *Batman Forever?*"

—BRANDY HALL

As a skilled carpenter, I have plenty of work. One September a customer contracted with me to build extra leaves for an antique table she had just purchased. She stressed that the job had to be done by Thanksgiving because she was expecting a crowd for dinner. Other jobs piled up, however, and I neglected her project.

One evening in mid-November, I received this phone message: "I'm calling to find out if I need to buy a small tablecloth or a large tablecloth for Thanksgiving dinner. Please call me back."

I started her job the next day.

—MARTIN G. ANTHONY

"It's an invitation to eat out in the cold in November. Sounds like a nut."

Thanksgiving is still a big family day in most homes— they get together during half-time.

—LESTER LANIN

Every Thanksgiving we play a Turkey Bowl football game to determine neighborhood bragging rights. One year our team was close to scoring a game-winning touchdown, so we all listened carefully as our quarterback explained a play to us in the huddle. "I'll look over the defense when we come to the line," he said. "If I call out a color, I'll hand the ball off and we'll run left. If I call out a fruit, I'll throw a pass into the end zone."

Wow, we're actually using strategy this year, I thought. How can we lose with such a wise team leader?

When our quarterback came to the line, he looked around, then barked out the signals: "15, 43, 18, orange, hike!"

—DAN DUGAN

I was reading a book aloud to my class about Squanto and the first Thanksgiving. Near the end, I came to the part about the great feast where people gathered together, partied, and celebrated for days. I paused to add, "And we all know the name of that special celebration...."

One student called out, "Woodstock!"

—CHRISTINE SWANSON

Having been an air force brat all my life, I'm used to moving unexpectedly to a new post. But even I was a bit shaken when, at college last November, I received a letter from my father bearing an unfamiliar postmark and saying, "Oh, son, did I tell you? Don't come home to Louisiana for Thanksgiving. We've been transferred to Madrid."

—TIMOTHY K. CORMANY

Our neighbor ranks in the top 10 on any list of the nation's most dedicated football fans. Every Saturday, Sunday, and holiday he digs in at the line of scrimmage, squarely in front of the TV set, and with unswerving devotion watches every game scheduled, from opening kickoff to final whistle.

On Thanksgiving morning his teenage daughter sat in my kitchen, listening gloomily as our children made eager inquiries about the status of our turkey: "When will it be ready?" "When do we eat?"

Hoping to cheer our young visitor, I asked brightly, "And what time are you having dinner?"

Her unhappy voice seemed to answer for all the football widows and orphans of America. "At half-time," she muttered.

—JAN WASHBURN

My son is ticket-taker, baggage carrier, and all-purpose expert for a small airline in Augusta, Maine. On Thanksgiving he was planning to take the last flight himself home to Boston. When the plane landed in Augusta, he unloaded the luggage of the arriving passengers, handed it out to them, checked in the new passengers, lined them up at the door, put their bags aboard, and escorted them to the plane. Then he closed up the office and climbed into the plane himself.

As he was shutting the door, one man who had been watching the proceedings carefully tapped him on the shoulder. "Look," he said, "if you're flying this thing, I'm getting off."

—MRS. WILLIAM O. NICHOLS

The windows of playwright Marc Connelly's New York apartment offer a perfect view of Macy's Thanksgiving Day parade. Connelly sends formal invitations to come and watch the parade to the children of his friends, with this postscript: "Parents optional."

—LEONARD LYONS

The day before Thanksgiving, one of the professors at pharmacy school presented the class with a surprise quiz. In addition to the usual A, B, C, or D answers, the multiple-choice test had options like R, S, T, and U on some questions. After completing the exam, I knew I had done well, for the letters of my answers spelled out: "Eat a lot of turkey."

—LARRY J. SULLIVAN

I was preparing my nursery-school class for Thanksgiving. Many years ago, I told them, the pilgrims survived a difficult voyage, arrived at Plymouth Rock, and met the Indians, who helped them prepare a great feast. The mother of one of my pupils came in the day after our class discussion. Her daughter had reiterated the story of the pilgrims, and the mother asked her what the menu for the first Thanksgiving had included.

The little girl replied, "I'm not sure, but you can ask my teacher—she was there!"

—JANICE SOFRAN

One Sunday I was scheduled to preach twice: first at my small church and then at a larger church, near the city. After finishing the early service, I left for the second. In my haste, and traveling in unfamiliar territory, I got lost. Finally reaching the church, I heard the strains of the opening hymn. I hurried in and took my place next to the pastor.

When the hymn ended, I stood up and gave the prayer of Thanksgiving. After I sat down, my colleague turned to me and said, "Who are you?"

After I told him, he informed me that I was at the wrong church. He then explained my gaffe to the congregation, and I again walked down the aisle, this time to applause.

—RICHARD J. HENDRY

Yuletide
Cheer

"Santa Claus has the right idea.
Visit people once a year."

—VICTOR BORGE

'Tis the Season

We make a lot of fruitcakes, and for special occasions we ice them with marzipan. Just before Christmas my daughter-in-law, Heather, called to ask me for the icing recipe. During our conversation, she mentioned that she'd told some friends about the cakes she was making, and one friend asked her how she learned to make them.

"It was easy!" Heather told her. "I called my mother-in-law. She's the queen of fruitcakes!"

—PAM NORTHCOTT

Last year in August, my wife, Louise, announced that she wanted a new stove because the timer on our 25-year-old model wasn't working. "Why do you need a new stove?" our son Wade asked. "You don't cook."

"I do," she countered. "I cook a turkey at Christmas."

In early September she got a new stove. In October, Wade asked, "When are you going to cook something on it?"

"Is it Christmas already?" she asked.

—DAVID HODGKINSON

The popular and busy men's clothing shop in a neighboring town employed a dedicated staff who always helped clients select just the right items. At Christmas every year, they added a festive touch—a bowl of mixed candies on the counter.

One day, after having made numerous purchases, an older woman leaned over the counter, smiled at the young clerk, and said, "Now, my dear, may I please have a kiss?"

Mindful of good customer relations, the young man leaned over and planted a kiss on the woman's cheek.

"No, no," the customer laughed. "I meant the candy kisses."

—CATHERINE J. BLENKHORN

When my husband and I were newly married, he received his first bonus check—for $15. I was duly impressed and asked what he intended to do with it. "Put it in the bank," he said. I protested that it was a gift and, since it was Christmas, he should get something special with it, something he wanted. "That's what I want," he replied. "Money in the bank."

—MRS. R. C. DARRE

This story is about Jack Straus, chairman of the board of Macy's. One Christmas Eve he returned late to his New York apartment, having worked until midnight ensuring that all Christmas orders were filled in the "world's largest store." He climbed wearily into bed, and at two o'clock in the morning the phone rang. He picked up the receiver.

"Hello, Mr. Jack Straus of Macy's?"

"Yes."

"Oh, Mr. Straus, I was in your store the other day, and I found the most adorable ski hat for my husband. It's in his stocking, and I just can't wait for him to see it."

"May I ask," he replied with chilling politeness, "what prompts you to call me at this hour of the night about a ski hat?"

"Because your darn truck just delivered it," came the shouted reply as the phone was slammed down.

—J. S. Z.

One December morning I headed down the steps to catch my subway, the L train. A sign on the platform declared that the line was not running, but there was bus service aboveground. I was rushing back up the stairs when I passed two women descending. "No L," I gasped as I ran by.

"And a Merry Christmas to you, too," they called out, continuing down the stairs.

—MIKE CAMPBELL

I work in the dress department of a large store, and each Christmas I watch for my favorite customer, a small, dignified elderly gentleman. He carefully examines every dress on the size 16½ rack and, after making his choice, moves to the size 22½ rack, where he selects the identical dress. I gift-wrap the size 16½ and hold the 22½ until the day after Christmas, when his smiling wife comes in to exchange sizes.

—ELAINE HALLIGAN

While packing a box to send to our son for his first Christmas in the air force, I decided to follow an old family custom and add a stocking full of toys and games. When he called home on Christmas Day, I asked nervously if the package had caused him any embarrassment.

"Well," he said, "right now two guys are up on the barracks roof flying the glider plane; there's a bet on who can keep the paddle ball up the longest; the wind-up cars are being raced; everybody's been shot with the water pistol. I haven't even had a chance to play with my own stuff."

—MRS. T. LESNICK

I enjoy dressing up for the holidays, so when my family gathered for dinner at a nice restaurant, I wore a sweater with five little Santas on the front. Each Santa had a real bell sewn onto his hat. When the waiter came to our table, he turned to me, "What a festive sweater. Do they jiggle?"

Red-faced, he corrected himself. **"I mean, jingle."**

—MOLLY D. SLOAN

"I'm pretty sure it was over the river."

We purchased an old home in northern New York State from two elderly sisters. Winter was fast approaching, and I was concerned about the house's lack of insulation. "If they could live here all those years, so can we!" my husband confidently declared.

One November night the temperature plunged to below zero, and we woke up to find interior walls covered with frost. My husband called the sisters to ask how they had kept the house warm. After a brief conversation, he hung up. "For the past thirty years," he muttered, "they've gone to Florida for the winter."

—LINDA DOBSON

Man to man: "All I expect for Christmas is my wife's relatives."

—EARL WILSON

Last Christmas my wife, Laura, was counting calories to minimize the inevitable holiday pounds. She asked me to hide her favorite snacks in a cupboard too high for her to reach, even with a chair. When I came home from work that evening, I saw the nearly empty bag of Bugles sitting on the counter.

"How'd you get those down?" I asked, surprised.

"With a little eggnog," Laura sheepishly replied.

—JARRETT SYLVESTRE

To lighten the postmen's load during the Christmas rush, Toronto postal authorities arranged with strategically located residents to leave sacks of mail on their porches. The first day one postman arrived to collect such a sack on his route, he found none there and supposed none had been left. But when it happened again the next day, he reported it to his supervisor.

Mail had been left, so an investigator called on the householder and asked if she hadn't agreed to have the mail left there during the Christmas season.

"I did," said the woman. "And it's the last time, too. I don't mind helping out, but the last bag you left took me two and a half hours to deliver."

—ROSEMARY BREW

Just as I began my Christmas Eve service, the electricity in the church failed. The ushers and I found some candles and placed them around the sanctuary. Then I reentered the pulpit, shuffled my notes, and muttered, "Now, where was I?"

A tired voice called out, "Right near the end!"

—REV. DOUGLAS C. WOODS

It was the Sunday before Christmas, and our young new pastor was sharing with the congregation the somewhat ambitious goal he had set for himself the previous December: to visit every church family in their homes before the year ended. Apologizing for not quite achieving his aim, he asked that anyone desiring a visit before the year's end please raise his hand. We all looked as one person raised her hand. It was the pastor's wife.

—SHARON MACY

The local minister was fond of an occasional tipple, so the owner of a bar offered him a crate of cherry brandy for Christmas in exchange for a free advertisement in the church newsletter.

The minister reluctantly agreed and ran the following message in the next issue: "The pastor would like to thank Patrick O'Reilly for his kind gift of a crate of fruit and for the spirit in which it was given."

—WILLIAM ROSS

As an instructor, I try to lighten the stress of important exams by sticking in a lighthearted question at the end. Before Christmas break one year, the last question read: "Your instructor wishes you: (a) an enjoyable holiday; (b) a happy New Year; (c) a restful vacation; (d) all of the above."

One of my students, correctly anticipating his low grade on the exam, added a choice of his own: "(e) Had studied more!"

—LINDA PAYNE

How many reindeer does it take to change a lightbulb?

Eight. One to screw it in, and seven to hold Rudolph in place.

"Some people are squeamish about raising their own holiday turkeys—but not me. Back in January we bought a turkey who became like a member of the family. We kept him in the house, fed him, and took him for walks. But when the time came, there was no nonsense about it. We had him for Christmas dinner. He sat on my right."

—ROBERT ORBEN

I was a vegetarian until I got married. One Christmas, as our children and their families gathered around the table, my husband, Cyril, announced,

"Your mother didn't know what a turkey was until she met me."

—LORRAINE LARKIN

One December, when I was assistant manager of a children's bookstore, we set up a special rack of small holiday books. Looking at a few of the Hanukkah books on display, a customer remarked to the counter clerk how well priced they were.

"Yes," the clerk agreed. "And they make great stocking stuffers, too!"

—KIMBERLY C. PETERSEN

I bought three additional strands of exterior Christmas lights. As my husband and son were busy when I wanted them put up, I decided to do it myself. I climbed up the ladder to the roof, hung over the edge, and secured the wires under the eaves. Back on the ground, with knees still quivering, I flipped the switch and stood back to admire the effect. Seventy-five empty light sockets stared back at me.

—LYNNE BAUMANN

In the midst of the most chaotic traffic, my husband, late and impatient, put his hand full on the horn and left it there, honking away. A woman in the car next to ours leaned over and asked me, "And what else did he get for Christmas?"

—MARIA NATAL CARVALHO

A friend of mine married a fellow named Sherlock. Easy to remember, I thought. I'll just think of Sherlock Holmes. Not long after, however, I sent out my Christmas cards, and my friend called me, laughing.

I had addressed their card to Mr. and Mrs. Holmes.

—SONYA CARSWELL

While Christmas shopping, I asked a pretty college freshman working in our local bookstore during the holiday rush for a copy of Dickens's *Christmas Carol*. Smiling sweetly, she said, "Oh, he didn't write songs. He wrote books."

—ANNABEL COWAN

As a new minister, I wanted my first holiday services to be both attractive and meaningful. The Christmas Eve service included a candle-lighting ceremony in which each congregant lit a candle from his neighbor's candle. At the conclusion of the ceremony, the congregation sat hushed, pondering the beauty of the moment.

I rose to announce a hymn and was taken completely by surprise when laughter broke out in response to my invitation: **"Now that everyone is lit, let's sing 'Joy to the World.'"**

—DAVID PINCKNEY

Shortly before Christmas my niece Carolee took her dog Tippy to the groomer. When she picked Tippy up, they sent her home with a beautiful gingerbread man wrapped in holiday cellophane, tied with a red bow. Once home, Carolee put the cookie on a table.

A few days later she returned from work and saw that half the cookie had been eaten.

When Carolee asked her husband about it, he said, "That was Tippy's? No wonder it tasted like liver."

—EDITH HENRY

My friend Shirley had written her last Christmas card and wearily moved on to writing checks to the phone company, the electric company, and a department store. After the holidays the extent of her pre-Christmas exhaustion became apparent when the bank returned one of her checks with an "incorrect signature" notation. She had signed it "Shirley, Bernie and the girls."

—BETH MCMASTER

Married 37 years, my brother- and sister-in-law, Jake and Fran, were chatting with another couple. Jake admired his friend's ornate gold-and-diamond ring and lamented that all he had was a gold washer, indicating his plain gold wedding band.

The following December a small jeweler's box appeared under the Christmas tree for Jake. When he opened it, he found an expensive gold-and-diamond ring. Thanking Fran for the beautiful gift, he added, "You really shouldn't have spent so much money on me."

"Oh, I didn't," she replied. "I took it out of your top dresser drawer. It's the ring I gave you for our twenty-fifth wedding anniversary."

—V. K. HOEPPNER

Working at the post office during the Christmas rush, I saw these words boldly scrawled across a large package: "Nonperishable, unbreakable—have fun!"

—LOWREY MCNEEL

Attending our church's Christmas program, I noticed that many other men there had full beards. Knowing my wife's aversion to facial hair, I teasingly whispered to her, "How do you think I'd look with a beard and mustache?" She whispered back,

"Lonely."

—ROBERT C. BAPTISTA

Under a cultural-exchange program, my family was host to a rabbi from Russia at Christmastime. We decided to introduce him to a culinary treat that was probably not available in his country: We took him to our favorite Chinese restaurant.

Throughout the meal, the rabbi spoke excitedly about the wonders of our country in comparison to the bleak conditions in his homeland. When we'd finished eating, the waiter brought the check and presented each of us with a small brass Christmas tree ornament as a seasonal gift. We all laughed when my father pointed out that the ornaments were stamped "Made in India."

But the laughter subsided when we saw that the rabbi was quietly crying. Concerned, my father asked him if he was offended because he'd been given a gift for a Christian holiday. He smiled, shook his head, and said, "*Nyet.* I was shedding tears of joy to be in a wonderful country in which a Buddhist gives a Jew a Christmas gift made by a Hindu!"

—ALAN ABRAMSKY

"It was just gonna be too difficult to untangle."

As Canadians living in Miami, we often drove back to Canada for vacations. One year we decided to drive up for the Christmas holidays. When we reached the border, the customs official took one look at our Florida license plates and said, "Anyone dumb enough to leave Florida this time of year can't be smart enough to smuggle anything. Go on through!"

—MRS. M. T. SMITH

Every Christmas, composer Giacomo Puccini would send a coffee cake to each of his friends. One year, after he had given his baker the list, which included the name of Arturo Toscanini, he and the conductor had one of their frequent quarrels. It was too late to recall the cake, but Puccini wanted Toscanini to know how he felt. So he sent him a telegram saying: "Cake sent by mistake."

The conductor replied: "Cake eaten by mistake."

—E. E. EDGAR

We were expecting holiday guests, and I was eager to make our house as festive as possible. Every time I came back from the mall, the miniature Dickens-era village under our Christmas tree grew.

I added a train station, chocolate shop, toy store, and bakery. Then I enhanced the cultural life of the village with a school and a gazebo for band concerts.

After one especially productive shopping trip, I put in a restaurant, where the imaginary villagers could have Sunday brunch after attending services at the new church. I happily rearranged the newest pieces and said to my husband, "Do you know what this village really needs?"

"Yes, I do," he answered crisply. "It needs a board of trustees to enact zoning laws to contain expansion."

—JANET PRZYBORSKI

Hoping to make some money on sales commissions, I took a job as a telemarketer. With a prepared script and a list of 300 names, I started my calls.

"Congratulations," I'd say. "You've just won a Christmas ham."

For four hours, as soon as I got the opening pitch out of my mouth, the prospects hung up. Meanwhile, the other telemarketers were making sales right and left. When my supervisor came by to check on my progress, I asked what I was doing wrong.

"Perhaps it's the list," he said, handing me another one. "You've been calling the members of Temple Israel."

—LARRY SOLOMON

Rich, my husband, and I had a hectic holiday schedule encompassing careers, teenagers, shopping, and all the required doings of the season. Running out of time, I got the stationer to print our signature on our Christmas cards instead of signing each one individually.

Soon we started getting cards from friends signed: "The Modest Morrisons," "The Clever Clarks," "The Successful Smiths."

Then it hit me. I had mailed out a hundred cards neatly imprinted "Happy Holidays from the Rich Armstrongs."

—PATRICIA MEES ARMSTRONG

My creative mother enjoys doing crafts, such as making potpourri boxes decorated with ribbon and lace. Sometimes she gets so involved she disappears into her upstairs workroom for hours, forgetting about more mundane things—like making dinner.

One evening I arrived home to find the kitchen empty again. But this time I found a note: "Warning! Small craft advisory: Buy yourself a pizza."

—JANICE DECOSTE

Two weeks before Christmas my mother was searching for a Precious Moments ornament. After what seemed like hours, we found a Hallmark store. Mom approached the sales clerk, who looked more like a linebacker than a cashier, and asked if they had any Precious Moments. "Aren't we having one now?" he replied.

—KAREN HOLTZ

After their wedding on December 23, a Galena, Kansas, couple went directly to the farm where they would live instead of taking a honeymoon trip. There on the farm gate they put a huge red ribbon and a sign: "Do not open until December 25."

—A. M. HEISTAND

It was Christmas Day, and we had all gathered for the holiday meal at the home of my husband's parents. After dessert my mother-in-law left the table and returned carrying a bowl filled with slips of paper. Each adult was instructed to take one. Excited, we did so, wondering what surprise she had thought up for us.

My slip of paper instructed me to dry the dishes; another person was told to wash them. Others had to do pots and pans. Then, with all the parents out of the way, Grandma and Grandpa went into the living room and enjoyed their grandchildren.

—MERNA ALEXANDER

Winters have been hard in our part of Ohio, and my husband's spent many an hour shoveling out our long driveway. He often admired our neighbor's snow blower, so one fall day I decided this would make a perfect Christmas gift. I bought one and hid it away for the holidays.

When snow was predicted for December 15, I broke down and gave my husband his present early. He was thrilled. That night, he made sure his new machine was fueled and ready to run. Then he carefully laid out his thermal clothes in preparation for the next day's adventure. He was so excited, he slept fitfully all night.

In the morning, my eager husband dressed quickly and glanced out the window on his way to the door. Sure enough, the ground was covered with a blanket of snow—but not one inch in the driveway. It had been cleared by our neighbor doing us a favor.

—KIM TERLECKY

Two months after Christmas, our post office had finally recovered from the rush of cards, letters, and packages. I was working at the canceling machine when I noticed that a collection of card-size envelopes had been dropped through the mailing slot.

"Could these be Christmas cards in February?" I thought to myself as I reached for the stack. As I shuffled through the envelopes, my suspicion was confirmed, for on the back of each card was handwritten: "Don't ever trust your husband to do anything."

—REG ALEXANDER

When my mother began teaching, she was known as Miss Smeed to her grade 1 students—or so she thought. She found out differently when she met one of the dads the following January.

"I'm so glad to meet you," he said warmly. "Do you know it was Christmas before I found out your name wasn't Mincemeat?"

—NOREEN AULD

"This one can't promise us the video game. What's your Santa say?"

The nice thing about a gift of money for Christmas is that it's so easily exchanged.

—ARNOLD H. GLASOW

My mother always resists our attempts to simplify her life with modern conveniences. She claims it's more relaxing to wash dishes by hand and just as easy to use a knife as a food processor. Last Christmas, however, we surprised her with a microwave oven.

"Look, Mom," I said, "these brownies took only four minutes to bake. Isn't a microwave marvelous?"

"Just what I need," she retorted. "A machine to make me fat faster!"

—CARRIE S. BROWN

While driving in New York City one evening during the pre-Christmas rush, I was startled when a police officer blew his whistle and motioned me to stop. I certainly couldn't be speeding! I was relieved when the officer, pointing first to my darkened headlights and then to the brilliant Christmas lights and decorations, said, "Madam, won't you help us illuminate Fifth Avenue?"

—DOROTHY L. BONNER

When my wife returned from a shopping trip, she complained that she was having trouble finding the items on my Christmas list. She began naming them: a hydraulic jack, a lug-all hoist, a circular saw, a green toolbox, and a power drill. Baffled, I asked to see the Christmas list. I am a city policeman, not mechanically inclined, and live in an apartment. The problem, I discovered, was that my wife had taken a page from my police notebook—a list of the items in a recent burglary.

—JAMES WEISS

My sister-in-law, sending some homemade cookies to brighten my Christmas in Vietnam, wasn't taking any chances with my health. A note on the outer wrapping read: "If this package arrives after January 10, give it to the enemy."

—DONALD M. NAGEL

Two desperate days before Christmas, I was buying gift wrap when I saw a crumpled piece of paper on the counter. It was a Christmas list—almost a twin of the one I was clutching—crossed out, scribbled over, and packed with question marks.

My heart went out to the harried list maker as I read: "Harry—bourbon? Paperweight? Get embroidery hoop and gold paint for Judy's halo. New bills from the bank for mailman. Order pies today." But the last notation was the real heart-wrencher. In big print, it read: "Don't lose list!"

—BEE HARGROVE

When the bishop of Chester, England, declared that there should be a religious message on Christmas stamps, *Punch* magazine suggested, "Lord, deliver us."

—KENNETH THOMAS

One week before Christmas last year, Connecticut was hit by a storm that gained the honor of being the worst ice storm in memory. Over a quarter of a million households were without electrical power or heat. In many houses there was no water. Freezing temperatures drove families to emergency shelters. In some areas five or six days passed before the lights came on. When we returned home six days later, there was one holiday greeting card waiting in the mailbox. It read: No lights, no heat, Noel.

—MARIA C. JOHNSON

Have you noticed how all the new toys need batteries? Years ago, your biggest problem on a cold Christmas morning was getting the car started. Now it's getting the toys started.

—ROBERT ORBEN

Dad doesn't waste words when he writes a letter. One he sent to me at Simmons College was enclosed with airfare home for Christmas vacation.

The letter read: "Dear Sue, here's some bread so you can get back to the breadbox."

—SUSAN MINOR

The ecumenical spirit of goodwill to all men was never brought to my attention more vividly than on a brisk December day in New Haven, Connecticut. As I pressed through the crowds of holiday shoppers, I chanced to hear a warm-hearted matron taking leave of her friend.

"So," she said, "if I don't see you before Hanukkah—have a merry Christmas!"

—WILLIAM FRANCIS

Having reached the far side of 40, my tastes have become somewhat conservative. So when my teenage daughter presented me with an above-the-knee bright-yellow shift as a Christmas gift, I was a bit stunned. I told her the dress was pretty, but added, "This is the kind of dress a woman wears to attract a man, and I already have my man."

With a sidelong glance at her father, she said, **"Well, attract him."**

—JANE A. PENSON

Posted notice: "Give something warm and fluffy for Christmas. Five groovy puppies."

—ROBERTSON F. SMITH

I was in line at the post office early in December. The man in front of me had a package that he was mailing to his sister in Brazil. After weighing the package, the clerk handed him a mailing form and said the postage would be $6.36. The man looked at the package, then at the form. He hesitated a moment.

"Have you a knife?" he asked. The clerk handed him one. The man slit open the package and unwrapped a delicious-looking fruitcake. After cutting the cake into pieces, he pushed it toward the postal employees and said, "The cake isn't worth that much. Merry Christmas!"

—JUNE BROCK

We spent an enjoyable Christmas holiday in New York City, but battling the crowds became too much one day, and we sought refuge in a quiet museum, where I sat writing postcards. It was surely weariness that moved me to add on one card: "New Yorkers are rude people." And it was weariness that caused me to leave the cards, ready for mailing, on a bench.

When we returned home, my family showed me a card that, in addition to my message, said: "Mailed by a rude New Yorker."

—LINDA PRAGER

I was sitting on a bench outside the post office licking stamps for our Christmas cards when I noticed a lad about nine on a nearby bench doing the same job. But this enterprising youth had recruited a helper. He was rubbing the stamps across the waiting tongue of his obedient Saint Bernard.

—W. R. SHIRLEY

My wife of six months and I spent a long time selecting the card we would send to friends on our first Christmas together. We chose a card with a distinctive abstract design and a meaningful message and proudly mailed early. Shortly after the holiday, we received a silver baby rattle from a generous, elderly aunt who apparently misunderstood the message: "A child is born and peace descends."

—DOUGLAS E. LAM

Our daughter, Cindy, who remained in California after graduating from college, has developed an acute sense of things distinctly southern Californian and occasionally sends them back to us in Ohio.

One Christmas she sent gifts in colorful wrapping paper that showed angels with harps on a background of blue sky and billowing clouds. It was traditional holiday wrapping in every respect—except for one thing: All the angels wore sunglasses.

—LEONARD F. WAITE

In preparation for a Christmas Eve performance, some of the members of our church were rehearsing a group of carols. All went well except for one song, which sounded slightly off. After listening carefully, I finally located the source of trouble. One girl, who came from the Deep South, had been singing: "O lil' ol' town of Bethlehem . . ."

—TENA MOHAUPT

 ## Why was the little pointy-eared guy down in the dumps?

He had low elf-esteem.

On Christmas morning my sister opened a large box from her husband. Inside she found a card that said: "Merry Christmas and Happy New Year." Under a second wrapper was a card: "Be my valentine." More paper and strings came off to reveal "Happy Easter," "Happy Birthday" and Mother's Day greetings.

Finally she worked her way through "Happy Wedding Anniversary" to the gift, a beautiful mink stole, and the final card, which read: "Gal, you've had it for this year."

—J. V. RHODES

Excited over the success I'd had with my new diet, I optimistically projected several months into the future and announced to my husband that I was giving him a 110-pound wife for Christmas.

"Oh, good," he answered. "Whose?"

—MARY A. JOHNSON

To show our admiration for his imaginative and interesting lectures, we bought the professor a box of his favorite cigars for Christmas. On the last day of class, the present was on his desk, but much to our surprise he didn't seem pleased. In fact, he acted somewhat annoyed when he unwrapped the box. He said nothing about it, however, until the end of the period.

"Gentlemen," he announced, "the university strictly forbids faculty members accepting gifts from the students. I appreciate your sentiments, but we must obey the rules."

He took the box of cigars and tucked it under his arm. "There is only one course open to me. I shall take them home and burn them."

—BRUCE BROWN

"Don't worry. It's very common for fruitcakes to have self-esteem issues around the holidays."

Like most families, we exchange Christmas cards with some people who are quite unremembered acquaintances. Once on our list, the names seem to stay. The fact that we were no more remembered than they were was evident the year we sent out cards showing a busy family engaged in holiday activities. Printed on them was: "Greetings from the harried Parkers."

To our surprise, we received in return a number of cards addressed to Mr. and Mrs. Harried Parker.

—PATRICIA L. PARKER

Greetings of the season were expressed in a special way by the officers of one city's police station. A sign in front of the station read: "Christmas greetings from the fuzz."

—MRS. PIERRE PALMENTIER

A church choir was singing Christmas carols at a neighborhood shopping center, and at the entrance a sign read: "Park, the herald angels sing."

—ANGIE PAPADAKIS

As the number of sons of our friends Dick and Marge Hitt increased, their Christmas cards carried the signature: "Dick and Marge and the 3 Hitts" or "4 Hitts" or "5 Hitts," depending on the current score. Finally a long-awaited baby girl arrived, and the signature changed to: **"Dick and Marge, 5 Hitts and a miss."**

—MRS. L. R. TJENSVOLD

The Christmas season is really over when you finally get the pins out of your new shirt.

—JACK HERBERT

Facing possible dismissal from West Point because of our low scholastic standing, my roommates and I were forced to spend our Christmas leave at the academy studying for re-exams. We decided it might be appropriate to send the dean of the academic department, Brig. Gen. Harris Jones, a Christmas card. Using the numbers representing our class standings, we signed the card: "#470, #492, #517, class of 1955."

After mailing it, we began to have misgivings. But a few days later a card arrived addressed to the three of us, reading: "Merry Christmas and Happy New Year, from #1, class of 1917."

—J. W. NAPIER

Red's Rite Spot, a diner on the University of Michigan campus, was gay with Christmas decorations. When Red had served a pretty blond coed sitting at the counter, he leaned over and gave her a big smack on the cheek. Before she could protest, he pointed to a twig of mistletoe hanging above her. The mistletoe was attached to a convenient pulley system that ran the length of the counter.

—PAUL CAMPBELL

During the Christmas season, I walked along Chicago's state street with a friend who is a minister. We stopped to look in a store window that displayed a choir of buxom angels dressed in filmy gowns. My friend gazed into the window for a long time. Then he sighed and said, "Oh, my. If they look like that, we're going to have trouble up there, too."

—G. EUGENIE MAFFIOLI

One Christmas card I received was a snapshot of a relative all bundled up in a bathrobe, with a towel around his neck and clutching a hot-water bottle as he soaked his feet. It was inscribed: "No well."

—R. J. KAPSCH

A weary middle-aged woman on a Philadelphia subway during the Christmas rush was struggling to hang on to a strap as well as an armload of packages. She was standing in front of three men who were occupying space for four, and no one made any effort to move. Suddenly a big, burly fellow pushed her aside, thrust his ample posterior into the narrow space, and wiggled in. Then he rose to his feet.

"Merry Christmas," he said as he gallantly offered her the newly won seat.

—NORMAN A. TAYLOR

Grandfather had always been a problem at Christmas—nothing seemed to please him. This year the children and I decided to chip in and give him a $50 bill to spend as he wished. We watched expectantly as Grandfather opened the envelope. He studied the crisp new bill for a moment and then growled, "Humph! General Grant! Worst president we ever had."

—HOWARD W. LUNDGREN

A cartoonist and I, both attached to a special-service unit, teamed up to print Christmas cards, which we sold for 10 cents apiece to our fellow enlisted men and for 25 cents to officers. We were doing a flourishing business, when the officers learned of the price difference. I was called in by our captain to explain.

"There is a 15-cent sir-charge," I announced.

—I. GOLDSTEIN

A young medical student we know received a very expensive microscope from his parents for Christmas. The card was signed: "Mama and Pauper."

—VERREE WAYNE

When an Iowa girl attending college in Alabama was unhappy because she couldn't afford to return home for the Christmas holidays, her many southern friends presented her with a round-trip ticket accompanied by a large handmade card inscribed: "Yankee, go home!"

—MRS. BEN M. HERR

Could I get my husband to address Christmas cards? I wondered. The family was coming. There were shopping, gifts, the tree, cooking and cleaning *ad infinitum*. I arranged cards, stamps, and address book on the table, then hopefully pulled up a chair and said, "Come on, dear. Let's get these out of the way."

He glanced at the array on the table, turned away, and went into his den, while I looked daggers at his back. I heard a drawer jerked open, banged shut. He returned with a high stack of cards, stamped, sealed, and addressed.

"They're last year's," he said. "I forgot to mail them. Now let's go out to dinner and relax—you've been working too hard."

—MARGARET RICE

When our no-particular-breed dog presented us with eight puppies in November, we knew we would be hard put to find homes for all of them. So we enclosed with our Christmas cards this gift certificate: "Redeemable for one puppy after weaning. Accept this gift in the spirit in which it is given—pure desperation." All the puppies got a good home.

—IRA KELSO

"Help me with this. How did the Wakemans get off our card list but stay on our re-gift list?"

Sign in hospital bacteriology lab: **"The staph wishes you a merry Christmas."**

—MRS. DAVE MADDUX

Shortly before Christmas a Texan dropped in at an exclusive New York art gallery and bought three Van Goghs, five Picassos, six Lautrecs, and an assortment of Monets, Manets, and Corots. "There, my dear," he said to his wife. "That takes care of the Christmas cards. Now let's get on with the shopping."

—LEONARD LYONS

During the Christmas season, when I went to the clinic for a checkup, there was an air of gay excitement as doctors and nurses, carrying beribboned packages, hurried by me toward a certain room. Finally my curiosity got the better of me, and I asked my nurse if there was something special going on.

"No," she explained, laughing. "It's just that when anyone on the staff gets a 'Do not open until Christmas' present, they bring it down here to the fluoroscope machine so they can see what's in it."

—RITA R. IRWIN

One hectic afternoon shortly before Christmas, a harried young mother came to my window at the post office with an energetic small boy in tow. While she purchased a large number of stamps, the mischievous youngster ran helter-skelter through the lobby. A little later I glanced across the lobby and saw that the mother had found a way to keep the boy quiet. He was perched on a writing desk, his tongue sticking out. The mother was methodically tearing off stamps, one by one, moistening them on the handy tongue, then applying them to the Christmas cards in her pile.

—LORRAINE B. HERR

The traditional English folk song "The Twelve Days of Christmas" was revised for a school Christmas program in Donna, Texas. The gift list: twelve fields of cotton, eleven owls a-hooting, ten deer a-running, nine jacks a-jumping, eight bonnets-blue, seven doves a-mourning, six armadillos, five oil wells, four prickly pears, three ruby reds, two Brahman bulls, and a mockingbird in a magnolia tree.

—J. BAILEY

We were studying the Book of Proverbs in our Bible study class, and our minister had included the proverb "Better to live on a corner of the roof than share a house with a quarrelsome wife."

There were a few grins and nudges among the husbands, which turned to laughter when my friend, Terri, turned to her husband and said, "While you're up on that roof, take down the Christmas lights."

—KATHY GALE

One Christmas I visited a friend who has eight children. As we picked our way through the cluttered living room, he said, "To many people, certain sounds are symbolic of Christmas—the tinkle of bells, carol singing, the shouts of happy children. To me it's the unceasing crunch, crunch, crunch of plastic toys."

—J. H. BARNES

We had been out of town for the Christmas holidays, and when we returned, we found in our mailbox a note from friends, saying, "We left you a gift in your milk chute." Eagerly we went to the milk chute—and there found a note from our milkman, thanking us for the good bottle of scotch.

—A. M.

The Christmas card we found on the front seat of our car a couple of weeks before Christmas was from the boys at the garage where we park nightly. We were pleased that they should remember us with a greeting. A week later we found another card from them. It read: **"Merry Christmas. Second notice."**

—VIRGINIA ANGEL

During the usual confusion on Christmas Day, I was putting away the dishes when my son rushed up to me and held out a glass of water and a pill. In a voice of authority he said, "Here, take this!"

Without thinking, I swallowed the pill and then, feeling quite foolish, asked what it was.

"A tranquilizer," he replied. "Now come into the living room and see what your grandson and his toy truck have done to your favorite table."

—MRS. ROBERT SCHAEFER

Why is it that nothing makes you feel more wicked than disobeying a "Do not open until Christmas" seal, and that you're always sorry afterward?

—KATHARINE BRUSH

Bride-to-be to friend: "It was Christmas when I first realized that Tom was getting serious. He gave me an electric blanket with dual controls."

—MAGDALENE WIEL

Doing last-minute Christmas shopping, I was loaded down with bulky packages and heading for my car parked several blocks away. I noticed that a car seemed to be following me, and sure enough the driver offered me a lift. As I climbed in, I thanked him.

"Oh, don't thank me," he said with a sigh. "With all that stuff you've got there, I was sure you must be heading for your car—and I've been looking for a parking place for the last thirty minutes."

—TED F. LANGE

A young friend of mine, wondering what to buy his fiancee for Christmas, heard via the grapevine that she longed for a white negligee. This presented a problem, for he was too shy to shop in the lingerie departments for such a garment. But he found a solution. He telephoned several shops and finally heard about a garment that sounded both glamorous and within his price range.

"Would it be possible for you to put it on one of the mannequins in the window?" he asked. The startled salesgirl agreed that it would be. Half an hour later the young man strolled past the shop window. He eyed the filmy creation furtively, turned, and strolled past once more. Then he hastened to the nearest telephone and rang the salesgirl. "I'll take it," he said. "Please have it gift wrapped, and I'll stop in to pick it up at noon."

—ARTHUR J. ROTH

My Christmas cards from A to G have long and chatty notes from me. My lines get briefer by and by; all T to Z receive is "Hi!"

—ELINOR K. ROSE

QUOTABLE QUOTES

"Christmas is the season when people run out of money before they run out of friends."

—LARRY WILDE

"Most Texans think Hanukkah is some sort of duck call."

—RICHARD LEWIS

"Marry an orphan: You'll never have to spend boring holidays with the in-laws."

—GEORGE CARLIN

"I wrapped my Christmas presents early this year, but I used the wrong paper. See, the paper I used said 'Happy Birthday' on it. I didn't want to waste it so I just wrote 'Jesus' on it."

—DEMETRI MARTIN

"A lovely thing about Christmas is that it's compulsory, like a thunderstorm, and we all go through it together."

—GARRISON KEILLOR

"Christmas is a time when kids tell Santa what they want and adults pay for it. Deficits are when adults tell the government what they want—and their kids pay for it."

—RICHARD D. LAMM

"The one thing women don't want to find in their stockings on Christmas morning is their husband."

—JOAN RIVERS

"One of the most glorious messes in the world is the mess created in the living room on Christmas Day. Don't clean it up too quickly."

—ANDY ROONEY

The Big Man

My nine-year-old son, Roman, had received the latest video game console from Santa Claus, but found several months later that he couldn't load any games into it.

Recalling that a warranty had come with the console, I told him, "I have the receipt, so we can take it back to the store."

Roman gave me a puzzled look. Then his eyes widened and he exclaimed, "Santa gives receipts?"

—SUE PENNINO

Christmas was fast approaching when my friend Dawn reminded her eight-year-old son, Ken, that he would soon be visiting with Santa Claus. He seemed unusually resistant to the idea.

"You do believe in Santa, don't you?" Dawn finally asked her son.

He thought hard, then said, "Yes, but I think this is the last year."

—PENNY HARRISON GILL

Our son and his wife took their two children to the store to see Santa Claus. However, when it was time for three-year-old MaKenna to go up and talk to Santa, she became shy and wouldn't go.

Several times, Santa asked her to come to him, but she refused.

Finally, he asked, "Would you like a present?"

"Yes," MaKenna replied.

"Can you come get it?" Santa asked.

MaKenna thought about this for a moment, then said, "Can you throw it?"

—MAE SIBA

"**And remember, no texting while driving!**"

While in the car, my three-and-a-half-year-old son, Nick, asked me, "Mommy, how does Santa Claus get into all the houses?"

"He goes down the chimney," I answered.

"But we don't have a chimney," he said in a worried voice.

"Oh," I replied, "if there's no chimney, he goes through the front door."

"But what if it's locked?" he persisted.

Thinking fast, I explained, "Yes, that could be a problem, but happily, Santa made a magic key that opens all the doors of all the houses in the world."

He brightened at once. "Oh, like in the song: 'Glory to the new door key'!"

—ALICIA EAKINS

As part of his job as a driver for a florist's shop, my husband, Michael, would dress as Santa for the holiday season. He was a great hit when making flower deliveries.

Once, Michael popped into a drugstore for a last-minute purchase of his own and was asked by the clerk if he had air miles.

"What do I need air miles for?" he laughed. "My reindeer are parked on the roof."

—SUSAN THORN

As we were putting out cookies for Santa on Christmas Eve, I accidentally dropped one. "No problem," I said, picking it up and dusting it off before placing it back on the plate.

"You can't do that," argued my four-year-old.

"Don't worry. Santa will never know."

He shot me a look. "So he knows if I've been bad or good, but he doesn't know the cookie fell on the floor?"

—KELLY LEDOUX

I love playing Santa at the mall. But parents often have trouble getting young children to sit on my knee. It took a lot of coaxing for one little girl to perch there, so I got straight to the point. "What do you want most of all for Christmas?" I asked. She answered, "Down!"

—MORLEY LESSARD

My nine-year-old son, Gabriel, had heard some rumors at school that Santa wasn't real. He approached me with a big question: "Dad, tell me the truth. Is Santa real?"

I decided to tell him it was us who had bought his latest Nintendo Wii game.

"Really?" he said. "You should have let Santa bring it. That way, it would have been free."

—MARIO RODRIGUEZ

I became aware of the changing times when I asked my six-year-old granddaughter whether she had written her letter to Santa Claus yet. She gave me a rather puzzled look and then said: "No, Gran. I e-mailed him."

—JANE MINAKER

My four-year-old daughter knows that Santa Claus brings presents to children on Christmas Eve. One day, when we were going into a shop, she asked me for a gift, to which I replied that I couldn't because I had to start saving money for Christmas presents. Confused, she asked:

"Why? Do you have to pay Santa Claus?"

—CLARA RIBEIRO

"You see me when I'm sleeping and know when I'm awake? Wow, Santa. Get a life."

Our daughter announced that she no longer believed in Santa Claus and flatly refused to leave milk and cookies out for him on Christmas Eve. Upset at losing a four-year tradition, her father tried bribing and cajoling her. Nothing worked.

Later that evening, to my surprise, she walked into the living room carrying a bowl of oatmeal. Her father helped her put the bowl under the tree, next to eight others just like it. "What on earth are you doing?" I asked. "I thought she didn't believe in Santa."

"She doesn't," he said, beaming. "But the reindeer—they're a different story!"

—KAREN DWYER

I overheard my seven-year-old son and his friends discussing the Tooth Fairy, Easter Bunny, and Santa Claus.

"Steven says it's the parents who bring the toys," he said skeptically, "but I know my parents wouldn't know how to drive the reindeer."

—SHARON PRICE

Kelsey, my seven-year-old daughter, surprised me when she said she couldn't wait for her first confession so she could wipe her soul clean.

"Then," she added, "there's no way I can be on Santa's naughty list!"

—MELISSA HARVEY-DANIELL

What does a teacher call Santa's little helpers?

Subordinate Clauses

My husband took our two sons, six-year-old Devin and four-year-old Chase, to a party where Santa would be handing out gifts. The instructions from the organizers were to bring our own gifts, so I brought beach towels with the kids' names printed on them.

Upon arriving, Devin said he couldn't believe the skinny Santa was actually Santa. His doubt turned to belief when he opened his gift.

"He has to be the real Santa!" he said. "How else would he know my name?"

—PAULETTE RYAN

Both male and female reindeers grow antlers in summer, but males drop theirs at the beginning of winter. Females retain their antlers until after they give birth in spring.

This means that all of Santa's reindeers are females. We should have known that only women would be able to drag a fat man in a red velvet suit around the world in one night without getting lost.

—GRAHAM CAHILL

While working as a mall Santa, I had many children ask for electric trains.

"If you get a train," I would tell each one, "you know your dad is going to want to play with it, too. Is that okay?"

The usual answer was a quick yes. But after I asked one boy this question, he became very quiet. Trying to move the conversation along, I asked what else he would like Santa to bring him.

He promptly replied, **"Another train."**

—GEORGE T. FAURE

Youngster singing about Santa Clause:
"He's making a list—and checking his wife."

—LIDA YARBROUGH

It was the first year that our son, Adair, was old enough to tell Santa what he wanted for Christmas. Before we left for the mall, we asked him what he would ask Santa for, and he confidently replied, "A drum!"

Perched on Santa's knee, Adair was asked what he wanted, and he quietly said, "A drum." Santa then asked what else he wanted.

Unprepared for this opportunity, Adair looked uncertain, then enthusiastically replied, "French fries!"

—JANE-ANN DALE-HUNTER

When my husband, Bill, was stationed in Germany, our four-year-old son, Darren, would often help me think of gifts to send him. So on learning that Bill would be coming home in late fall, I told Darren we should have a Christmas surprise waiting for him.

But I was taken aback by the gift Darren requested for his father from the mall's Santa Claus. "Please, Santa," he asked, "bring me a little brother so we'll have a surprise for Daddy when he comes home."

—JUNE B. SCHUH

I was in the post office just before Christmas, where the wait in line seemed too much for an energetic boy named Josh. He was causing a commotion. Needing to make a call, I took out my cell phone.

When Josh looked at me, his mother said, "Look, she's calling Santa." Josh stood silently by his mom for the rest of the wait.

—VICKI BROWN

🎁🎁🎁🎁🎁🎁🎁🎁🎁🎁🎁🎁🎁🎁🎁🎁🎁

To: Santa. Re: Where Are My Gifts?!

If you fear that letter to Santa won't get to the North Pole in time, try e-mailing him. EmailSanta.com sees more than a million missives every year, and each one gets a response, including these:

- I'm sorry, but I don't have a chimney. . . . I'll leave the cat flap unlocked for you, but please watch out for the litter box! *Jon, 4*

- Mommy and Daddy say I have not been very good these past few days. How bad can I be before I lose my presents? *Christian, 7*

- Did you really run over my grandma? *MacKenzie, 11*

- I'm sorry for putting all that Ex-Lax in your milk last year, but I wasn't sure if you were real. My dad was really mad. *Bri, 7*

- You really don't need to send me the motor home. I know that you won't be able to fit it in your sleigh. I know that the elves won't be able to reach the pedals, and anyway, my mom said I can't get my driver's license yet. *Kyle, 5*

- Pleease! Don't bring me any new clothes. *Kayla, 9*

- Thank you for the remote-control car last year, even though it broke the day after. I know you tried, and that's what counts. *Alex, 8*

- Do you know Jesus is the real reason of Christmas? Not to be mean, but he is. *Rosanne, 11*

—SUBMITTED BY ALAN KERR

How many elves does it take to change a lightbulb?

Ten. One to change the bulb, and nine to give him a boost.

At Purdue University, shortly before Christmas vacation, I saw a pair of pantyhose dangling from a window in one of the men's dorms. Then I realized that there were pantyhose hanging from almost every window. A sign on the building read: "Dear Santa, please fill these appropriately."

—LEZLIE DOUTHITT

On Christmas Eve my nine-year-old son, David, put out milk and cookies for Santa, plus an extra treat—a beer. The next morning, David came tearing into our room. "Santa came!" he shouted. Holding up the half-full bottle of beer, he said,

"See? There really is a Santa, because Dad would have drunk the whole thing!"

—KAREN BELLAMY

Because of my fluency in American Sign Language, I was hired to be a Santa Claus in a large suburban mall. My employer wanted to provide deaf children with a Santa who could communicate with them.

I sat for hours, performing for the children who came to visit. But none of them were deaf. Then two girls approached shyly. One explained that her sister was deaf and could not speak.

"What is your name?" I signed slowly.

"J-A-S-M-I-N-E," she replied with her fingers, grinning from ear to ear.

I was bubbling over with pride when I absentmindedly signed, "My name is H-E-N-R-Y. Nice to meet you."

The startled child pulled back and furiously began signing, "I thought your name was Santa Claus!"

—HENRY E. LOWE

Why does Santa Claus come down the chimney on Christmas Eve?

Because it soots him.

— CHRISTOPHER WALTER

My four-year-old was sitting on Santa Claus's knee at the shopping center and was asked, "And what's your name, little boy?" Aghast, Adrian replied, "Don't you know?"

—ROSALIE NISSEN

"Santa, have you lost weight?" . . . "Mrs. Claus is looking exceptionally pretty." . . . "Your toys look wonderful this year."
—Rudolph's cousin, Larry the Brownnose Reindeer

—DAVE WEINBAUM

While doing some Christmas shopping, I overheard a clerk ask a young customer what he wanted Santa to bring him for Christmas. The little boy's face lighted up as he answered enthusiastically, "A baby brother." Upon hearing this request, his mother patted him on the head and replied sweetly, "I'm afraid there just aren't enough shopping days left, dear."

—DANNIE HAMMETT

When he returned home from his office, my husband, Peter-John, a small-town doctor, told me that one of his patients had handed him a letter and asked his advice on what she should do. The letter was from her small son, written to Santa Claus, and it read: "Dear Santa, please phone me. My number is . . ."

Later that night, I overheard Peter-John on the phone. In his deepest voice, he said: "Ho! Ho! Ho! Hello, Andrew! Do you know who this is?"

—JUDY PACE

I had wondered if my seven-year-old daughter was starting to doubt about whether there was a Santa—until Christmas Eve night. She woke up at 2:30 a.m. and again at 4:00 a.m. Each time she woke me up, I told her that if she didn't go back to sleep, Santa wouldn't come.

At 4:30 she could contain herself no longer. She woke me up and declared: "I can't take it! I've got to go see if I've been good!"

—COLLEEN V. GAZDEWICH

A coworker of mine, Cheryl, had done some last-minute shopping on Christmas Eve, leaving her two young sons with her husband. Over the course of the evening, the boys asked for some chocolate milk and Dad obliged, helping them mix the powder into their milk.

Later that night, Cheryl's unusually excited boys were in their parents' bedroom, almost hourly asking if Santa had arrived yet.

Cheryl learned why when a day or so later the boys asked her for some chocolate milk. She told them they had none. But they did, the boys insisted, and showed her what their Dad had made for them on Christmas Eve—Swiss Mocha coffee.

—BILL HARRISON

On a trip to see Santa, my friend's young son Danny climbed onto St. Nick's lap and shared his wish list. Later that day, in another store, there was Santa again.

"And what would you like for Christmas?" he asked Danny.

Shaking his head, Danny sighed, **"You really need to write these things down."**

—RUBY POPP

Oh, Christmas Tree!

Every December it was the same excruciating tradition. Our family would get up at the crack of dawn, go to a Christmas tree farm, and tromp across acres of snow in search of the perfect tree. Hours later our feet would be freezing, but Mom would press on, convinced the tree of her dreams was "just up ahead."

One year I snapped. "Mom, face it. The perfect tree doesn't exist. It's like looking for a man. Just be satisfied if you can find one that isn't dead, doesn't have too many bald spots, and is straight."

—CHRISTY MARTIN

Getting the lights on the Christmas tree can be a production that ranks right up there with hanging wallpaper. Throughout the process, I usually direct my husband as he secures the lights on each branch.

One Christmas, however, when we finally stood back and flicked on the light switch, I noticed that one branch obscured our prized angel ornament. I grabbed the pruning shears, mounted a stool, snipped once, and the lights went out. My ever patient husband, bless his heart, quietly said, "You don't have your glasses on, do you, dear?"

—LYNN KITCHEN

Knowing that my Jewish coworker, Morris, had married a Christian girl, I wondered how they would celebrate Christmas. As I approached their house, I could see reflections of a brightly lighted tree, and I knew that Morris's new wife had had her way. But Morris had the last word: The tree was topped by a brilliant Star of David.

—FRANCIS HANGARTER

"You gotta admit, it's straight now."

My brother Paulo decided to go camping with his family and asked his son and wife to get the box with the tent in the basement and put it in the car.

After a trip filled with great expectations, they arrived at the camping site and amidst great excitement they opened the tent box, from where a beautiful Christmas tree emerged.

—LUIZA AUGUSTA ROSSIGNOLLI SATO

At a Christmas tree lot in Toronto: **"Buy your wife a fir for Christmas."**

—MARY LE GROW

At first sight we knew it was the perfect Christmas tree. Tall, full and lush, and with no bare spots. Even our grown children were impressed.

"Wow," said my son, "if you didn't know it was real, it could easily pass as artificial."

—ROBERT PIEL

A customer walked into our store looking for Christmas lights. I showed her our top brand, but—wanting to make sure each bulb worked—she asked me to take them out of the box and plug them in. I did, and each one lit up.

"Great," she said.

I carefully placed the string of lights back in the box. But as I handed them to her, she looked alarmed.

"I don't want this box," she said abruptly. "It's been opened."

—GLENN PETTY

Just before Christmas, I was shopping at a local mall with my sister and her children. In the parking lot was a fellow selling Christmas trees from a camper trailer.

"Hey, look, Mom!" three-year-old Nick exclaimed. "That guy's camping. He even brought his own woods!"

—CHERYL GILLESPIE

Forget roses or ferns, Jay Leno tells guys on *The Tonight Show*. A Christmas tree is the perfect houseplant for them. "Because it's already dead," he explains, "you cannot screw it up more."

A Nashville grandfather took his four-year-old grandson out in the woods to select a Christmas tree. They tramped all over, but the boy couldn't find a tree that suited him. Finally, it began to get dark and cold, and the grandfather said they would have to quit looking.

"We'll have to take the next tree," he said flatly.

"Even if it doesn't have any lights either?" asked the boy.

—RED O'DONNELL, *NASHVILLE BANNER*

Some of my favorite childhood memories involve our family's annual trips to the local Christmas-tree farm. Although we have an artificial tree at our house, my children are still able to partake in the tradition by accompanying my parents when they cut down their tree.

When I announced we would be helping them pick a tree the following weekend, I expected Ethan, my six-year old, to be excited about the outing.

Instead, he furrowed his brow, puzzled, and asked, "What did they do with the one we got them last year?"

—SARA DAUB

One of my students told me she was happy because her family had got their Christmas tree the night before. "Is it real?" I asked.

"Yes," she replied, then paused for a second before continuing. **"Actually, I don't know. We haven't taken it out of the box yet."**

—TANIS MARSHALL

What Your Christmas Tree Says About You

- **White lights:** You ask houseguests to remove their shoes.
- **Multicolored lights:** You're an extrovert.
- **Blinking Lights:** You have attention deficit disorder.
- **Homemade ornaments:** You have lots of children.
- **Strung Popcorn:** You have too much time on your hands.
- **Red balls only:** You wish you lived in a department store.
- **Yellow star on top:** You're traditional.
- **Glowing Santa on top:** You shop at Kitsch 'R' Us.
- **Cutoff top:** You didn't measure the tree.
- **Vague evergreen smell:** You bought a healthy tree.
- **Strong evergreen smell:** You sprayed your tree with Pine-Sol.
- **Just plain smelly:** There's a dead bird in your tree.

—REBECCA MUNSTERER

You can tell a lot about a person by the way they handle these three things: rainy days, lost luggage, and tangled Christmas tree lights.

—EDWARD THOMPSON

I've always wanted a beautiful shawl to wear with my winter dresses. So when I opened the present from my sister Wanda and saw that it was a white-and-silver shawl, I squealed in delight.

"I love it!" I told Wanda that evening. "I wore it all morning."

"You wore it?" she asked, smiling. "It's a skirt for the Christmas tree."

—KAY PRZYBILLE

Sign on a Christmas-tree lot across the street from several posh shops in Troy, Michigan: **"Firs by Frederick."**

—DAVID W. CHUTE

An uncle of a friend of mine was reminiscing about Christmas during the Depression, when he was just a boy. "We couldn't afford fancy Christmas tree ornaments," he said wistfully, "so we had to settle for apples and oranges to decorate the tree."

Thinking nostalgically of the old days, my friend asked, "Would you like to do that this year?"

"Heck, no," came the answer. "Can't afford to."

—E. B. WINSTON

To decorate our Christmas tree, my eight-year-old daughter, Traci, wanted to string cranberries, so I sent my husband out to buy some for her.

I was putting up the tree when he returned with the cranberries. Not long after, I could hear Traci moaning and groaning that the cranberries wouldn't stay on the thread and her fingers were numb. After admonishing her a couple of times to stop complaining, that this was her idea, I finally turned around.

Cranberries were everywhere except on the thread, and juice was dripping off her hands. Her father had bought frozen cranberries.

—GRETA WOODCOCK

From the *Westfield* (Massachusetts) *Evening News* police log: "A caller reports that her neighbors are having another argument. The responding officer reports the resident was alone and not intoxicated but was having a disagreement with his Christmas tree, which was giving him trouble as he was taking it down."

—DOROTHY CUSSON

Deck the Halls with Office Follies

A waitress at our restaurant had a change of clothes stolen from the break room. Making matters worse, she'd planned on wearing them to the Christmas party.

As a brand-new employee, I didn't know any of this backstory, so I was a bit surprised to find this indignant note posted on the community board: "It has been two weeks since the Christmas party, and I still have not found my clothes."

—DAVID BUTTS

I share an office with three coworkers, one of whom loves to chat. She was scheduled to appear on a local TV show to promote our company's products as gift ideas for the Christmas holidays, and she was telling us about it.

"Eight minutes is a long time for an interview," she commented. "Imagine if I were to talk nonstop for the next eight minutes."

"I agree," one of my officemates replied. "It would feel like an eternity."

—ANITA HELMUS

As luck would have it, I drew the name of my principal at our school's Secret Santa Christmas party. A first-year teacher, I had no clue what to get her. I threw out a few ideas to some colleagues, but they always responded the same: "She already has one."

Desperate, I asked a doctor friend, "What do you give to a woman who has everything?"

He thought a moment before telling me what he gives in such situations: "Penicillin."

—DALE DAVIS

"I heard a rumor the boss may hand out holiday bonuses this year!"

Business merchant: "Dashing through the dough."

—RALPH M. WYSER

On the job as a legal secretary, I accompanied a lawyer to court just before Christmas. The attorney was representing a young defendant who was feeling very confident, almost cocky, obviously expecting leniency from the judge because of the season.

Suddenly the defendant started singing under his breath, "I'll Be Home for Christmas."

The judge, quick on his feet, sang back, "When You Wish Upon a Star." Our client waited for St. Nick behind bars.

—GEORGIA BENJAMIN

At our office Christmas party, a new female executive managed to break the ice and bridge the generation gap in one sentence. We had talked about how she would introduce her longtime live-in boyfriend to her boss, a conservative known to have strong opinions about the morality of the younger generation.

While she didn't intend to lie about her lifestyle, she also didn't want to jeopardize her position or embarrass anyone with views different from her own. When the time came for introductions, she led the young man to the boss and said, "I'd like you to meet Arthur Holt, my person to contact in case of emergency."

There was a slight pause. Then the boss laughed, shook the young man's hand, and invited the couple to join him in some holiday cheer.

—S.D.S.

Two executives, Gary and Bill, staggered out of their company's holiday party in New York City. Bill crossed the street, while Gary stumbled into a subway entrance. When Bill reached the other side; he noticed Gary emerging from the subway stairs. "Where've you been?" Bill slurred.

"I don't know," replied Gary, "but you should see the train set that guy has in his basement."

—WILLIAM ONORATO

The casino where I worked went through a round of layoffs just before the holidays. But it wasn't all bad news. In a memo, management stated, "During the Christmas season, laid-off casino employees will not have to wait the normal mandatory seven days before they are allowed to gamble."

—BOB TREBIL

In January my wife, a physician, met with an elderly patient. "So was Santa good to you?" she asked.

"Real good," he said. "I got an SUV."

"Nice."

"Yeah. . . . Socks, underwear, and Viagra."

—BRUCE NOBLE

The contest was simple: Which department in the hospital where I worked as a nurse could create the best Christmas decorations?

While they didn't win first prize, the members of the proctology department did receive high honors with their distinctive sign: **"Christmas is a good time to look up old friends."**

—PAT INGELS

Announcement in our church bulletin: **"All singles are invited to join us Friday at 7 p.m. for the annual Christmas Sing-alone."**

—JENNIFER BURLEY

Our office Christmas party was a week away, and I had purchased a gorgeous off-the-shoulder floor-length gown for the occasion. But since the weather was so cold, I decided I would need something to cover my shoulders.

I was excited to discover several shawls at one store and went into the dressing room to try them on. One over-the-shoulder cape perfectly matched the material of my dress. However, there was something about it that seemed a bit odd, but I couldn't quite put my finger on it—until I looked at the tag. It read: "tree skirt."

—SHANNON FIDDLER

It was Christmastime, and I was having a difficult day running my home business. While I was downstairs working, our home phone rang. Since I had forgotten to bring the portable with me, I ran upstairs to answer it. The caller gave up while I was searching for the phone, so I called our home number from my business line to find the handset.

I finally located it when I heard one of my son's gifts ringing under the Christmas tree. I had wrapped the phone with it by mistake.

—DONNA RAUSCHENBERGER

Why is Christmas like a day in the office?
You do all the work and the fat guy in the suit gets all the credit.

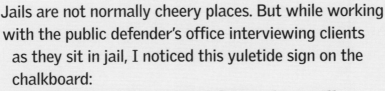

Jails are not normally cheery places. But while working with the public defender's office interviewing clients as they sit in jail, I noticed this yuletide sign on the chalkboard:

"Only 10 more shoplifting days till Christmas!"

—SUSAN CARMAN

Employer: "Here's the official letter on your raise, John. I hope you're satisfied with it."

John: "Thank you very much, Boss. And here's the tape recording of our last Christmas party."

—JOSEPH LOZANOFF

I know my company has made a big effort to be family friendly, but I was baffled when I read this holiday announcement posted on the bulletin board: "All employees are invited to the annual Christmas party. All children under the age of ten will receive a gift from Santa. Employees who have no children may bring grandchildren."

—KRISTIN BAYHAN

My mother writes a column for more than 200 newspapers, and Dad, now retired, helps her answer the mail. They follow a very businesslike procedure—I didn't realize how businesslike until last Christmas Eve. Mother was in her office, and Dad called her to the kitchen. When she came into the room, she saw an array of hors d'oeuvres and a bottle of champagne. "It's our office party," Dad explained, popping the cork.

—SUSAN M. STEIN

The Art of Gifting

When I picked up my son at the airport a few days before Christmas, I was surprised to see him waiting with only his backpack—the airline had lost his luggage. After filling out some forms, we headed home, updating each other on what was new. Knowing he was the typical financially strapped student, I asked what he was giving his mother and brother for Christmas. "Well," he replied, "if they really have lost my bags, all my presents were in them. If they find them, then I have to go shopping tomorrow."

—GORD WADDINGTON

We spend most Christmases with my husband's family, so my mother celebrates Christmas with us two weeks earlier. Once, after a wonderful day opening presents, eating turkey, and seeing other family members, my mother handed me a present. "Please open this Christmas morning. I want you to have a gift to open from me," she said.

Even as a child, I'd never been able to wait to open a gift. With my mom's present, I really, really tried—but lasted two days. Finally, I unwrapped it, lifted the lid of the box, and read the note on top of the present: "What are you opening this for? It's not Christmas yet!"

—DONNA FORD

My 13-year-old grandson David was excited to learn his aunt had sent a check for his mother to buy Christmas presents for him and his brother. David craned his neck to see the check, which his mother hid, saying, "It's the thought that counts."

"I know," David replied. "I just want to see how big the thought was!"

—CAROL CHARTERS

My husband went to the mall with my "Dear Santa" list. One item was perfume. Not having a fragrance in mind, I'd written that I would like something subtle.

Hours later I got an exasperated call. "I'm having a very hard time finding Something Subtle," he told me. "The sales clerk wants to know who makes it."

—JEAN FITZGERALD

Our family drove to a nearby shopping center one morning to buy Christmas presents for one another. In order for the four of us to keep our purchases secret, we decided to split up and meet back at the car.

"Let's all synchronize our watches," Dad said, "so we'll be back here at the same time."

We adjusted our watches and were beginning to go our separate ways when Mom turned to Dad with her hand outstretched and said, "Now let's all synchronize our wallets!"

—BEVERLY BREWER

One week before Christmas, my wife, Theresa, and I discovered we'd each bought the same gift for each other—The Beatles' Number One CD. My wife suggested I return mine, but I suggested whoever paid the most for theirs should be the one to deal with the return.

After she told me how much she had paid—$18.99—I said, "Well, I paid only $16.99, so I guess you'll have to return yours."

"How could you get me such a cheap gift?" she asked indignantly.

—PAUL ROTH

"Don't make it look too nice, I want her to think I did it myself."

What I like about Christmas is that you can make people forget the past with the present.

—DON MARQUIS

My friend reviewed her young son's fill-in-the-blank homework.

One line: "At Christmas we exchange gifts with____."

His response: "Receipts."

—CAROL SCHNELL

Last autumn I found a bargain-priced pair of slippers, size 12, and gave them to my husband, David. But he said he didn't wear slippers, so I set them aside for our family's "White Elephant" gift exchange at Christmas.

The way it works at our get-togethers is you choose a gift marked "man" or "woman" from among the presents when your number is called. When the time came, I watched David choose the gift-wrapped box I had added to the pile. "Look at these nice slippers," he said to me after he opened it. "I can't believe they're the right size, too!"

—IRENE MYERS

My grandfather passed away not long before Christmas, and at almost the same time, my mother's friend lost a close relative.

When they exchanged presents a week later, Mom wrote a sensitive message on the gift tag: "May God give you peace at this difficult time."

Mom was expecting a note of condolence from her friend, but she had evidently chosen not to dwell on the bereavement: Mom's present—a hedgehog garden ornament—came with a tag bearing the words, "I hope you have room for him in your garden."

—MARK SHEARMAN

I spent days searching for the perfect Christmas gift for my husband. Finally, I decided on a hooded full-length purple terry robe and could see from his face on Christmas morning that I'd made the perfect choice. With great enthusiasm Ed put on his robe just as our youngest daughter walked into the room.

She stopped, stared, and said, "Why are you dressed like Barney?"

—LINDA ATMANIK

My four-year-old daughter Sarah received a Christmas gift from her pet goldfish. I could tell she was perplexed. At dinner she asked, "Dad, how did Happy get me a gift?"

Caught off guard, I improvised, "Well, Happy wanted to show you he loves you, so he got you a present."

Not satisfied, she pressed on, "Yeah, but how?"

I started conjuring up an elaborate tale about how Happy had done mail-order shopping, but changed tactics and put the ball back in her court. "Why do you find it strange that Happy would get you a gift?"

"Dad," she shot back, "everyone knows goldfish can't wrap."

—JOHN BARRY

For Christmas my niece and her husband bought a toy parrot that repeats everything you say. Trying it out, they accidentally knocked it off the table. It didn't look broken, but the wings would no longer flap. Hoping to return it to the store, my niece boxed it back up and advised her husband, "Don't tell the clerk it fell off the table; just tell him it was defective."

Immediately the bird inside the box began to chant, "Fell off the table! Fell off the table!"

—BECKY McGLAUFLIN

One Christmas my husband put an assortment of beauty products in my stocking. I tried one of the facial masks and was about to wash it off when my eight-year-old son, Callum, walked in. I explained to him that it was a present from his Dad and it would make me beautiful.
He patiently waited by my side as I rinsed and patted my face dry. "Well, what do you think?" I asked.

"Oh, Mom, it didn't work!" Callum replied.

—LYNN THIBODEAU

Our daughters, Rebecca, 10, and Sabrina, 12, love to try to guess what their presents are by shaking them. On Christmas morning my wife secretly switched the tags on two gifts. The girls were thoroughly confused, until the truth was revealed and the presents they had predicted they would receive were in the right hands.

"What a relief," Rebecca said. "I thought that I was losing my powers!"

—BRIAN PRICE

Husband: "On the twelfth day of Christmas, my true love gave to me—all the bills."

At a variety store, I overheard this conversation between a husband and wife who were obviously rethinking their Christmas list.

"We've bought her a couple of gifts, but do you think she will have enough?"

"Well, I sure don't want her to feel left out."

"Maybe we should just forget it."

"No. I want to buy her just one more. Which do you think she'd rather have, a new collar or one of these chewy bones?"

—ROBERT F. DANNER

I received a box of chocolates for Christmas, and as sweets were abundant in the house, I placed it in the freezer to be enjoyed later.

Recently, longing for some chocolate, I rooted around in the freezer and finally spied the holiday box. I lifted it out, opened it, and found that I'd preserved a plaid scarf and gloves.

—HELEN FLAIG

A friend and his wife decided that letting their young son open all his gifts at once on Christmas morning always turned into present overload. So last December they decided to hold back the big gift—a bike—until after lunch. Unable to figure out how to wrap it, they tied a balloon to the handlebars.

Christmas Day arrived, lunch was eaten, and then the boy's mother announced, "Look what else Santa brought you." And with that, my friend wheeled in the bike.

"Yippee," the boy shouted. "A balloon!"

—JIM WATT

"There's nothing in any of them.
Like he's going to know the difference."

I was going shopping to buy a gift for my wife and asked for her sizes. "If it's clothes, I wear small," she said. "If it's diamonds, I wear large."

—WENDELL W. FENN

Pre-Christmas payments of application fees to several graduate schools had left my son Brian's bank balance low. On Christmas morning each member of the family received a token gift from him, along with a card carrying the following announcement: "Congratulations! In lieu of a gift, a graduate school has been applied to in your honor." The name of a different school was written on each card.

—DOROTHY G. JONES

I thought it would be nice to send a Christmas package to my in-laws in Florida. I went shopping at a local department store and found the perfect gift to send: gourmet coffee, shortbread, and a selection of jams in a festive candy-cane basket.

I called my in-laws on Christmas Day to wish them a merry Christmas. They told me that instead of festive jams, I had sent body frosting complete with a set of instructions.

—BLAIR MCLAUGHLIN

In our home we celebrate Hanukkah, but in keeping with the holiday spirit, my husband and I delivered a box of cookies to a neighbor, saying, "Ho! Ho! Ho! And a very merry Christmas!"

Two days later the neighbor's two children stopped by to reciprocate. The mother had coached her children with the proper greeting, so when I opened the door, the four-year-old handed me a gaily wrapped package and proudly exclaimed, "Merry Christmas and a happy harmonica!"

—ROBERTA COLETON

At day care my grandson and the other children drew names for a gift exchange. When he got home, Mitchell asked his mother to read him the piece of paper.

"It says that you got Christopher's name for Christmas," she said.

Mitchell looked uneasy. "Will everyone call me Christopher from now on?"

—HAZEL HUSZAR

Doing my Christmas shopping, when I was stationed at one of our continental Marine Corps air stations, I ran across a toy bagpipe. It seemed an ideal present for the young son of one of my brother officers on the base, so I sent it to him with a card: "Love to Peter from Uncle Jock."

About 10:00 on Christmas morning, I was awakened by a knock on my door at bachelor officers quarters. There stood my young friend, dressed in his Sunday best, with suitcase and bagpipe. From his neck hung a card: "To Uncle Jock, with love from Peter's parents."

—JOHN T. L. D. GABBERT

Our oldest son had his heart set on a new two-wheeler for Christmas, and our youngest wanted a tricycle. Money was tight, so we decided to buy a bicycle and fix up the old red tricycle as a gift for son number two.

One night I brought the trike in from our driveway and set to work. Four hours later a gleaming blue wonder stood there, complete with new pedals, handle grips, seat, and tires. Just then my wife came into the garage with a funny expression on her face. She was pushing another old red three-wheeler. I had worked my Christmas "miracle" on a tricycle belonging to the child next door.

—WILLIAM R DRUMMOND

"... And our 'Holiday Scented' candle smells just like credit cards."

Sign in department store: **"Make this a Christmas he won't forget—charge everything."**

—WINTON BURRHUS

My six-year-old daughter had chosen the perfect Christmas present for me at a craft sale early in November. When it was time to put our presents under the tree, she found everything she had hidden, except the gift for me. "I don't know what could have happened to it, Mommy," she said. "I put it where I thought you'd never look."

"Where did you put it?" I asked.

"In the garbage can," she replied.

—JANET ROBINSON

We bought my mother a shelf for Christmas, and I asked my husband if he'd hang it as part of her gift.

"Sure," he agreed. "Just remind me to take my tools."

I scribbled a note and stuck it on the gift.

"Holidays getting you down, Mom?" my daughter said.

She pointed to my Post-it: "Take items to hang self."

—BEVERLY WOLF

All the family gathered around the Christmas tree, and as the magic moment for present distribution arrived, wrapping paper was torn asunder and oohs and aahs greeted each gift.

Mom had chosen a box containing two exquisite silk ties for Dad, and rather than saying a simple "Thank you, dear," he quietly slipped away to their bedroom. There he changed from his casual attire into a crisp white shirt and his best suit before parading in front of Mom wearing one of the ties.

She looked at the tie, then asked, "Don't you like the other one?"

—WINSTON WADE

When I found out the price of the lovely powder-blue dressing gown my husband gave me for Christmas, I took it back to the store to exchange it for two less expensive ones. The clerk to whom I explained what I had in mind stared at me wide-eyed.

"Was that man really your husband?"

"Yes, of course," I replied. "Why?"

She called to another girl, "Remember the man who had you model all those robes? Well, he really was buying it for his wife! Imagine!" Turning to me, she asked, "How long have you been married?"

"Twenty-seven years."

The girl shook her head. "Lady, if I were you I wouldn't exchange that robe for anything. I've been selling a long time, and I never saw a man who chose a gift for his wife with such care. You sure are lucky."

I really enjoy wearing that robe.

—RUTH JOHNSON

My husband doesn't buy me intimate apparel, so I was delighted when his grandmother sent me a semi-slinky nightie for Christmas. Meanwhile, he received a much-needed set of plastic storage drawers, which he put to use right away.

He expressed his appreciation to his grandmother in these words: **"I have filled the drawers and emptied the nightie. Thank you for both!"**

—TANIA LEIGH

My 17-year-old son asked me if he could have two of my trading-stamp books to buy a Christmas present for his grandmother. I was quite surprised and told him so.

"What makes you think that you should buy a present for Grandma with my trading stamps?" I asked.

"Well," he replied, "you wouldn't have all those stamps if I didn't eat so much."

—JANE E. BLAINE

Just before their second Christmas as a couple, my sister and her husband were discussing their wish lists. "Do you remember the lovely drill bits you gave me last year?" he asked

"Do you think that this year I could get the drill?"

—JACQUELINE MCGANN

The quilt store where my wife, Donna, shops has a men's shopping night before Christmas, where husbands can fill their wives' wish lists. Last year I attended, and this year, to keep Donna's gift a surprise, I pretended I had a prior engagement the night of the sale.

That night, I stopped at the quilt store, bought Donna a Christmas present, and entered a door-prize draw.

The next day, when I got home from work, Donna said I had a phone message. We listened to the message together: I won a prize at the quilt store the night before.

—HUGH WOLLIS

The minister reluctantly agreed and ran the following message in the next issue: "The pastor would like to thank Patrick O'Reilly for his kind gift of a crate of fruit and for the spirit in which it was given."

—WILLIAM ROSS

Shortly before Christmas, I almost stumbled over a little boy in the middle of the sidewalk who was so busy playing with a toy merry-go-round, a waddling duck, and a walking man that he was oblivious to the crowd milling around him. His obvious pleasure made me think the same toys would delight my own youngster. I asked the little boy where he got them.

"In there," he said, pointing to a shop behind him.

I went in and asked for the toys the small boy was playing with. "Who is he?" I asked as the proprietor wrapped my purchases.

She smiled. "You might say he's my Christmas present. A few days ago he came in and stood staring longingly at the merry-go-round. 'Would you like it for Christmas?' I asked. 'Mother says there isn't any money for Christmas this year. We lost Dad last spring,' he explained, and turned to go.

"It had been a lean season for me—but it was the week before Christmas. I gave him the merry-go-round, and he was so delighted that he got no farther than the sidewalk before he sat down and wound it up. Then the most amazing thing happened. People stopped to talk to him—and I've never had so many customers. I kept count of the merry-go-rounds I sold, and when he got up to go, I called him in and gave him a twenty-five percent commission. I asked him to come back the next day and added the duck and the man to his playthings. Yesterday his commission amounted to eleven dollars!"

—G. C. HENLEY

QUOTABLE QUOTES

"There is a remarkable breakdown of taste and intelligence at Christmastime. Mature, responsible grown men wear neckties made of holly leaves and drink alcoholic beverages with raw egg yolks and cottage cheese in them."

—P.J. O'ROURKE

"Guilt: the gift that keeps on giving."

—ERMA BOMBECK

"Oh, volunteer work! That's what I like about the holiday season. That's the true spirit of Christmas. People being helped by people other than me."

—JERRY SEINFELD

"Oh, joy, Christmas Eve. By this time tomorrow, millions of Americans, knee-deep in tinsel and wrapping paper, will utter those heartfelt words: 'Is this all I got?'"

—KELSEY GRAMMER ON *FRASIER*

"The main reason Santa is so jolly is because he knows where all the bad girls live."

—GEORGE CARLIN

"No matter how carefully you stored the lights last year, they will be snarled again this Christmas."

—ROBERT KIRBY
IN THE *SALT LAKE TRIBUNE*

"Christmas: It's the only religious holiday that's also a federal holiday. That way, Christians can go to their services, and everyone else can sit at home and reflect on the true meaning of the separation of church and state."

—SAMANTHA BEE

"What I don't like about office Christmas parties is looking for a job the next day."

—PHYLLIS DILLER

"Where's your little brother?"

The Very Merry Things Kids Say

Just before Christmas, my five-year-old grandson, Jacob, said, "Could you put away all the decorations, Dad? I want Christmas to be over with."

"But why?" asked his father.

"I'm just so tired of being good!"

—DAVID GRIFFITHS

"You know, I'm not sure I believe in Santa Claus anymore," said my five-year-old nephew a few days before Christmas.

"Oh!" I said laconically, unsure how to respond to this revelation that surely marked a turning point in Louis's existence.

Without reacting to my slight uncertainty, my nephew continued his line of thought: "Almost every time I ask him for something, he sends it to me. So I think I'll go on believing in him for one more year."

—JEAN LAMBERT

Early in December I was racing madly around the house to get my three boys dressed for a children's Christmas party. I wanted them to look just so for their picture with Santa. I was proud of the results when I inspected them before leaving.

Then my middle son piped up, "Aren't we supposed to wear underpants to parties?"

—DENISE SEMOS

A little girl was saying her prayers in a very loud voice and adding what she'd like from Father Christmas. "You needn't shout," her mother admonished her. "God isn't deaf."

"I know," her daughter replied, "but Grandma is."

—PAT ELPHINSTONE

Four-year-old to her two-year-old sister: **"Let's play Christmas. I'll be Santa Claus, and you be a present and I'll give you away."**

—MRS. KENNETH LABAUGH

One Christmas I was teaching a class of ten-year-olds. We talked about how important it was to send cards to people who might be lonely.

The pupils were absorbed in silent contemplation, so I pressed on and asked, "What about giving a card to someone you don't even like very much?"

The children pondered this for a minute or so before one girl walked up to my desk, handed me an envelope, and said, "Merry Christmas, sir."

—UNKNOWN

My five-year-old son, Jordan, had been asking for an Easy-Bake oven for months, so when he received money for Christmas from his grandparents, I told him he could use the money to buy it.

The following week, we purchased the oven, and then we stopped by the grocery store to pick up the turkey.

"Don't worry about Christmas dinner, Mom," Jordan said excitedly. "I'll do the turkey!"

—KAREN LUCIAK

For 98 percent of the students at the school where my wife teaches, English is a second language. But that didn't stop them from giving her Christmas cards. Still, their enthusiasm for the occasion sometimes exceeded their grasp of English. Among the many cards that flooded her desk were: "Happy Birthday, Grandma," "Get Well Soon," and "Congratulations on Passing Your Driving Test!"

—JOHN HYDE

On the afternoon of Christmas Eve, one of my four daughters, Lizann, wanted to show me what she had bought for Holly, her youngest sister. We went to her room while the other girls got ready for the evening church service.

While we were sitting on the bed, door closed, looking at the gifts, Holly came to the door, wanting to come in. We told her she couldn't.

"But I have to ask you something," she said.

"Ask me through the door!" Lizann yelled.

After a moment, Holly called out, "How do I look?"

—SANDY GAGNON

One evening I arrived home from work to find the lights out. My wife had prepared a lovely candlelit dinner, and our two young sons, Garett and Seldon, were dressed in their suits.

"Hey," I joked, "didn't we pay our hydro bill?"

A few months later, during the Christmas Eve candlelit procession, the church was packed and silent when Garett asked, "Hey, Dad, did they not pay their hydro bill, too?"

—SYLVIO GRAVEL

On the last day of school before Christmas vacation, I sent my son to the bus stop with a box of chocolates for the driver. Three weeks later I was getting his school bag ready to return to classes when I unearthed the box. "Why didn't you give the driver her chocolates?" I quizzed.

"I did, Mom," he protested. **"I gave her one!"**

—LYNN AUBIN

When my niece was a student, her class of six-year-olds sang, "Hark, the Herald Angels Sing" at a Christmas concert. The line "God and sinners reconciled" was a tricky one for this age group.

One little boy, with a voice that completely drowned out the rest of the choir, happily belted out, "God and sinners dressed in style!"

—JESSIE ROBERTSON

A few days before Christmas, just as we were about to leave for the visitation at the funeral home, we tried to explain to our children what had happened to Nana.

"Wow!" exclaimed four-year-old Alex. "Nana picked a good time to die." When he saw our confused faces, he explained, "She's going to heaven just in time for Jesus's birthday party."

We were humbled by his sweet response. "You know," he continued, "there are only four very, very lucky people invited to Jesus's birthday party."

"Who are the four?" we asked.

"You know, Nana and the Three Wise Men."

—ANGELICA HILDEBRAND

Our four-year-old son, Gerald, was thrilled with the electric train set he got for Christmas. As I was in the kitchen preparing dinner, I heard him say, "Dad, isn't it neat that I got an electric train from Santa?"

My husband, busily getting the train set up, did not respond. Then I heard Gerald say, "Dad, isn't it neat that we got an electric train from Santa?"

My husband still did not respond. Then Gerald said, "Dad, isn't it neat that you got an electric train from Santa?" I laughed so loudly, my husband finally looked up.

—WILMA VAN DUNGEN

"Come on, Rusty . . . you know they mixed up our presents."

"What is Christmas a time for?" I asked my Sunday school class. Came the usual answers: Jesus's birthday, a time of joy, a time for presents, etc.

But one 11-year-old's answer was unique: "Christmas is a time for sportsmanship, because you don't always get everything you want."

—DONALD POSTEN

My mother cast one of her students as the innkeeper for the Christmas pageant. All the third-grader had to do was tell Joseph, "There is no room at the inn."

But during the performance—after Joseph begged for a room for his pregnant wife—the boy didn't have the heart to turn him down.

"Well," he said, **"if it's so urgent, come on in."**

—ALEX DOMOKOS

When my son, Terrence, was four years old, he piqued everyone's interest when he placed a childishly wrapped package under the tree for each family member.

On Christmas morning, Terrence looked on with joy and expectation as we opened his gifts. There were exclamations of "I thought I'd lost that!" and "So that's where that went!"

When we asked Terrence why he had wrapped our favorite items, he replied, "Because I knew it was something you would really want!"

—SANDI REIMER

I was watching television, and my seven-year-old brother was reading aloud the Christmas list he was sending to Santa Claus. "I would like a Pokémon video game and some Pokémon cards . . ." His voice became louder and louder, until he was almost screaming.

"Jack," I said, "you don't have to scream. Santa can hear you anyway."

"I know," he replied, "but it's better if Dad hears me, too."

—MICHAEL VEZINA

About a week before Christmas, I found signs that mice had got into the house. Each night before bed, I put down traps to try to catch the intruders. On Christmas Eve, as I went to get the traps, my daughter Josephine said, "You don't need to do that tonight, Dad."

"Why not?" I asked.

"Well, after all," she replied, "it's the night before Christmas."

—PETER J. PERRIN

For Christmas I gave my six-year-old nephew, Josh, a pair of *Iron Man* pajamas. Later in the evening, while helping him put them on, I asked if he liked them.

"I would wear anything you gave me, Auntie!" Josh exclaimed. "Except a bra!"

—JANICE HICKEY

During Christmas shopping, my son, Daniel, lost his wallet. I learned how different his reaction was to losing a wallet, compared with me.

"Oh, no!" he said. "Someone might use my library card, return the books late, and not pay the late fee."

—GARY O'LEARY

It was Judy's first Christmas pageant, and like all five-year-olds, she was thrilled to be in the manger scene. She came onstage clutching her gift and gazed in awe at the scene before her: Mary, Joseph, the resplendent wise men, shepherds, animals, all grouped around the simple cradle. Her face shone with eagerness as she approached the crib, and her eyes grew wide in wonder. With uncontainable joy she turned toward the congregation and called out: "Mommy, Daddy—Mary's had her baby. It's a boy!"

—ROBERT A. DOUGLAS

Every Christmas, my father makes a large and complex nativity scene with moss, branches, and many clay figures. He is as meticulous about it as he is with the garden. In fact, when my younger cousins came over, he would spend the whole afternoon outside making sure nobody stepped on the grass or flowerbeds.

One Christmas he caught my younger cousin leaning over the nativity scene removing figures from the moss and placing them in the sand path leading to the stable where baby Jesus was born.

"What's going on here?" he asked.

To which my cousin replied serenely: "You said you didn't want anybody stepping on the grass!"

—GONÇALO PIMENTEL SERRA

Even after they moved to their own homes, both our daughters and their families would either stay at our place Christmas Eve or arrive early Christmas morning to open Santa's gifts.

Last Christmas, during the opening of gifts, our telephone rang. We asked our oldest daughter, Jennifer, to grab it, as she was closest to the phone. She picked it up and walked into the hallway, where it was a bit quieter. Suddenly we heard a crash as the phone fell off the end table.

"Good grief!" Jennifer exclaimed. "It has a cord!"

—JIM MCLEAN

I phoned my four-year-old grandson Tyler shortly after Christmas and asked him what his favorite gift was.

"A drum set, Nan. Want to hear me play?"

He dropped the phone and started banging. After a few long minutes he returned. "Did you hear me play, Nan?"

"Yes, Tyler," I said. "But Nan is phoning long distance."

"It's okay," he reassured me. "I can come closer to the phone."

—MAUREEN PERRY

When school resumed after the Christmas break, my aunt asked my eight-year-old cousin: "Who is mom's dearest son that's going to do very well in school next term?"

To which my cousin immediately answered: "I'm the dearest son, but I don't know who is going to do very well at school."

—CATARINA FERNANDES

Just before Christmas, my son asked,
"Is there really a Santa Claus?" As he was in sixth grade,
I felt he was ready for the truth, so I told him.
Later, at bedtime, I asked how he was feeling.

"I'm sad," he said, tears welling up, "but I'm glad I know the truth. If I didn't and had kids someday, they wouldn't get anything."

—LYNN WINTER

In our house, Advent begins with the family assembling a Nativity scene on our mantel. We unwrap figurines one by one from their storage box and set them in place while retelling the story of the first Christmas, and we conclude by singing, "Away in a Manger."

The year our son, Douglas, was four, we finished and stood back to admire the angels, shepherds, Wise Men, animals, and Holy Family.

"But Mommy," Douglas complained, "you forgot the fish."

"The fish?" I responded. "What fish?"

"You know, Mommy," he said. "A whale in a manger."

—MARGARET HAMMOND

"That's my list so far. But be sure to check my Twitter updates for any changes."

While my five-year-old son Caleb played in his nightly bath, I quizzed him on a new book for "young and inquiring minds" that he had received for Christmas.

"What's the difference between a caribou and a reindeer?" I asked.

"That's easy, Mom," he replied. "Reindeer fly."

—DIANE WHITE

Close to Christmas, I arrived at the babysitter's one day to pick up my five-year-old daughter, Kelly, only to learn that she had been bouncing around on the furniture and had broken the coffee table. She seemed remorseful on the way home and asked me, "Will Santa Claus know?" I said I didn't think so.

"Will God know?" she then asked.

"God knows everything," I replied.

She thought for a moment, then asked, "Does God know Santa Claus?"

—PAT CONNOLLY

On the way to our children's school Christmas performance, our six-year-old daughter was uncharacteristically quiet. As we approached the school, she announced: "I don't really know my lines, so you might want to watch another kid."

—IAN TISDALE

Before the Christmas gathering of our French class, each student had written what he or she wanted most in the world on a slip of paper for the grab bag. When gifts were exchanged, many got cardboard models of sports cars or fake airline tickets. But a student who had requested an A in French unwrapped his gift to find this sign: "Freanch."

—PHILLIP F. KING

Corey, my seven-year-old son, asked me why people celebrate Christmas. Wanting him to know there are many religions, I began to explain that some people do not have Christmas.

"I know," he interrupted me, and in a world-weary tone stated, "I know. Some people celebrate Harmonica."

—JERRY WAUGHTAL

Our daughter was chosen to play the role of Mary in a Christmas pageant. The morning of the first rehearsal, we overslept and got her there late.

The director wearily dismissed our apologies. "It doesn't matter," he said. "The shepherds have hockey practice, and Joseph went ice fishing."

—T. BRADLEY HAYS

I was packing away Christmas ornaments in their boxes when my three-year-old son, Dylan, sat down beside me. Out of the blue, he asked me if we had bought our house. I thought it an odd question, but I said yes, we had bought it.

"Was it new when we bought it?" he wanted to know.

"Brand new," I answered.

Eyes huge, Dylan asked, "Where's the box?"

—MARY LEWIS

Helping me sort clothes into "save" and "give away" piles, my six-year-old daughter came across a garter belt. "What's this?" she asked.

"It's a garter belt," I said. Seeing that meant nothing to her, I added, "It's for holding up stockings."

"Ah," she said, carefully placing it in the "save" pile. "We'll use it Christmas Eve."

—NANCY HALL

It was December 21, and I was frantically preparing for Christmas. All day I complained that I didn't have time to do everything I had planned.

My four-year-old son watched me come and go as he played in front of the TV. Suddenly a TV announcer commented that this was the shortest day of the year.

Sébastien stopped playing and said to me with great compassion: "Oh, Mom, you're really not lucky!"

—FRANCE RODRIGUE-TESSIER

The hymnbooks in our church are designated G or R, depending on the color of their covers (green or red). As we were waiting for the service to begin on Christmas Eve, our nine-year-old son was reading the bulletin. He turned to his uncle and said, "We can't sing the hymns today; they're rated R."

—PATRICIA KIM

Last Christmas one father gave his boy a battery-operated tank, a battery-operated gun, and a battery-operated train. The child loved them. All day he sat around trying to make towers out of the batteries.

—ROBERT ORBEN

In fourth grade my daughter had to write a 200-word essay. She chose the subject "My Grandma, My Heroine."

I suggested she e-mail a copy to her grandma, which she did immediately, adding this postscript:

"Did you get my Christmas wish list last week?"

—YOKE KENNEDY

What do you call a reindeer wearing earmuffs?

Anything you want—he can't hear you.

Visiting Montreal with my daughter Morgane, age 5, we silently entered Notre-Dame church and stopped in front of a statue of Christ.

"Who is that man?" she asked.

"Jesus," I replied.

"That's impossible!" she exclaimed. "At Christmas he was only a baby."

—VALÉRIE ANZALONE

At Christmas I took my son and my four-year old niece to the church to see the manger. There were the three Wise Men, numerous shepherds with their sheep, and a lot of ordinary people. Baby Jesus, Saint Joseph, and the Virgin Mary had an arch over their heads to symbolize halos. I heard my son say to his cousin: "Have you noticed that not all of them have a satellite dish?"

—MARIA EMÍLIA NOGUEIRA MARTINS

All my relatives know that I refold the wrapping paper from my Christmas presents for reuse later.

"Auntie," asked one of my young nieces, "why do you save all that paper?"

"I'm doing what's best for the environment," I replied, "so I'm recycling."

"Good thing you didn't ask that question five years ago," my daughter interrupted. "Then she was just plain cheap."

—OKSANNA GUDZ

On a drive home from visiting family over the holidays, my children and I stopped off at a corner store. The cashier turned to my four-year-old daughter and asked, "Was Santa good t' ya?"

My five-year-old son, not used to the Ottawa Valley accent, piped up, "Her name's not Tia."

—TRISTA FENNELL

I live next door to a four-year-old girl named Jayla. After Christmas she was showing her grandmother the new nativity scene they had gotten.

"These are the kings, Grandma," she said. "They brought Jesus gifts."

"Oh, how nice of them," said her grandma. "What did they bring?"

"Banana bread," Jayla replied.

—ESTHER PALFY

While Christmas shopping with my two young kids, I found myself listening to an enthusiastic preschooler singing Christmas carols in front of us in the checkout line.

"On the first day of Christmas, my true love gave to meeeee," he sang, "a bar fridge in a bare treeeee!"

—KATRINA BATEY

Our discussions at home about politics and world affairs had more impact on our children than we realized. At the end of our church's Christmas Eve service, the minister leaned across the pulpit to address the restless youngsters in the congregation: "Who is the good-natured, plump man who goes all over the world on Christmas Eve working miracles?"

Our ten-year-old son answered, "Henry Kissinger!"

—JUDITH B. AYERS

During the holidays, one fourth-grade class wrote, directed, and acted in a Christmas pageant at the second Presbyterian Church in Charleston, South Carolina. It opened with the scene at the inn. Joseph and Mary ask for a room overlooking Bethlehem.

Innkeeper: "Can't you see the 'No Vacancy' sign?"

Joseph: "Yes, but can't you see that my wife is expecting a baby any minute?"

Innkeeper: "Well, that's not my fault."

Joseph: "Well, it's not mine, either!"

—ASHLEY COOPER

I was surprised when my teenage son handed me a Christmas gift, because I knew he had little money to spend. Opening the wrapped box, I found two AA batteries with a note: "gift not included."

—CHET ROGOWSKI

Our daughter chose to go to college 1,400 miles away from home. As Christmas approached, we decided to dispense with gifts for one another so we could send her the airfare to spend the holidays with us. At the close of the joyous visit, we asked our daughter to phone us when she got back to college.

Our teenage son answered the phone that evening. I asked, "Who is it?"

He replied, "The Grinch who stole Christmas."

—MRS. W. B. LOWE

When my former landlady stopped by to visit one day, she told me about a group of Boy Scouts who had come to see her at the masonic home during the holidays. One boy said, "Mrs. B, you are my troop's problem for this Christmas."

—MRS. W. O. CAMPBELL

"Be careful opening it. He doesn't like being cooped up so long."

We had moved to Seattle from Texas, and each of us missed our old home. That December, when I went to pick up our first-grade son, Madison, from school, his teacher told me about a conversation she overheard.

One boy said, "We're Catholic, and we are going to Christmas Mass."

"We're Jewish," said another child. "And we're going to have a Hanukkah celebration."

Madison chimed in, "We're Texans, and we're going to have a barbecue."

—STEVE MOORE

When my four-year-old son got home from school, I asked him what he'd done that day. He told me that he'd learned a new Christmas song called "Dick the Horse."

"I've never heard of that one," I said, and asked him to sing it for me.

Taking a deep breath, he began to sing, *"Dick the horse with boughs of holly, fa la la la la la la . . ."*

—P. SECCOMBE

When my daughter, Laura, was three, she wanted a violin for Christmas more than anything in the world, and we were successful in finding one for her.

She unwrapped the instrument with great pleasure, then tucked it under her tiny chin, serious and solemn. She slowly ran the bow across the strings, and there was a squeal of discord. She looked up at us in surprise: **"Where's the music?"**

—KERRIN MONIZ

Elementary teachers in Nome, Alaska, subscribe to the same professional publications as their colleagues in other states, but their problems are sometimes different. The third-grade teacher, a newcomer to Alaska, had just received her latest project magazine and was discussing with the class the suggestions for a Christmas pageant. For the children playing Santa's reindeer, there should be brown cambric outfits, and passable reindeer horns could be made of bare branches, trimmed to the proper shapes and painted. She looked out at the barren, treeless landscape.

"Well, children," she sighed regretfully, "I guess we'll have to do something else. We can't make horns of branches, because there isn't a tree for miles."

The children looked disappointed. Then one little boy spoke up. "We haven't any trees, teacher," he said, "but we do have lots of reindeer horns."

—EDITH M. JARRETT

On Christmas morning I was telling the story of the Nativity to a group of youngsters in an armed forces Sunday school. To test their attentiveness, I began to ask questions. Expecting a reply of either "the shepherds" or "the wise men," I asked, "Who was the first to know of Jesus's birth?"

Immediately a five-year-old waved her hand and shouted, "Mary!"

—JAMES L. JENSEN

My small daughter was addressing Christmas cards to a few carefully selected girls in her class at school. Casually I suggested, "Why don't you send a card to everyone in your class? That's the democratic thing to do."

"Why?" she exclaimed, looking up from her writing in surprise. "I thought being nice like that was republican."

—MARTHA WOLFE

Our seven-year-old son received a set of two-way radios for his birthday. On several occasions he has breathlessly reported picking up the conversations of helicopter pilots, truck drivers, etc., with the set. A few evenings before Christmas, on his way home from the office, my husband had one of the units in the car with him, and I had the other one turned on at home, with our son nearby.

As my husband neared home, he began saying, "Ho, ho, ho, Richard, this is Santa Claus."

After several "Ho, ho, hos" with no results, there was heard a very distinct reply: "Ho, ho, ho, license tag 18w 1678, this is not Richard. This is police car 67 behind you, and you are doing a pretty fair job of driving with one hand. Merry Christmas."

—CAROL T. DEBOEST

After listening to Christmas carols interspersed with news broadcasts on the radio, my three-year-old recited this version of *'Twas The Night Before Christmas*: "Now Dasher, now Dancer, Prancer and Vixen! On Comet, on Cupid and President Nixon!"

—MARCELLA LECKY

While lounging in the battalion aid station one evening, I suddenly realized that Christmas in the jungles of South Vietnam was going to be a meaningless and depressing event. My melancholy was interrupted when the company clerk walked in dragging a mail sack bulging with Christmas cards.

"Grab one, sir," he said. "They're all addressed to the unit from people back in the states."

I picked up an envelope that had fallen to the floor and casually opened it. As I read the labored penmanship, I felt my spirits brighten and Christmas became merry indeed, for the moment. The card said: "Dear soldier, if you think things are bad there, I just got my report card. Good luck, Terry. Fourth grade."

—JOHN C. ANDREONI

> Sitting at the kitchen table one evening in December, I told my husband, "I can't seem to get into the holiday spirit. I feel there is something I have to do, but I don't know what it is."
>
> My seven-year-old son piped up, **"Maybe you should vacuum."**
>
> —JACKIE WHITE

One day after church I asked our three-year-old daughter about the lessons and music she had learned that day. She told me they were singing Christmas songs. I was puzzled, because this was Easter, so I asked her to sing one.

In her clear voice she sang: "Ho-Santa, Ho-Santa!"

—PATTI HINZ

During the Christmas holidays, my niece, Justine, who had been staying with us, asked me, "Who is older, Grandpa or Grandma?"

I replied, "Grandpa is older. Why do you ask?"

"Well, if Grandpa is older," said Justine with a confused look on her face, "how come he always follows what Grandma says?"

—REYNANTA FERNANDEZ

My 11-year-old son had the role of Joseph in the Sunday-school Christmas program. We were discussing what he should wear on his feet. I suggested sandals, but he wanted to wear his cowboy boots. When I said it was unlikely that Joseph wore western boots, my son replied, "Yes, but then he didn't have braces on his teeth, either." He wore the boots.

—MRS. ROBERT D. OLSON

Ringing in the New Year

"An optimist stays up until midnight to see the New Year in. A pessimist stays up to make sure the old year leaves."

—BILL VAUGHAN

✳ ✳ ✳ ✳ ✳ ✳ ✳ ✳ ✳ ✳ ✳

"This year just flew by."

✳ ✳ ✳ ✳ ✳ ✳ ✳ ✳ ✳ ✳ ✳

The Big Night

My mother-in-law was going to spend the holidays with us. Before her arrival, my husband, Barrie, and I debated whether or not she should accompany us to a party on New Year's Eve. Barrie wanted her to attend, but I worried she might feel out of place.

I turned to my 21-year-old son, who had been listening. "I agree with you, Mom," he said. "You shouldn't take her."

Surprised, as he always agrees with his dad, I was basking in his approval, when he added, "That would be like me taking you to a party with me."

—BEV FERGUSON

At a New Year's Eve celebration, tycoon to waiter about to fill his glass: "No, thank you. I do all my celebrating at the end of the fiscal year."

—UNKNOWN

On New Year's Eve at the turn of the millennium, our four-and-a-half-year-old little girl got very sleepy. So I said to her, "Don't go to sleep, Sandy. We'd so like to enter the new millennium with you!"

Half asleep, Sandy replied, "You go on ahead. I'll come after you on my bike!"

—MRS. GÁBOR TÓTH

On New Year's Eve we raised our champagne glass to the new year. A few weeks later my partner's daughter asked him for juice in one of the glasses we had used that night. Luc didn't understand what she meant, so she explained: "You know, Daddy. The pretty glasses with the high heels."

—SOPHIE GUÉNETTE

✳ ✳ ✳ ✳ ✳ ✳ ✳ ✳ ✳ ✳ ✳ ✳

Anything goes on New Year's Eve. It's when old acquaintances are forgot—along with hats, coats, and wives.

—ROBERT ORBEN

The hostess at a New Year's Eve party was blond, beautiful, buxom—and in a low-cut gown. My husband and another man sat on a sofa watching as she passed the fortune cookies. Bending low, she treated them to quite a spectacular view.

When my husband broke open his cookie, he convulsed with laughter. Wiping his eyes, he passed his fortune to me. It read: "One good look is worth 10,000 words."

—MRS. PAUL O. SNYDER

On New Year's Eve my neighbor telephoned her newlywed daughter—and was surprised to find her at home. "I thought you and Doug would be out celebrating," she said.

"No, Mom," her daughter replied. "We spent the day painting our bedroom. Then I put on the hostess gown you gave me for Christmas, Doug put on his tux, I set the table with our good china and silver, and we dined by candlelight. After dinner we changed our clothes and started painting again. It's been a wonderful evening!"

—JACK JOYCE

My husband and I hardly ever had an opportunity to stay out late. Having outgrown parents' deadlines and college-dormitory curfews, we now find ourselves confronted with babysitters' deadlines. On New Year's Eve I heard my husband plead with the sitter, "Couldn't we stay out past midnight tonight? All the other parents are doing it."

—MARGARET RALPH

✳ ✳ ✳ ✳ ✳ ✳ ✳ ✳ ✳ ✳ ✳

My daughter, her husband, and their three children planned to meet us at the Wilmington, Delaware, railroad station. My husband phoned and told them we were arriving on the 5:11 p.m. train. And, he added with a chuckle, "We want to be met by a brass band."

When we got off the train, we did not get our usual reception—no grandchildren came running to meet us. But as we approached the station, there stood our family, each one holding a musical instrument, one grandson conducting the band to the tune of "Seventy-six Trombones."

Passengers stood, smiling and laughing at the reception. The music, we discovered, was coming from a tape recorder—for not one of the family can play an instrument. Since it happened to be New Year's Eve, our family performance added a special aura of happiness to the train station.

—MRS. PHILIP GOODMAN

On Christmas Day all five of my sisters and their husbands were excitedly discussing their New Year's Eve plans. For the first time in many years, I was going to be alone that night, and anticipating that I might feel lonely, I asked one of my sisters if I could go to her house on New Year's.

"Of course you can!" she said enthusiastically.

And before I had a chance to thank her, she added, **"And if we're not home, the key will be above the door."**

—AUDRIE VANDER WERF

✳ ✳ ✳ ✳ ✳ ✳ ✳ ✳ ✳ ✳ ✳ ✳

My eldest daughter, Katherine, was home from college for the holidays and held a New Year's Eve party for her old high school friends. Billy arrived with all the makings of an Italian meal, which he had prepared in advance, including a large pot of sauce. The meal was a huge success.

A few days later, just before she returned to school, Katherine, her two younger sisters, and I went out for dinner.

"Oh," one of the girls said to Katherine in the car, "I forgot to tell you Billy called and left a message."

"What is it?"

"I can't tell you," she said. "Mom's here."

"Oh, come on," I protested. "Nothing can shock me."

"No way!" she said. "There's no way I'm repeating this."

After a lovely dinner, we returned home and the girls darted downstairs. A moment later Katherine came back up, laughing. "Do you know what Billy's message was? He said, 'Tell your sister I'm coming over to pick up my pot.' "

—WENDY STEWART

The party was getting under way, and our hostess, who had never before opened a bottle of champagne, was struggling with the cork. It popped out suddenly, dousing the gown of one guest.

The hostess was completely flustered until the soaking-wet woman saved the day by announcing gaily, **"At last I've been launched!"**

—MEGAN ADAMS

✳ ✳ ✳ ✳ ✳ ✳ ✳ ✳ ✳ ✳ ✳ ✳

Overheard: "I have three trophies—two are for golf and one my wife gave me last New Year's day for watching only two out of three bowl games."

—ANGIE PAPADAKIS

A snail made its way into a lounge one New Year's Eve and hopped up onto the bar. "What do you want?" the barman asked.

"I want a cocktail so I can celebrate with everyone else," the snail replied.

"I'm sorry, but we don't serve snails here. I'm going to have to ask you to leave."

"Only one drink, sir, and I'll be on my way," the snail pleaded.

"No. Furthermore, if you don't leave immediately, I'll be forced to evict you."

The snail persisted. "Just one—"

The barman, forming a circle with this thumb and finger, flicked the snail out the open window.

New Year's Eve arrived the next year, and the same barman was serving in the same lounge. To his surprise the same snail appeared on the bar. "What, you again? What do you want this time?" he shouted.

The snail replied, "What did you do that for?"

—BRAD GIESBRECHT

With a party going full bore in the apartment above his, my friend could forget about getting any sleep. The next day, he spotted the offending party giver.

"Didn't you hear me pounding on the ceiling?" he asked.

The woman smiled pleasantly. "That's okay. We were making a lot of noise ourselves."

—RALPH WARTH

QUOTABLE QUOTES

"New Year's Day is every man's birthday."

—CHARLES LAMB

"The proper behavior all through the holiday season is to be drunk. This drunkenness culminates on New Year's Eve, when you get so drunk you kiss the person you're married to."

—P. J. O'ROURKE

"Every new year is the direct descendant, isn't it, of a long line of proven criminals?"

—OGDEN NASH

"People are so worried about what they eat between Christmas and the New Year, but they really should be worried about what they eat between the New Year and Christmas."

—AUTHOR UNKNOWN

"May all your troubles last as long as your New Year's resolutions."

—JOEY ADAMS

"January is the month when we start paying on December bills and on November election results."

—JAMES HOLT MCGAVRAN

"Be always at war with your vices, at peace with your neighbors, and let each new year find you a better man."

—BENJAMIN FRANKLIN

"Youth is when you're allowed to stay up late on New Year's Eve. Middle age is when you're forced to."

—BILL VAUGHAN

✳ ✳ ✳ ✳ ✳ ✳ ✳ ✳ ✳ ✳ ✳ ✳

Starting on the Wrong Foot

Last New Year's Eve found me in the hospital scheduled for an operation to remove hemorrhoids. So while others donned party hats and sipped champagne, I wore a hospital gown and swigged painkillers.

That's not to say the holiday spirit was completely absent. The next day, January 1, I woke up to a banner on my bedroom wall. It screamed: "Happy New Rear!"

—MARILYNN BELLMANN

Having just moved into a new neighborhood, I wanted to start out on the right foot and not disturb anybody with the New Year's Eve party I had planned. To test the sound from the television, I turned it on full blast, walked out of the house, closed the door, and listened. An awful amount of noise came through, and I tried to open the door to turn it off. But I was locked out. Since my wife would return soon, there was nothing to do but wait in the car, although I felt more like crawling under it.

Soon a neighbor came tearing out of his house and headed toward me. As he approached, he shouted above the racket, "Look, Mac, if you'd turn the damn thing down, you wouldn't have to sit out here to listen to it!"

—GROVER DUNN

George, an old friend, is an unusually calm, serene individual. One day he told me his secret. "Aunt Hildy," he said, "is an old lady in my town who is a great worrier. She fusses and frets over everything. So every New Year's Day I pay her a visit and hire her for one dollar a year to do all my worrying. She's an expert at it, and the price is right."

—FERN GREENWOOD

✳ ✳ ✳ ✳ ✳ ✳ ✳ ✳ ✳ ✳ ✳ ✳

My friend's parents run a big business and have little time for her. She always complains about that to me, and I always advise her to tell her parents how she feels. On New Year's Eve her parents asked what she wanted for New Year's.

My friend thought this was the perfect opportunity to talk with her parents. "I just want some time and warmth from you," she said.

As it turned out, her father gave her a watch, and her mother gave her a water heater.

—SIRIKANYA PHATHANAKUL

A drunk staggered into a bar shouting,
"Happy New Year, everybody!"
The fellow closest to him said,
"You turkey, it's the middle of May."
The bewildered drunk looked at him and cried,
"Oh, my gosh. My wife is going to kill me.

I've never been this late before."

—B. K.

After spending an excessive amount of money on Christmas, my husband decided to finish up the holiday week with one last grand flourish, and on New Year's Eve he gave me an exquisite white orchid. Attached was this card: Let the whiteness of this flower attest the purity of my love for you. Let the price of it measure in millions the joy you bring to me. Let the cellophane on the box represent the window of the poorhouse, where I'll soon be if this keeps up!

—BEATRICE J. STURM

✳ ✳ ✳ ✳ ✳ ✳ ✳ ✳ ✳ ✳ ✳

One New Year's Eve my wife and I decided to celebrate the advent of the new year in a rather sedate manner with two neighborhood couples. After a few rounds of bridge, a couple of highballs, and a midnight toast in champagne, however, I got a sudden urge to phone people in faraway places.

First, I called some good friends in Bermuda and wished them a Happy New Year. Then, feeling even more venturesome, I decided to call a first cousin in Germany, Dr. Hans Koehl. The operator told me that all circuits to Europe were busy, so I went to bed.

At 3:30 a.m. I was awakened by the message that the operator was still trying to put through my call. At that point, I was delighted. But at 6:30 a.m., when I wasn't feeling much like getting up, the phone rang again, with the news that the operator was ready with my call to Germany.

Reluctantly, in the freezing-cold bedroom and cold gray dawn, I said okay, whereupon I heard my cousin's voice saying in German: "Dr. Hans Koehl speaking. This is a recorded message. I will be away until Tuesday. In the meantime, please call my colleague, Dr. Max.

—ALBERT E. KOEHL

A professor was lecturing on the age of our planet and man's relatively recent appearance here. "If you were to telescope the entire history of the Earth into just a calendar year," he explained, "humans wouldn't show up until a few minutes before midnight on New Year's Eve." **"Hey,"** a student shouted, **"at least we made it for the party!"**

—CAROLYN VAN COTT

Why didn't the calendar go to the New Year's party?

No one wanted to date it!

— ANONYMOUS

Driving home in thick traffic on New Year's Eve, our car dented the bumper of the vehicle ahead of us. As the driver started to get out of his car shouting at us, my friend who was driving our car leaned out and said with a smile, just helping you to start the new year with a bang.

The offended man accepted the apology, smiled, wishing us in return and drove off.

—N. MULLAN

My mother and sister were chatting on the telephone on New Year's Day but were persistently interrupted by crackling and other people's voices. "This line is terrible," remarked my mother.

"Yes," my sister agreed. "I'll call the telephone company to complain."

"There's no point. They won't be working today," said Mom.

"Yes, we are," interrupted a third voice. "We're trying to fix this crossed line."

—HUGH SLEIGHT

Some people's idea of celebrating the holidays is to have a Christmas they'll never forget and a New Year's Eve they can't remember.

—MAURICE SEITTER

✳ ✳ ✳ ✳ ✳ ✳ ✳ ✳ ✳ ✳ ✳

Weather reports from our previous hometown told of severe cold spells and heavy snows. Feeling a little smug over the warm, sunny climate we now live in, I couldn't resist sending a snapshot back to a good friend and former neighbor. It showed gay flowers blooming along a rustic fence and me in a light shirt and shorts, leaning casually against my lawn mower. On the back of the picture I wrote: "Taken on New Year's Day."

His reply arrived within the week—an indoor color shot of himself sitting by his fireplace, open book in lap, feet on a hassock, pipe in one hand, the other hand resting on the head of his big shepherd dog, who was lazily stretched beside the easy chair. The enclosed note read: "A darn shame you're still cutting grass in January."

—MARK HAYES

When my husband and I were teenagers, we went out on our first New Year's Eve date in the car he had recently bought. It was his first car, and he was enormously proud of it. At midnight, amid noisy horns and kissing, I waited eagerly for his romantic words. He looked into my eyes and said, **"Darn—my car is a year older now."**

—MARILYN MONDROSKI

✳ ✳ ✳ ✳ ✳ ✳ ✳ ✳ ✳ ✳ ✳

Hard-Working Holidays

My son's first job took him to Shenzhen, China. During the Chinese New Year, I asked Todd why it was called the Year of the Pig.

"I'm not sure," he wrote back. "A few months ago it was the Year of the Dog, and I'm still writing Dog on all my checks."

—PHAMA WOODYARD

During my years in Paris as a foreign correspondent, my wife and I came to expect a steady procession of visitors to our apartment the week between Christmas and New Year's. Every person who had served us in any way came then to ring the bell and hold out his palm for his "gift." There was the man who swept the gutter, the woman who sold flowers, the delivery boys, the postman, even the higher agent of the postes, who made a specialty of delivering nothing but registered letters. We doled out francs to them all.

One year, just when we thought there couldn't possibly be anyone else left to tip, the bell gave an imperious summons. I opened the door to a resplendent man in a tailcoat and a derby. I'd never laid eyes on him, and I thought he must be the chief assistant to the mayor of the arrondissement, at least. But no, he used the set formula: *"Bonjour, monsieur,* a happy New Year to you. A little present, if you please."

"Pardon me," I said, "but I can't remember ever having had the pleasure of seeing you."

"No," said the little man. "Monsieur has never viewed me, but I have served Monsieur and Madame and looked after their safety all through the long year. I, Monsieur," he said dramatically, "am the person who greases the elevator."

—BEN K. RALEIGH

✳ ✳ ✳ ✳ ✳ ✳ ✳ ✳ ✳ ✳ ✳

And then there was the psychiatrist who put a sign on his door that read: **"And a well-adjusted New Year to you all."**

—RUTH MACKAY

At a New Year's party of foreigners in Moscow, there was a champagne-fueled debate as to how the invisible Soviet agents manning the various "bugs" and tape recorders might be spending the holiday.

"Imagine the poor devils down at the KGB sitting around listening to all the parties tonight and not a drop to drink," said one Western diplomat, raising another glass.

A few minutes later the phone rang and the host answered. He heard no voice—only the unmistakable pop of a cork and the glug-glug pouring of champagne. Then the callers, anonymous as ever, hung up.

At the start of a new year, an employee came into the payroll office and asked, "Who do I talk to about changing my number of dependents?"

Before I could answer, my supervisor suggested, "How about your wife?"

—SANDRA L. GLAHN

At the army printing plant where I was assigned, much of the printed material was classified. All around the facility were reminders stressing the importance of maintaining secrecy. Visitors were given carefully supervised tours, and signs indicated areas that were off limits.

One day, just before Christmas, a beautiful banner was hung near the front entrance proclaiming, "Merry Christmas and Happy New Year." But after careful scrutiny, I noticed a hand-scrawled message below it: "To authorized personnel only."

—THOMAS J. VERBRUGGE

✳ ✳ ✳ ✳ ✳ ✳ ✳ ✳ ✳ ✳ ✳

Punts, Passes...

New Year's Day, and I had planned on spending it watching football. My wife, however, had other ideas, which resulted in my serving time at a family dinner. But when the coast was clear, I sneaked away and turned on the ball game. A few minutes later my wife came by with a cup of coffee for me.

"What's the score?" she asked.

"Zero-zero at the end of the third quarter," I told her.

"See?" she said, walking away. "You didn't miss a thing."

—HUY NGUYEN

It was the young bride's first New Year's Day in the married state. Her husband had spent all day sitting in front of the TV set, watching football games. The only time he said anything was when he demanded another beer.

At last she could bear it no longer. "I am going over to Mother's," she announced. "Maybe she will talk to me."

A shock awaited the bride, however. When she got to the home of her parents, her father was there alone, engrossed in the football games. Her mother was over at her mother's.

—ROBERT MCMORRIS

Not only did I have the usual Christmas and New Year's football games to contend with, but we had a new color television set as well. Finally, the Sunday after New Year's, I said in desperation to my husband, "Look, Bob, it's either me or this football game. Make your choice!"

He didn't take his eyes from the set. "Listen, Sal," he said. "Could we wait until half-time and see what we can salvage?"

—MRS. R. D. RUD

"I'm just picking up some New Year's Day football provisions."

✳ ✳ ✳ ✳ ✳ ✳ ✳ ✳ ✳ ✳ ✳ ✳

. . . and Promises

I made a resolution to start jogging again and needed to replace my running shoes. My sister Rebecca found a great deal on an expensive pair of shoes and bought them for me.

Later my boyfriend, Kyle, decided to come over and lend his support by jogging with me. So I put on my new shoes, and we went out. But I started to feel self-conscious, as he kept looking sideways at me.

Finally I stopped and said, "Okay, I know I don't run as much as you, but I'm trying my best here. So could you please stop staring at me like that?"

"Oh, that's not it at all, honey," Kyle said. "I'm just trying to figure out why you're jogging in cleats."

—SAMANTHA TOMICKI

On my list of New Year's resolutions was: "Be more patient with my daughter, Janet. No matter how irritating she is, remember that, after all, she is only 15 and is going through the exasperating period of adolescence."

Imagine then my feeling when, quite by accident, I came across Janet's New Year's resolutions and saw at the head of her list: "Try and be more patient with mother."

—MRS. C. R. KNOWLES

Last year when I called my parents to wish them a happy New Year, my dad answered the phone. "Well, Dad, what's your New Year's resolution?" I asked him.

"To make your mother as happy as I can all year," he answered proudly.

Then Mom got on, and I said, "What's your resolution, Mom?"

"To see that your dad keeps his New Year's resolution."

—JEANETTE CASE

" QUOTABLE QUOTES

"He who breaks a
resolution is a weakling;
He who makes one is a fool."

—F.M. KNOWLES

"Good resolutions
are simply checks
that men draw on
a bank where they
have no account."

—OSCAR WILDE

"A New Year's resolution is
something that goes in one year
and out the other."

—UNKNOWN

"New Year's Day now is the accepted time to
make your regular annual good resolutions.
Next week you can begin paving hell
with them as usual."

—MARK TWAIN

"Never tell your resolution beforehand,
or it's twice as onerous a duty."

—JOHN SELDEN

"Now there are more
overweight people
in America than
average-weight people.
So overweight people
are now average . . .
which means you have
met your New Year's
resolution."

—JAY LENO

"New Year's Resolution:
To tolerate fools more
gladly, provided this does
not encourage them to take
up more of my time."

—JAMES AGATE

"One swallow doesn't make a summer, but it
sure breaks a New Year's resolution."

—WILL ROGERS, JR.

"Would you like me to make a list of New Year's resolutions for you?"

Some of those New Year's Eve hangovers last longer than some of those New Year's Eve resolutions.

—EARL WILSON

Hoping to excite student interest in our reading center, I asked each teacher to write a New Year's resolution on a special form and send it to me. After I posted the resolutions on the bulletin board in the reading center, one young teacher stopped by, looked at them for a few minutes, then left abruptly.

Passing two other teachers on their way in, she stormed, "My resolution isn't posted—and mine was one of the first ones in!"

I couldn't help but overhear, and the tone of her voice sent me flying to my desk in search of a misplaced resolution. Looking rapidly through stacks of papers, I uncovered hers. It read: "I resolve not to let little things upset me."

—JACKIE DAY

The trouble with making too many New Year's resolutions is that, if you stick to them, you could become impossible to live with.

—TONY ZARRO

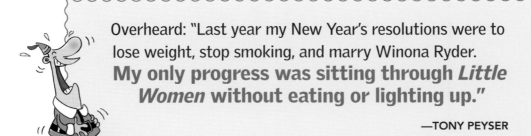

Overheard: "Last year my New Year's resolutions were to lose weight, stop smoking, and marry Winona Ryder. **My only progress was sitting through *Little Women* without eating or lighting up.**"

—TONY PEYSER

Seasonal Silliness

"Once again, we come to the holiday season, a deeply religious time that each of us observes, in his own way, by going to the mall of his choice."

—DAVE BARRY

That's Snow Funny!

Snow was falling heavily the day I decided to visit a car dealership. I was confident I'd get a great deal, figuring the salesmen would be desperate for customers on such a lousy day.

Sure enough, when I entered the showroom, I was the only client.

But my hope of getting a good deal quickly faded with the salesman's first words. "Boy," he said jovially, "you must want a new car real bad to come out on a day like this."

—TOM CARTER

My husband and I are from the "Live Free or Die" state, New Hampshire. Once, while visiting an island in the Caribbean, we started chatting with a resident, and our home state came up.

"I spent the coldest winter of my life in New Hampshire," he told us. "Your state motto really fits—'Live, Freeze and Die.'"

—CHRISTINA MCCARTHY

Returning to the University of Notre Dame after winter break one year, I was greeted by a freshly snow-blanketed campus. While admiring the scenery, a strange figure looming in the shadow of a campus building caught my eye. Directly under the words "Radiation Laboratory" on the side of the edifice stood a perfectly sculpted two-headed snowman.

—JESSICA WARD

During a storm, my wife's car became stuck in a snowbank. Our obstetrician saw her spinning her wheels, trying to get out. When he offered to help, my wife could not resist telling him, "Okay, Doctor. Now, when I count to three, push!"

—H. STEINBERG

"So much for the lemon. Let's try a carrot."

❄ ❄ ❄ ❄ ❄ ❄ ❄ ❄ ❄ ❄ ❄ ❄

Skiing is best when you have lots of white snow and plenty of Blue Cross.

— EARL WILSON

One October my wife and I spent a vacation on Washington's Olympic Peninsula. We were eager to visit the rain forests near the coast, but we heard that snowslides had made some of the roads impassable. Although apprehensive about the conditions we might run into, we drove on.

Sure enough, we had gone only a short way up the Hoh Rain Forest road when we saw a sign: "Ice 10 miles."

Five miles farther on, there was another: "Ice 5 miles."

The next one was: "Ice 1/2 mile."

We crept that half mile, then came to the last sign. It was outside a small grocery, and it read: "Ice 50¢."

—GIFFORD S. WALKER

Friends of ours, Sam and Ruth, from Maine had just bought a car when winter hit with all its fury. "I wonder if the car has seat warmers," Ruth wondered.

"It does," said Sam, looking through the owner's manual. "Here it is: rear defrosters."

—DALE DUTTON

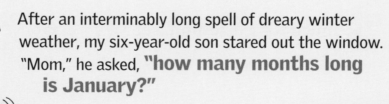

After an interminably long spell of dreary winter weather, my six-year-old son stared out the window. "Mom," he asked, **"how many months long is January?"**

—NANCY CASTILOW

QUOTABLE QUOTES

"I grew up thinking of snow as a luxury you visit."

—JOHN LANDIS

"To appreciate the beauty of a snowflake, it is necessary to stand out in the cold."

—UNKNOWN

"Each snowflake in an avalanche pleads not guilty."

—STANISLAW J. LEC

"When it snows, you have two choices: shovel or make snow angels."

—ANONYMOUS

"Getting an inch of snow is like winning 10 cents in the lottery."

—BILL WATTERSON

"Snow and adolescence are the only problems that disappear if you ignore them long enough."

—EARL WILSON

"Kindness is like snow— it beautifies everything it covers."

—ANONYMOUS

"Snowmen fall from heaven . . . unassembled."

—UNKNOWN

"A lot of people like snow. I find it to be an unnecessary freezing of water."

—CARL REINER

❄ ❄ ❄ ❄ ❄ ❄ ❄ ❄ ❄ ❄ ❄ ❄

Just getting out of the driveway was a major feat during last year's snow and ice storms. One coworker was relating how he used his seven-year-old son's baseball bat to smash the slick coat of ice on his driveway. He got cold and went inside for a cup of coffee before attempting to clear the car. Several minutes later his son, who had been outside with him, came in.

"Dad," he said, "I got the ice off the car."

"How did you do that?" his father asked.

"Same way you did," the boy shrugged, "with the baseball bat."

—JANINE JAQUET BIDEN

While traveling through Wyoming one winter day, I was experiencing what's called a horizontal blizzard. The snow that had fallen the day before was blowing across the road.

When I stopped for fuel, I remarked on the condition to a man at the gas station. He was obviously a local who had seen a lot of winters.

"Yeah," he said, nodding. "We don't get much snow, but what we do get, we use a lot."

—R. WAY

After I had attended a weeklong business meeting in sunny Orlando, Florida, my return flight to Philadelphia was canceled because of yet another snowstorm. My wife was not sympathetic when I called to report that I was spending another night in Orlando.

Arriving home the next day, I was greeted by a large sign on our garage door: "Dear 'Stranded in Orlando,' welcome to reality." Next to the sign was our snow shovel with a smaller sign attached. It read: "Reality."

—J. ROBERT BANKS

❄ ❄ ❄ ❄ ❄ ❄ ❄ ❄ ❄ ❄ ❄ ❄ ❄

Did you hear about the guy who froze to death at the drive-in? **He went to see "Closed for the Winter."**

—UNKNOWN

For several days mother had noticed a bulky parcel among the neat packages in our new quick-freeze chest but had been too busy to investigate. When she finally unwrapped it, she was amazed to find three dozen carefully shaped snowballs.

Inquiry about them was greeted by a wail from seven-year-old Billy. "Oh, Mother! Please don't throw them out! I'm going to make a lot of money selling genuine January snowballs on the Fourth of July."

—ELINOR M. CURD

Louie and his wife are listening to the radio when they hear the weather report: "A snow emergency has been declared. You must park your cars on the odd-numbered side of the street." So Louie gets up and moves his car.

Two days later, same thing. "A snow emergency has been declared," blares the radio. "Park your cars on the even-numbered side of the street." Louie gets up and does what he's told.

Three days later: "There will be a foot of snow today. Park your cars on the—" and then the power goes out.

"What should I do?" a confused Louie asks his wife.

"This time," she says, "why don't you just leave the car in the garage?"

—UNKNOWN

How do snowmen travel?
By icicle

Festive Follies

Late shoppers were frantically completing their Christmas purchases. The streets were filled with cars, and the sidewalks had barely enough room for shoppers. At one corner a middle-aged couple stood waiting for the light to change. The husband was so loaded down with packages that he could hardly see where he was going.

"Get back on the curb, George," his wife told him as he inched his way out into the street. But he paid no attention. Finally, in a voice that carried above the street noise, she said, "Well, if you're going to stand out there, let me carry the packages."

—THOMAS ARKWRIGHT

My six-year-old niece, Diana, often picks up minor illnesses in nursery school which means she has to stay at home for one or two weeks. So that she wouldn't be ill over Christmas, her parents didn't send her to nursery school from the middle of December

One day while out shopping, a kind acquaintance addressed her: "Why aren't you in nursery school, Diana. I hope there's nothing wrong," she said.

"No, nothing," was the reply. "I can't go, because I'm healthy."

—MARIANN SZAMOSI

Two kids are on their way to Sunday school when one says to the other, "What do you think about this Satan stuff?"

"Well, you remember Santa? This could turn out to be your Dad, too."

—PAT RUZSBATZKY

"It's very nice, but I asked for *boughs* of holly."

❄❄❄❄❄❄❄❄❄❄❄

Sign in a weight-loss center: **"24 shaping days until Christmas."**

—MRS. C. M. SWENSON

My grandmother has lived all her 80 years in northern New England, where what she sees from November until April is mostly snow. When my husband and I moved to California in January, we couldn't wait to phone and tell her about our green lawns, green trees, and flowers that bloom all winter long. "It sounds lovely, dear," she replied. "But doesn't it look terribly artificial?"

—MARGARET HEAGY

One of the rural community's biggest social events of the year was the Christmas program at the school, and my first-grade grandson was very excited about "speaking a piece" for this great affair. School was dismissed early that eagerly awaited day so everyone could be rested for the evening's events.

When Buster arrived home, he noticed that his sister had her hair up, his mother was pressing his dad's suit, etc. "Where are you all going?" he asked, concerned.

"To your Christmas program, dear," replied his mother. "Didn't you think we were going?"

"Well, I didn't think you'd have to come to the schoolhouse," he said. "I thought you'd be watching it on TV."

—MRS. WILLMA M. VEUM

I was recently talking with a friend who bemoaned her family's lack of holiday rituals. "My family doesn't have any traditions," she complained. "We just do the same thing year after year after year."

—NATALIE EDGE

To help our four-year-old son Eric learn to ski, I bought a harness that allows him to ski slowly on a leash. After a few practice runs on the rope tow, he and his father rode up the gondola with two experienced skiers.

"You must be a good little skier," one said to Eric.

"Yes," he said, "but I have to drag Dad along."

—VIRGINIA VICKERS BRAUN

A small boy in kindergarten was assigned by his teacher to make a Christmas drawing of the three Wise Men riding their camels across the desert. When the drawing was finished, the youngster took it to the teacher for her approval. She studied it and then pointed to an item—a square box with a couple of wires sticking out of it—that was being carried by one of the men.

"What's that?" she asked.

"Oh, that," said the boy. "That's the portable TV set. I didn't want them to miss *Gunsmoke!*"

—DAN BENNETT

My mother is a cleaning fanatic. One Saturday she told my brother and me to get down to the playroom and straighten it up. We had had a party there the previous evening, and she was none too happy about the mess.

As she watched us work, it was clear Mom was completely dissatisfied with our cleaning efforts and let us know it.

Finally my brother, exasperated with having to do it all over, reached for a broom and asked, "Can I use this, or are you planning to go somewhere?"

—MARK BERMAN

❄ ❄ ❄ ❄ ❄ ❄ ❄ ❄ ❄ ❄ ❄

The road by my house was in bad condition after a rough winter. Every day, I dodged potholes on the way to work. So I was relieved to see a construction crew working on the road one morning.

Later, on my way home, I noticed no improvement. But where the construction crew had been working stood a new, bright yellow sign with the words "Rough Road."

—SARAH KRAYBILL

Heavy snow had buried my van in our driveway. My husband, Scott, dug around the wheels, rocked the van back and forth, and finally pushed me free. I was on the road when I heard an odd noise. I got on my cell and called home. "Thank God you answered," I said when Scott picked up. "There's this alarming sound coming from under the van. For a moment I thought I was dragging you down the highway."

"And you didn't stop?"

—PAIGE FAIRFIELD

Our minister was discussing various holidays and traditions with a flock of his young parishioners. "At Christmas," he said, "we traditionally use a plant called the poinsettia for decorating and giving, symbolizing Christmas. Can anyone tell me what plant we use to symbolize Easter?"

A hand shot up, and a small boy piped earnestly, "An eggplant?"

—GAIL P. HURST

❄ ❄ ❄ ❄ ❄ ❄ ❄ ❄ ❄ ❄ ❄ ❄ ❄ ❄

Sign posted in office: **"This year's Christmas party has been canceled due to last year's Christmas party."**

—ROBERT SYLVESTER

Over the years, I've tried to thank Mom for all her support throughout my college days at Illinois Wesleyan University. A chance to repay her came last winter. During her Christmas break from Depauw University in Indiana, where she is a fraternity housemother, Mom came to visit me in Florida. The morning after her arrival, I was late opening my art shop. The student waiting to buy supplies looked confused when I apologized and explained that my mother was home from college and I had been doing her laundry.

—BARBARA KLEIN CRAIG

My frugal aunt believes in buying paper napkins on sale, no matter what is printed on them. Thus, our family has become used to seeing Santa's face at Easter and wedding bells at Thanksgiving. But at one family reunion this practice puzzled a new in-law.

"Congratulations," he read on his napkin. "Congratulations for what?"

"Congratulations," my aunt said tersely. "You got a napkin!"

—F. R. KRANS

My son, Brian, was a theater major at Shenandoah University in Winchester, Virginia. He got a part in a local production and the director was telling the cast they would be doing a holiday musical called Yes, Virginia, There is a Santa Claus.

"Are you familiar with it?" he asked the cast members.

"Not really," Brian answered, completely serious. "I'm from New Jersey."

—NANCY CURL

Sign in a men's clothing store: **"Make him feel like an astronaut—buy him long underwear for Christmas!"**

—IRVING KUPCINET

During the holiday season, my husband, Gordon, called one day to say we had been invited to a party that night at a client's house. A little later he phoned back. "Honey, I'm going to have to meet you at the party. I'm running late."

"But I don't know these people," I protested.

"Just tell them you're Gordon's wife."

It was snowing heavily, and many street signs were covered. But I eventually found the street and spotted cars and a party in full swing.

I was greeted warmly at the door, plied with food and beverage, and met everyone. After some time I went to the host and asked him if he'd heard from Gordon.

"Gordon? Who's Gordon?"

My heart sank. "You're not Reed, are you?

"No," he laughed. "He lives five houses down."

—DENISE LEAVITT

With the Christmas season over, two ministers in our town began teasing a third because the stable for a nativity scene was still standing on the lawn at his church. The figures had been removed, but the wooden shed and bales of straw remained. Toward the end of January, with the stable still there, the two ministers decided to act. On the empty stall they placed a large sign proclaiming: **"Gone to Egypt."**

—MRS. EDWARD R. JAEGER

❄ ❄ ❄ ❄ ❄ ❄ ❄ ❄ ❄ ❄ ❄ ❄ ❄

As I was leaving a formal dinner party in the early hours of the morning, I remembered that the motor of my new Mercedes-Benz had been hotter than it should have been. Realizing that I might not find a service station open, I asked my host for a bucket of water. No bucket was available, but my resourceful host handed me a large paper sack containing three champagne magnums filled with water. Once on the street, I felt rather ridiculous as, dressed in my tuxedo, I proceeded to empty the water into the radiator. Then two passers-by stopped in amazement, and one said to the other, "These Mercedes owners really do pamper their cars, don't they?"

—Y. YOGASUNDRAM

For years my mother and aunt had exchanged ten-dollar bills at Christmas. When they both became widows, they reduced the exchange to five dollars. This year, to cut expenses even more, they decided not to exchange gifts at all!

—JACK I. KIBBEN

To add a personal touch to his Christmas cards, a friend of ours decided to have the local ones delivered by hand. He told his son he would get two cents for each card delivered. Later the boy returned. "Some people said they had enough Christmas cards," he said. "Others paid the two cents, and Mr. Jones only had a nickel."

—CINDA WARNER

I asked my mother-in-law if she enjoyed the flight back from her vacation.

"Yes," she said, "but we had to keep our seat belts on because of all the flatulence."

—MERVYN SAUNDERS

"Room 721, sir. Ah, yes . . . the Nutcracker Suite!"

❄ ❄ ❄ ❄ ❄ ❄ ❄ ❄ ❄ ❄ ❄ ❄ ❄

People sometimes have trouble believing that the name of our town is George. Last New Year's Day, for example, my brother, about 150 miles away in Seattle, telephoned us. We had just begun our conversation when we were cut off.

My brother immediately dialed the long-distance operator and pleaded, "Operator, I was talking to George, Washington, and you cut us off."

Apparently, she thought someone was still celebrating, for she replied, "Anyone who's been gone that long, we only allow thirty seconds."

—MRS. AUBREY STRONG

I was shopping in a large department store in mid-January. All the rush of the holiday and post-holiday sales was over, and the place seemed quite empty. One saleswoman, however, was swamped in packages. As she went by me with an armload of boxes, she explained, "MacArthurs."

A few minutes later she passed me again with another batch of cartons. "More MacArthurs," she said. Then I saw her again—and again—with still more packages. "Full of MacArthurs," she said, smiling.

When I saw her for the fifth time, I asked, "Miss, could you tell me what in the world MacArthurs are?" As she carried away yet another armload, she winked at me and said, "I shall return."

—RENNY HARTMANN

 ## Why are there only snowmen and no snowwomen?

Because only men are crazy enough to stand out in the snow all winter.

❄❄❄❄❄❄❄❄❄❄❄❄❄

Sign on a St. Louis church bulletin board:
**"Merry Christmas to our Christian friends.
Happy Hanukkah to our Jewish friends.
And to our atheist friends, good luck."**

—WILLIAM E. BURKE

At our traditional Christmas family gathering, relatives who hadn't seen one another for a year were catching up on news. One loud voice above the babble commented, "Looks like you've put on a little weight."

The remark was addressed to my youngest son. However, all conversation in the room stopped as everyone responded, "Oh, maybe a couple of pounds."

—PAT RICE

While shopping in a Bowling Green, Kentucky, drugstore one January day, I noticed an old man approach the counter, hat in hand, and ask the druggist for one of the store's free almanacs.

Receiving the almanac, he thanked the druggist and added, "I sure appreciate this. Last year I didn't get a copy and had to take the weather just as it came."

—W. E. FINCH

Ice-fisherman Floyd Colburn, of Grand Rapids, Michigan, got tired of catching and throwing back small perch. Finding a Christmas ribbon in his pocket, he began tying pretty red bows on each perch before throwing it back. It wasn't long before another fisherman came dashing up to him, wide-eyed, and cried, "You won't believe what I'm going to tell you!"

—JIM KIMBALL

Last Christmas I put up colored lights in the form of the word PEACE on the side of the barn. The lights were still in place several weeks later, although we had not turned them on since New Year's.

One evening I turned into my drive and saw the word PEACE glowing on the barn. I wondered what the occasion could be, until I got out of my car and saw that my wife had put a fresh dent in the family station wagon.

—BERNARD J. WEISS

To entertain a business partner from England last winter, my father took him to a restaurant in Butte, Montana. They ordered red wine, which arrived icy cold, seemingly straight from the refrigerator.

"Oh, Miss," my father's guest said, gesturing to the waitress. "Red wine should be served at room temperature."

"Is that right?" she replied. "Then maybe you should come visit us again in July."

—RAMONA RADONICH

I was getting a little exasperated with my four-year-old daughter, Eloise, and her constant questions about Mary, Jesus, and the nativity story.
After explaining to her that I wasn't sure of Mary's exact features, Eloise suggested I add her as a Facebook friend to find out.

—AMANDA WEBSTER

❄ ❄ ❄ ❄ ❄ ❄ ❄ ❄ ❄ ❄ ❄ ❄

Four-year-old, bursting into song:
"Hark! The hairy angels sing,"

—LIDA LARKIN

"Save during our January white sales," read a sign visible for blocks in Grosse Pointe, a wealthy suburb of Detroit. We drove up to the sign expecting to find the usual window display of linen but instead found Grosse Pointe's version of the white sales—an automobile showroom filled with white Cadillacs.

—MRS. PETER J. THOMAS

On a chilly winter evening, my husband and I were snuggled together on the floor watching television. During a commercial break, he reached over and gave my foot a gentle squeeze.

"Mmmm," I said. "That's sweet."

"Actually," he admitted, "I thought that was the remote."

—STEPHANIE EELE

As a financial-aid counselor at a state university, I work with many students. Recently a young woman named Noel came to my office. Thinking to put her at ease, I asked if she had been born around Christmas.

"No," she replied. "Actually, my birthday is September 25." Then her expression brightened, and she added, "But I suppose originally I was a Christmas present."

—MILFORD JOHNSON

What do you get when you cross a snowman with a vampire?

Frostbite

——————————————————————— DUSTIN GODSEY

CALDWELL.

"Uh, oh. Gotto run, Dave. Here comes the ol' ball and hook."

When testing our hospital's pharmacy computer system, we chose names such as Bugs Bunny and Buffy the Vampire Slayer for our fictitious patients so there would be no mix-ups with real people. Just before Christmas, the test name Santa Claus was used. It wasn't long before a preoperative medication for Santa was returned to the pharmacy with the notation: "Operation on hold until he finishes work on December 25."

—HELENE LAU

Jokes Around the Table

Lost in the desert for three days, a man suddenly hears, "Mush!"

Looking up, he sees what he thinks is a mirage: an Eskimo on a sled, driving a team of huskies. To his surprise, the sled comes to a stop at his feet seconds later.

"I don't know why you're here, but thank goodness," the man says. "I've been lost for days."

Panting, the Eskimo replies, "You think *you're* lost?"

—ROBERT LUTZ

Although fighting the enemy is considered normal, the army frowns upon fighting among the troops. So much so that after one too many battles royal, my uncle was ordered to undergo a psychiatric evaluation in which he had to endure some odd questions.

"If you saw a submarine in the Sahara, what would you do?"

"Well, I'd throw snowballs at it," he answered.

"Where'd you get the snowballs?" the doctor asked.

"Same place you got the submarine."

—HANNAH ETCHISON

Longtime friends were celebrating their 50th anniversary. One of their sons gave a loving toast, finishing with, "And thank you for having such a beautiful marriage."

"Thank you for making it necessary," the father joked.

In the silence that followed, his wife whispered, **"Not him. He's the second son."**

—DOT WILSON

A man suffering from a miserable cold begs his doctor for relief. The doctor prescribes pills. But after a week, the man's still sick. So the doctor gives him an injection. But that doesn't help his condition either.

"OK, this is what I want you to do," says the doctor on the third visit. "Go home and take a hot bath. Then throw open all the windows and stand in the draft."

"I'll get pneumonia!" protests the patient.

"I know. That I can cure."

—UNKNOWN

❄ ❄ ❄ ❄ ❄ ❄ ❄ ❄ ❄ ❄ ❄ ❄ ❄ ❄

Fatherhood is pretending the present you love most is soap-on-a-rope.

—BILL COSBY

Late one foggy night, a Yankees fan and a Red Sox fan collide head-on while driving across a bridge. Fortunately, both are unhurt, but their cars are pretty banged up.

"This is a sign," says the Yankees fan, "that we should put away our differences and live as friends instead of rivals."

"You're right," says the Red Sox fan. He pops open the trunk and takes out a bottle of bourbon. "Let's toast our newfound friendship."

The Yankees fan takes a big swig and hands back the bottle. "Your turn!"

"Nah," says the Sox fan, tossing the bottle into the river. "I think I'll just wait for the police to show up."

—FRANK BACHARD

"Mom, is God the one who puts food on our table?"
"Yes, He is, my child."
"Is Santa Claus the one who brings us gifts at Christmas?"
"Of course."
"Did the stork bring me?"
"Yes, it did, sweetheart."
"Then what good is Daddy?"

—FABIANO SANTOS DUARTE

How do you fix a broken tomato?

A twelve-step program to keep it from getting sauced.

JIM RAU

When I tell people that I am an explosive ordinance disposal technician, I usually need to go into further detail about what I do. Once I was with my eight-year-old son when I was explaining my job to someone. "I defuse live bombs," I said.

"Yeah," my son added. **"If you see him running, you'd better catch up!"**

—THOMAS LIGON

"I was at a dinner party the other night, and one woman had on a dress that was cut so low, you had to look under the table to see what she was wearing."

—JOEY ADAMS

Eve, in the Garden of Eden, called out, "Lord, I have a problem."

And the Lord said, "What's the matter, Eve?"

"I know you created me and this beautiful garden. But I'm lonely—and I'm sick of eating apples."

"Well, in that case," replied the Almighty, "I'll create a man for you."

"What's a man?"

"He's a flawed creature with aggressive tendencies, an enormous ego, and an inability to listen. But he's big and fast and muscular. He'll be really good at fighting and kicking a ball and hunting animals—and not bad in the sack."

"Sounds great!" replied Eve.

"There's one condition," added the Lord. "You'll have to let him believe that I made him first."

—MONICA HYSON

"Oh sure!! Run away when there's work to do!"

Spotted outside a church in Michigan:
"Honk if you love Jesus. Keep on texting while you drive if you want to meet Him."

—GINA VESELY

I stopped by my church in time for Communion. As I left my pew to approach the altar, I spotted this sign on the wall: "Please don't leave your personal things unattended lest someone assume that these are the answers to their prayers."

—BIENVENIDO GONZALEZ

After reading up on the finer points of ice fishing, a young woman heads onto the ice. Just as she's about to drill her first hole, a booming voice from above bellows, "There are no fish under the ice!"

The woman is startled, but she keeps drilling.

Again the voice thunders, "There are no fish under the ice!"

Now the woman is shaking. But she takes a deep breath, and just as she's about to cut a new hole—

"There are no fish under the ice!"

The frightened woman looks skyward and asks, "Is that you, Lord?"

"No. This is the manager of the skating rink!"

—UNKNOWN

My wife took our three-year-old to church for the first time. Getting impatient while waiting for the Mass to start, he turned to her and asked,

"What time does Jesus get here?"

—UNKNOWN

❄ ❄ ❄ ❄ ❄ ❄ ❄ ❄ ❄ ❄ ❄

Head of household: We jingle the bells in December and juggle the bills in January.

—MARY H WALDRIP

Visiting a village in a Third World nation, an American dignitary tells the local inhabitants, "I bring you warm greetings from my people!"

The locals respond, "Kazanga!"

"We wish you prosperity!"

"Kazanga!" they bellow.

"I promise years of friendship and economic benefit!"

"Kazanga! Kazanga!"

As the dignitary leaves the podium, he tells the chief, "That went well."

"Uh-huh," the chief replies, adding, "Look out! Don't step in the kazanga."

—UNKNOWN

I've never understood the concept of the gift certificate, because for the same 50 bucks, my friend could've gotten me 50 bucks.

—UNKNOWN

Ten men and one woman are hanging on to a rope that extends down from a helicopter. The weight of 11 people is too much for the rope, so the group decides one person has to jump off.

No one can decide who should go, until finally the woman volunteers. She gives a touching speech, saying she will sacrifice her life to save the others, because women are used to giving up things for their husbands and children.

When she finishes speaking, all the men start clapping.

—MARGARET PITMAN

QUOTABLE QUOTES

"I once wanted to become an atheist, but I gave up—they have no holidays."

—HENNY YOUNGMAN

"Airport screeners are now scanning holiday fruitcakes. Not even the scanners can tell what those little red things are."

—DAVID LETTERMAN

"I'm glad that life isn't like a Christmas song, because if my friends and I were building a snowman and it suddenly came alive when we put a hat on it, I'd probably freak and stab it to death with an icicle."

—MATTHEW PERRY

"A good holiday is one spent among people whose notions of time are vaguer than yours."

—J. B. PRIESTLEY

"Nothing says holidays like a cheese log."

—ELLEN DEGENERES

"Happiness is having a large, loving, caring, close-knit family in another city."

—GEORGE BURNS

"At this time of the year, with the holidays upon us, nothing says she cares about how I am, where I am and what I'm doing as much as the restraining order."

—RANDY SAINT

"No self-respecting mother would run out of intimidations on the eve of a major holiday."

—ERMA BOMBECK

What sound does a grape make when an elephant steps on it?

None. It just lets out a little wine.

In the spring I planted a small vegetable garden and looked after it with great pride as it flourished. Then came the summer day when I said to myself, "The first thing in the morning, I'll harvest my crop."

But before I got outside, my small son dashed in, yelling, "Mama, the ducks are in our garden." What a feast my neighbor's fowl had! Not a bean vine was left standing. Squashed tomatoes were all over. I bawled. My neighbor apologized. Months later, after all was forgiven and forgotten, the neighbor came to wish us a merry Christmas. He handed me a package, which he said I must open right away.

We all burst into laughter when we saw the gift—a plump duck all ready to pop into the oven, with this note attached: "Enjoy your garden."

—MRS. PLEAS OVERBY

A Florida man protested a tax clerk's ruling that a baby born on January 24 was not deductible on last year's income. "Why not?" he asked. "It was last year's business!"

—DORA JANE DEMING

Mystery writer P. D. James told a college audience that her career path was laid out early in life. "My parents had an inkling of what I might become when I was five years old. When they read me 'Humpty Dumpty,' I asked, 'Was he pushed?'"

—SHIRLEY SAYRE

❄ ❄ ❄ ❄ ❄ ❄ ❄ ❄ ❄ ❄ ❄ ❄

A man walks up to an attractive girl in a disco and asks, "Would you like to dance?"

"I wouldn't dance with you if you were the last man on earth," she snorts.

"I don't think you heard me correctly," the man says. "I said, 'You look fat in those pants.'"

—SERRA ADALAR

A group of middle-aged people came into the roller-skating rink my wife and I own. One explained that none of them had skated in 15 years, but they thought it would be fun to give it a try. I had handed out eight pairs of skates before asking the last person in the group what size he needed.

"No, thanks," he said. "I'm the designated driver."

—MIKE WILLIAMS

Did you hear about the doctor who went on a ski trip and got lost on the slopes? He stamped out "help" in the snow, but nobody could read his writing.

—HAROLD ZUBER

My five-year-old son and I were discussing some of the differences between his childhood and mine. I pointed out that when I was young, we didn't have Nintendo, cell phones, computers, or even digital cameras.

I realized just how difficult this was for him to comprehend when he asked, **"Did you have fruit?"**

—MICHELLE PORTER

"Now, let me get this straight—four calling birds,
three French hens, two turtle doves,
and a partridge in a pear tree?!"

❄ ❄ ❄ ❄ ❄ ❄ ❄ ❄ ❄ ❄ ❄ ❄

Alice and Ted went snowboarding, and Ted brought along a quart-size thermos. Alice had never seen one and asked what it was. "It's a thermos," replied Ted. "The guy at the store told me it's used for keeping hot things hot and cold things cold."

"Sounds great," said Alice. "What do you have in it?"

"Three coffees and a Popsicle."

—JEANNE STANTON

My wife, a professor of medicine, has published five books. After she'd written her latest one, I stopped at a market to buy some chocolate and champagne.

"Are you celebrating something?" asked the clerk as he bagged my items.

"Yes," I replied proudly. "My wife just finished a book."

He paused a moment. "Slow reader?"

—DENNIS DOOK

A couple of fishing buddies from Alabama decided to travel to Minnesota one winter to try ice fishing. Just before they reached the frozen lake, they stopped at a bait shop to buy supplies. "Don't forget an ice pick," one of them said. They paid for their purchases and were off.

Two hours later, one of them returned. "We need another dozen ice picks," he said. He bought a whole box full and left. But in an hour, he was back.

The bait man asked, "How are you fellows doing?"

"Not too well," the fisherman replied. "We haven't even got the boat in the water yet."

—STANTON SEEPERSAUD

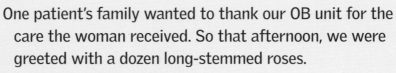

One patient's family wanted to thank our OB unit for the care the woman received. So that afternoon, we were greeted with a dozen long-stemmed roses. The included card began,

"To the Obese staff . . ."

—SHEREE CHRISTENSEN

According to the order form, if I wanted a school photograph of my first-grader, there was one simple rule I had to adhere to: "Your child must be present at the time the picture is taken."

—LEAH BANG

I was looking at the pies offered by a nearby café. They had cherry, apple, berry, peach, and Herman's.

"What type of pie is Herman's?" I asked the waiter.

"Apple," he said.

"Then why is it called Herman's pie?"

"Because Herman called in to reserve it."

—MARY SKORDINSKY

Just before Christmas, we had as visitors two young couples from Hong Kong, where it never snows. I decided to drive them to a mountain ski area and let them have the experience of being in deep snow and of riding the ski lift.

As we drove up the canyon through the green pines with their sparkling white mantle, our visitors were wide-eyed with the beauty of it all. One man said quietly, "I feel as if I'm right inside my own Christmas card."

—T. FRANK NELSON

❄ ❄ ❄ ❄ ❄ ❄ ❄ ❄ ❄ ❄ ❄ ❄

Seen in the window of a camping shop:
"Now is the winter of our discount tents."

—PAMELA KILGOUR

When a woman in my office became engaged, a colleague offered her some advice. "The first ten years are the hardest," she said.

"How long have you been married?" I asked.

"Ten years," she replied.

—TONYA WINTER

I answer a lot of questions at the information desk at Olympic National Park, in Washington State. But one visitor stumped me: "Do you have any trails that just go downhill?"

—MIKE PERZEL

During our church service one Sunday, a parishioner was speaking about an emotionally charged topic and had trouble controlling her tears. Finishing her remarks, she told the congregation, "I apologize for crying so much. I'm usually not such a big boob."

The bishop rose to close the session and remarked, "That's okay. We like big boobs."

—L.S.

The highlight of our zoo trip was a peacock showing off its plumage. My four-year-old son was particularly taken with it. That evening, he couldn't wait to tell his father: "Dad, guess what! I saw a Christmas tree come out of a chicken!"

—CAROL HOWARD

LAUGHTER
THE BEST MEDICINE®
THOSE LOVABLE PETS

Contents

A Note from the Editors   415

To the Dogs   417

They are dedicated, affectionate, and oh so lovable. When our canine friends cross paths with humans, they make us roll over with laughter.

Cunning Cats   461

Cat owner or not, the laugh-out-loud antics of these capering kitties give us an entertaining look inside the minds of these fabulous felines.

Tweety Birds   499

Their uncanny ability to bond with people has given rise to the popularity of parrots, parakeets, canaries, and other exotic birds. And the unlikely things they do—and often say—are priceless.

That's a Pet?   525

We open our hearts—and our home—to everything from fish and ferrets to rabbits, reptiles, and rodents. And the often hilarious trials and tribulations of these critters both great and small often leave us wondering why.

Not the "Vet"   561

Pets find nothing funny about an outing to the vet, and their diffidence often turns the trip into a riotous affair.

Dumb and Dumber   589

We're not just pointing fingers at our cute and cuddly friends, but pet owners, too, can easily tip the intelligence scales in the other direction when it comes to caring for pets—and the dumber, the funnier.

A Note from the Editors

People are funny, but so are the animals we love—and our day-to-day relationships with them can be even more entertaining. From cats fined for littering to dogs that tremble at the sight of their own "Beware of Dog" sign, this book is dedicated to the companions we hold so dear—our pets.

And it doesn't just stop with cats and dogs. Sure, these furry friends rule the comedic roost, but within the pages of *Laughter, the Best Medicine: Those Lovable Pets,* parrots, bunnies, hamsters, and even the occasional white rat are an endless source of amusement as well. Take, for instance, the scientist who crossed the carrier pigeon with a woodpecker and got a bird that not only delivered its message to the home of the designated recipient but also knocked on the door when it got there!

By way of funny tales, quotes, and cartoons compiled from more than eight decades' worth of *Reader's Digest* magazine, this book brings to life the often funny relationships we have with our animals—and promises to make you laugh your tail off.

To the
dogs

I think dogs are the most amazing creatures; they give unconditional love. For me they are the role model for being alive.

—GILDA RADNER

"Honey, the dog learned a new trick and now I owe him twelve dollars."

❤ ❤ ❤ ❤ ❤ ❤ ❤ ❤ ❤ ❤ ❤

I keep five dogs in my backyard, in four houses of various sizes. One day, during a heavy rainstorm, I went out to check on my pets. The big house was occupied by one dog, the middle-sized house held two, and the small houses had one pet each. Satisfied that they were all snug and dry, I left. A little later lightning streaked across the sky and thunder boomed. When I peeked out the back door, all the houses were empty except the big one. In it were all five dogs.

—JUNE CROSSLAND

Our happy little fox terrier, Cookie, had a game all her own. Every time we climbed into our car, she took a head start to race us to the bottom of the hill. Down the driveway she would scoot, across our near-neighbor's lawn, down the hill, across a basketball court, through a little gate, around our new neighbor's house, and through her front hedge just in time to grin at us as we caught up a half block from home.

Our new neighbor down the hill, upon meeting us for the first time recently, remarked, "We always know when you folks are going somewhere."

"How can you tell?" I asked.

"Well," she said, "it's strange, but always just before you drive past our house, our cat climbs a tree."

—MRS. W. T. BOONE

Our daughter was working as a telemarketer for a home-security firm. Once while she was reciting all the benefits of the system to a potential customer, he interrupted her and said, "We don't need it because we have a big dog."

"That's great," my daughter replied. "But can he dial 911?"

—EVELYNE DREEBEN

♥ ♥ ♥ ♥ ♥ ♥ ♥ ♥ ♥ ♥

"For sale: **Eight puppies from a German shepherd and an Alaskan hussy.**"

—RICHARD A. HARMS

Driving to work one morning, I heard an announcement on the radio about a lost dog. The deejay said the owner was offering a cash reward for its return. Getting to the traffic segment of his broadcast, the deejay asked the helicopter pilot who monitors morning rush hour what the roads were like. "To heck with the traffic," the pilot said on the air, "we're going to look for that dog!"

—SUZANNE DOPP

I'm a police officer and occasionally park my cruiser in residential areas to watch for speeders. One Sunday morning I was staked out in a driveway, when I saw a large dog trot up to my car. He stopped and sat just out of arm's reach. No matter how much I tried to coax him to come for a pat on the head, he refused to budge. After a while I decided to move to another location. I pulled out of the driveway, looked back and learned the reason for the dog's stubbornness. He quickly picked up the newspaper I had been parked on and dutifully ran back to his master.

—JEFF WALL

I was in a bank when a man entered with a rather large dog on a leash. When he asked if it was okay to bring his pet into the building, a bank official answered, "Yes, providing he doesn't make a deposit."

—JOHN REED

♥ ♥ ♥ ♥ ♥ ♥ ♥ ♥ ♥ ♥ ♥

The drive-up window at the bank where I'm a teller has an outside drawer to accept customer transactions. A woman once drove up with her dog in the front seat, and the pet eagerly jumped over onto the driver's lap when the car reached my window. He looked excited to see me. "Your dog is so friendly!" I said to the owner.

"He thinks he's at McDonald's," she replied.

—MARILYN BOURDEAU

As a mail carrier in Florida, I was attempting to deliver a certified letter when I heard a dog barking furiously on the other side of a front door. I stepped away from the door as the homeowner appeared, and asked that the dog be kept inside. It was too late. The little dog started yelping and jumping on me. I froze. As the customer signed for his letter, he kept saying, "Don't worry, he won't bite you." Just then the dog turned and bit its owner.

—RAMONA OCCHIUZZO

Whenever the alarm goes off after-hours at the municipal office where I work, the security company calls me at home and I have to go back and reset it. Late at night I got one of those calls. As I was getting ready to head out the door, my husband groggily said, "You're not going down there by yourself at this hour." Just as I was thinking, How thoughtful of him, he added, **"Better take the dog with you."**

—RUTH RODDICK

A new restaurant near our office boasted exotic fare. And exotic it was. When our dessert arrived, my coworker sniffed her chocolate dish and grimaced. "It smells like cocoa," she said.

"It's chocolate—shouldn't it smell like cocoa?" I asked.

More confused than I was, she answered, "Cocoa is the name of my dog."

—CYNTHIA ZHANG

My sister-in-law, a truck driver, had decided to get a dog for protection. As she inspected a likely candidate, the trainer told her, "He doesn't like men."

Perfect, my sister-in-law thought, and took the dog. Then one day she was approached by two men in a parking lot, and she watched to see how her canine bodyguard would react. Soon it became clear that the trainer wasn't kidding. As the men got closer, the dog ran under the nearest car.

—DANNY ARIAIL

My wife found this flyer taped to a neighborhood telephone pole:

"Found, male yellow Lab, very friendly. Loves to play with kids and eat Bubbles. Bubbles is our cat. Please come get your dog."

—ROBERT CHAPMAN

 What's the difference between a man and a dog running?

One wears trousers and the other pants.

MARIE TERRIEN

"When are you getting the windshield wipers fixed, Harold?"

Who could resist this sales pitch my ten-year-old daughter, Courtney, gave, describing what her future would be like. She told me she would have three dogs.

"Why three?" I asked.

Courtney said that when she slept, she'd have one big dog to rest her head on like a pillow, and a small one cuddled under each arm.

"Oh," I replied, "So if you're in bed with the three dogs around you and in your arms, what about your husband?"

Courtney was quiet for a moment as she thought this through. Finally she said, "He can get his own dog!"

—WALLY VOGEL

♥ ♥ ♥ ♥ ♥ ♥ ♥ ♥ ♥ ♥ ♥

Our dog, a Shih Tzu, was missing, and we advertised on the radio and in the paper. Several days later, a woman called.

"I think I have your dog," she told my wife, "but I don't know what a Shih Tzu looks like."

"Point your finger at the animal and say, **'Bang!'**" my wife told her.

In a few minutes the woman was back on the line. "The dog fell over," she reported.

We had found our pet.

—BILL MORRIS

Friends of mine sold their country home to move to the city after arranging for the new owners to keep their dog that they said was an excellent watch dog.

On their first night in the city, they received a frantic phone call from the new owners. "Please come back and collect your dog," they begged. "We've been out for the day and it won't let us back onto the property."

—NORMA KAWAK

At the end of the day, I parked my police van in front of the station house. My K-9 partner, Jake, was in the back barking, which caught the attention of a boy who was passing by. "Is that a dog you have back there?" he asked.

"It sure is," I said.

"What did he do?"

—CLINT FORWARD

A man and his dog entered the hardware store where I work. The man turned right, toward housewares. The dog turned left, toward pet supplies. The man returned to the checkout counter with kitchen tiling. The dog returned to the checkout counter with a fleece toy. The man paid for both, and they left, each carrying his own item.

—KENT MILLER

Once while riding the bus to work, I noticed a man at a stop enjoying a cup of coffee.

As we approached the stop, he finished drinking and set the cup on the ground. This negligence surprised me, since it seemed to be a good ceramic cup.

Days later I saw the same man again drinking his coffee at the bus stop. Once again, he placed the cup on the grass before boarding. When the bus pulled away, I looked back in time to see a dog carefully carrying the cup in his mouth as he headed for home.

—VALERIE A. HUEBNER

I was editing classified ads for a small-town newspaper when a man called to place an ad.

"It should read," he said, "'Free to good home. Golden retriever. Will eat anything, loves children.'"

—ELLEN YOUNG

Recently, my husband and I went to the movies. When the film ended, we sat for a few minutes discussing how disappointing it was. When we stood up, we overheard another couple having the same discussion. The man said, "For that we left the dog alone at home?"

—LOIS DAVIS IN *THE NEW YORK TIMES*

I had just come out of a store when the blast of a car horn scared me. When I turned to yell at the rude driver, I found a large white poodle sitting in the driver's seat of a parked car. When the impatient dog honked again, a man came scurrying out of a shop, shouting, "I'll be there in a minute!"

"Did you teach your dog to do that?" I asked the man.

"Yes," he answered in exasperation, "and now he won't let me go anywhere!"

—NANCY E. HAIGH

A truck ran a red light, almost sideswiping our car. As my husband veered away, he threw his arm across me, protecting me from a possible collision. I was ready to plant a big kiss on my hero's cheek when he apologized. In his haste, he admitted, he had forgotten it was me in the front seat and not our black Labrador, Checkers.

—APRIL COLE

QUOTABLE QUOTES

"So many of Lassie's fans want to ask: Is he allowed on the furniture? Of course he is—but then, he's the one who paid for it."

—JULIA GLASS

"I dressed my dog up as a cat for Halloween. Now he won't come when I call him."

—ROOFTOP COMEDY

"Dogs don't bark at parked cars."

—LYNNE CHENEY

"You own a dog; you feed a cat."

—JIM FIEBIG

"Don't accept your dog's admiration as conclusive evidence that you are wonderful."

—ANN LANDERS

"We give dogs time we can spare, space we can spare, and love we can spare. In return, dogs give us their all. It's the best deal man has ever made."

—MARGERY FACKLAM, AUTHOR

One dog to another: "What if the hand that feeds us is surprisingly tasty?"

—PETE MUELLER IN *BARK*

"If dogs could talk, it would take a lot of fun out of owning one."

— ANDREW A. ROONEY, FROM *NOT THAT YOU ASKED* (RANDOM HOUSE)

"I wonder if other dogs think poodles are members of a weird religious cult."

—RITA RUDNER

"He's a high-tech watchdog."

♥ ♥ ♥ ♥ ♥ ♥ ♥ ♥ ♥ ♥ ♥

My friend has a golden retriever that responds to music, and seems to especially like opera. The dog is appropriately named Poochini.

—JERRY SIMON

My sister's dog had been deaf and blind for years. When she started to suffer painful tumors, it was time to put her down. As I explained this to my seven-year-old son, he asked if Jazzy would go to heaven. I said I thought she would, and that in dog heaven, she would be healthy again and able to do her favorite thing: chase squirrels. Jacob thought about that for a minute then said, "So dog heaven must be the same as squirrel hell."

—JUDY SUTTERFIELD

As the stranger enters a country store, he spots a sign: "Danger! Beware of Dog!" Inside, he sees a harmless old hound asleep in the middle of the floor. "Is that the dog we're supposed to beware of?" he asks the owner.

"That's him," comes the reply.

"He doesn't look dangerous to me. Why would you post that sign?"

"Before I posted that sign, people kept tripping over him."

—L. B. WEINSTEIN

A French poodle and a collie were walking down the street. The poodle turned to the collie and complained, "My life is such a mess. My owner is mean, my girlfriend is having an affair with a German shepherd and I'm as nervous as a cat."

"Why don't you go see a psychiatrist?" asked the collie.

"I can't," replied the poodle. "I'm not allowed on the couch."

—JOHN W. GAMBA

♥ ♥ ♥ ♥ ♥ ♥ ♥ ♥ ♥ ♥ ♥

Did you ever notice that when you blow in a dog's face he gets mad at you, but when you take him on a car ride, he sticks his head out the window

—ROBYN CAMPBELL-OUCHIDA

Why It's Great to be a Dog

- No one expects you to take a bath every day.
- If it itches, you can scratch it.
- There's no such thing as bad food.
- A rawhide bone can entertain you for hours.
- If you grow hair in weird places, no one notices.
- You can lie around all day without worrying about being fired.
- You don't get in trouble for putting your head in a stranger's lap.
- You're always excited to see the same people.
- Having big feet is considered an asset.
- Puppy love can last.

—DAWN DRESSLER FROM *THE SUN*, BREMERTON WASHINGTON

We were going out of state for six weeks and asked the neighbors' nine-year-old son, Mike, to care for our dog. We explained that the job required feeding, grooming, walking and, most of all, plenty of love and playtime. Then we asked Mike what the job would be worth to him.

"I'll give you ten bucks," he said.

—JOAN KLINGLER

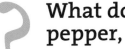 **What do you get when you cross a chili pepper, a shovel and a chihuahua?**

A hot diggity dog.

These guys, one a pessimist and the other an eternal optimist, had been friends for years. The optimist was always trying to get his pal to see the bright side of things. The optimist found a dog that could walk on water. This is perfect, he thought. There's no way that darn cynic can say anything negative about this. He took his friend duck hunting so he could see the dog in action. Mid-morning, they finally downed a bird. It fell on the other side of the lake, so the optimist sent the dog to retrieve it. The animal trotted across the water, grabbed the duck in his mouth, and ran back. "Isn't that amazing?"

"Hmmph," the cynic said. "That dog can't swim, can it?"

With a young child on the stand, the district attorney knew he needed to start with some simple questions. "If I were to tell you that this pen was red, would that be the truth or a lie?" he asked.

"The truth," said the child.

"Very good!" said the D.A. "And if I were to say that dogs could talk, would that be the truth or a lie?"

"The truth," said the child again.

"Really?" asked the D.A. "Dogs can talk? What do they say?"

"I don't know," the child answered. "I don't talk dog."

—LOS ANGELES COUNTY SUPERIOR COURT COMMISSIONER
MICHAEL A. COWELL IN *LOS ANGELES DAILY JOURNAL*

❤ ❤ ❤ ❤ ❤ ❤ ❤ ❤ ❤ ❤ ❤

An engineer, an accountant, a chemist and a bureaucrat are bragging about how smart their dogs are. The engineer called to his dog, "T-Square, do your stuff." The dog took out paper and pen and drew a circle, a square, and a triangle. Everyone agreed he was smart.

The accountant called, "Slide Rule, do your stuff." The pooch went to the kitchen, got a dozen cookies and made four stacks of three. Everyone was impressed.

The chemist called, "Beaker, do your stuff." The dog went to the fridge for a quart of milk, got a ten-ounce glass and poured exactly eight ounces without spilling a drop. Everyone agreed that was great.

The bureaucrat called, "Coffee Break, do your stuff!" Coffee Break ate the cookies, drank the milk, chewed the paper, claimed he injured his mouth doing so, filed a grievance for unsafe work conditions, put in for Workers' Compensation and took extended sick leave.

A Great Dane, a Scottie and a chihuahua were sitting in a bar, knocking back a few, when a beautiful French poodle walked in.

"Hi, boys," she said seductively, "I'll make a very happy dog out of whichever of you comes up with the best proposition using the words cheese and liver."

The Great Dane thought for a moment, and then declared, "I don't like cheese, but I sure like liver, and I like you, too!" The lady just looked away, obviously unimpressed. The Scottie immediately followed with, "I like cheese, and I like liver, and I like you!" He wagged his tail expectantly, but she ignored him.

Then the chihuahua stepped forward. "Liver alone!" he growled. "Cheese with me!" They left together.

"Word to the wise: Always check the cheese for pills."

An on-duty policeman and another gentleman were both interested in adopting the same dog at the SPCA where I work. I told both customers that they'd have to draw for the pet. The uniformed officer stepped back from the counter, put his hand on his hip just above his service revolver and with a grin drawled, "That suits me just fine."

—RICHARD A. CROOKES

♥ ♥ ♥ ♥ ♥ ♥ ♥ ♥ ♥ ♥ ♥

This ad in the *Bozeman Daily Chronicle* was obviously directed toward pet lovers only: **"Free to good home, a loving Jack Russell terror dog."**

—SARAH RUEFER

Because our dog, Dakota, travels with us in the car, my husband and I give him sugarless mints to sweeten his doggy breath. Soon he developed a taste for them. One day while my husband and I were out in the country, we let Dakota run off-leash. He began wandering away. I yelled for him to stop, stay, come. He ignored me and kept running. Finally, unable to think of anything else, I shouted, "Who wants a breath mint?" He stopped dead in his tracks.

—SUSAN NELSON

Driving back from Vermont, I stopped at a vegetable stand. It was deserted except for a sleeping German shepherd. I stepped over the dog, helped myself to some corn, then opened the cashbox to pay. Taped to the inside of the lid was this note: "The dog can count."

—CARLEEN CRUMMETT

One year on vacation I went to a resort in Wyoming. As part of the usual activities, a neighboring ranch invited guests from our resort to participate in a cattle drive. After watching 20 make-believe cowpokes whooping and hollering, I rode up to the ranch owner and asked her how many cowboys it normally takes to drive a herd of that size.

"One," she replied, "and a dog."

—DEBORAH BLITZ

❤ ❤ ❤ ❤ ❤ ❤ ❤ ❤ ❤ ❤

A couple of dog owners are arguing about whose pet is smarter. "My dog is so smart," says the first owner, "that every morning he waits for the paperboy to come around. He tips the kid and then brings the newspaper to me, along with my morning coffee."

"I know," says the second owner.

"How do you know?"

"My dog told me."

—SOURABH BHATIA

I dressed up my dog as a mailman for Halloween. He bit himself.

—CHRISTINA MELTON

Two dogs were out for a walk. One dog says to the other, "Wait here a minute. I'll be right back." He walks across the street and sniffs a fire hydrant for about a minute, then rejoins his friend. "What was that all about?" the other dog asks.

"Just checking my messages."

My dog plopped into my lap, accidentally speed-dialing an emergency number on the cell phone in my pocket. Moments later the phone rang. "This is Dallas Fire and Rescue. We received a call from this number. Is everything okay?"

Quickly I realized what had happened. "I'm fine. My dog must have punched your number."

The voice on the other end inquired, **"And how is your dog?"**

—CONSTANCE STROW

"He's a power pointer."

Irate man with dog, to pet-shop owner: "Of all the nerve! You sold me this mutt as a watchdog. Yesterday a robber broke into my home and stole three hundred dollars, and the miserable animal didn't make a sound."

Pet-shop owner: "My dear sir, this dog used to belong to very wealthy people. He doesn't react to such small amounts."

—FRITZ HERDI

❤ ❤ ❤ ❤ ❤ ❤ ❤ ❤ ❤ ❤ ❤

During their observance of Animal Week, the fourth-graders told about their kindnesses to pets. Asked what he had done, one little boy said: "I kicked a boy for kicking his dog."

—MARY WRIGHT

I was shopping in the pet section of my local supermarket when I overheard a woman singing the praises of a particular water bowl to her husband. "Look, it even has a water filter!" she concluded, holding the doggie dish out for her husband's inspection. He had a slightly different take on things: "Dear, he drinks out of the toilet."

—JAMES JENKINS

Butch, our boxer, hated taking his medicine. After a lot of trial and error my father eventually figured out the simplest way to get it into him: blow it down Butch's throat with something called a pill tube. So Dad put the large tablet in one end of the tube, forced the reluctant dog's jaws open, and poked the other end into his mouth. Then, just as my father inhaled to blow, Butch coughed.

A startled look appeared on Dad's face. He opened his eyes wide and swallowed hard. "I think I've just been de-wormed," he gasped.

—JOHN ROBERTSON

 Why are dogs such bad dancers?
They have two left feet.

❤ ❤ ❤ ❤ ❤ ❤ ❤ ❤ ❤ ❤ ❤

The 6 a.m. regulars at the dog run are, not surprisingly, a pet-oriented group.

Recently John started discussing his trip. "The flight was awful! We were delayed for a few hours, and when we finally boarded, the baby behind me didn't stop crying for the whole flight."

Another dog-run regular turned to him in surprise: "What did the owner do?"

—TOBY YOUNG

The Doggie Diner in Bellingham, Wash., has grossed $10,000 a month since opening last year. The eatery is so popular that reservations are a must for parties of more than two dogs. And, yes, the patrons are strictly canine. Says co-owner Taimi Gorham, "If a cat comes in, he's on his own. "

—THE CHRISTIAN SCIENCE MONITOR

On the last day of school, the children brought gifts for the teacher. The florist's son brought the teacher a bouquet. The candy-store owner's daughter handed the teacher a pretty box of candy. Then the liquor-store owner's son brought up a big, heavy box. The teacher lifted it up and noticed that it was leaking a little bit. She touched a drop of the liquid with her finger and tasted it.

"Is it wine?" she guessed.

"No," the boy replied.

She tasted another drop and asked, "Champagne?"

"No," said the little boy.

"I give up," she said.

"What is it?"

"A puppy!"

♥ ♥ ♥ ♥ ♥ ♥ ♥ ♥ ♥ ♥ ♥

When I was ill, my husband and I were stuck in the house for months. But I made a complete recovery and was so happy the day he bounded into the kitchen and asked, "Would you like to go out, girl?"

"I'd love to," I replied immediately.

We had a wonderful meal, culminating with my husband making a confession. "Remember when I suggested going out tonight?" he asked.

"Yes," I said.

"I was talking to the dog."

—ANITA SAUNDERS

Although legally declared blind, my friend Walter is able to see shadows, so he enjoys watching television. One day he was engrossed in one of his favorite programs when Joey, his guide dog, let him know that she needed to go out. "Okay, Joey, as soon as this program's over." She waited a few minutes, and then nudged his knee. "Wait until the program's over," Walter said impatiently. Joey sat a few more minutes, looking from Walter to the screen. Then she nudged him again and whined briefly. When Walter continued to ignore her, Joey calmly walked around behind the television, grasped the electric cord in her mouth, and unplugged the set.

—FLORENCE M. WEEKES

❤ ❤ ❤ ❤ ❤ ❤ ❤ ❤ ❤ ❤ ❤

"I've really had it with my dog. He'll chase anyone on a bike."

"So what are you going to do—leave him at the pound? Sell him?"

"No, nothing that drastic. I think I'll just take his bike away."

I arrived home from work to find all the windows and doors wide open. Apparently our puppy had had an accident.

"Yeah, it really stank," my daughter told me. "In fact, when we first walked in, I thought you had come home early and were cooking dinner."

—TIMOTHY SCOTT FOUBERT

After I completed a frantic afternoon of chores, I walked into the living room to find my husband reclining in his chair. He was looking bemusedly at our new puppy, who was napping.

"If I wanted to look at something lying around sleeping all day," he complained, "I would have bought a cat."

"Or you could have just bought a mirror," I said.

—TRACEY SMITH

We got a new dog, a dachshund. Next came the big question: what to call him. The winner came from our son, Brian.

"Hypotenuse," he suggested. Why? "He's got a long side between two shorter legs."

—JENNY ROWE

"If I had a cellphone you wouldn't have to whistle all the time."

QUOTABLE QUOTES

"The dog is mentioned in the Bible eighteen times—the cat not even once."

—W. E. FARBSTEIN

"A dog is the only thing on earth that loves you more than you love yourself."

—JOSH BILLINGS

"If your dog is fat, you aren't getting enough exercise."

—UNKNOWN

"Did you ever walk into a room and forget why you walked in? I think that's how dogs spend their lives."

—SUE MURPHY

"If you are a dog and your owner suggests that you wear a sweater... suggest that he wear a tail."

—FRAN LEBOWITZ

"The dog is a yes-animal, very popular with people who can't afford to keep a yes-man."

—ROBERTSON DAVIES

"A dog is the only exercise machine you cannot decide to skip when you don't feel like it."

—CAROLYN G. HEILBRUN
IN *THE LAST GIFT OF TIME*

"Dogs feel very strongly that they should always go with you in the car, in case the need should arise for them to bark violently at nothing right in your ear."

—DAVE BARRY IN *MIAMI HERALD*

♥ ♥ ♥ ♥ ♥ ♥ ♥ ♥ ♥ ♥ ♥ ♥

Whenever my family leaves the house, our Shetland sheepdog's animal instincts start to kick in. He runs circles around us and nips at our heels to keep us all together. Watching this display, my friend couldn't resist: "You always herd the ones you love."

—JOLENE HUEHOLT

Brownie was the last of a litter of pups in the window of the pet shop where I work. Although his looks were nondescript and he wasn't even a puppy anymore, his tail wagged jauntily, hopefully, at anyone who stopped to look. On the day that Brownie was to be transferred to the city pound, a pleasant young woman with several children in tow came in and bought him.

"I suppose it's an advertising gimmick," she said, "but it really got me."

I understood what she meant when I went to pull the "For Sale" sticker off the window. Someone had changed the 'l' to 'k' and added an 'n.'

—MARGARET WARK

My husband took our dog to the veterinarian and sat in the waiting room with the other dog owners. Suddenly the street door opened a few inches and an authoritative voice called, "Better get a tight hold on your animals!"

Everyone grasped his pet protectively, nervously wondering what sort of brute was to be led in. The door opened slowly— and in walked the mailman. He dropped some letters on a table, grinned, and walked out.

—MRS. ROY J. OLSEN

"Sometimes, you just have to let the stick go."

❤ ❤ ❤ ❤ ❤ ❤ ❤ ❤ ❤ ❤ ❤

Recently I ran into an old friend who told me he was trying to find a home for his Boston terrier. He was moving, and pets were not allowed in his new apartment. Since I had been thinking of getting a pet for my family, I agreed to take the dog.

"Fine," said Bill, happily, "I'll give you all her personal effects, too."

The next afternoon a friend of Bill's arrived at my home, explaining that Bill and his family had already moved. He then produced the terrier and her personal effects: chain, dish, collar—and three puppies!

—JAMES R. FINCH

A friend of mine, scheduled to move from Dunedin, New Zealand, to Sydney, Australia, sent his pet golden retriever ahead by air, and asked the kennel owner to let him know as soon as the animal arrived. He was relieved to receive a cable the next morning with the simple message: "Woof, Woof."

—JOHN MACKIE

During our show and tell period in the third grade, Mike mentioned that his pet beagle was expecting puppies. From then on, the class eagerly awaited the news of their birth. When the day arrived, Mike announced glumly, "Well, they're here." It was obvious that he was disappointed, but because of the intense interest of the class in the pups, I asked, "What's wrong, Mike? Tell us more."

"Well," he said, "I wanted a collie, and my sister wanted a poodle, but all we got were beagles—and we already have a beagle."

—NANCY NABBEFELD

♥ ♥ ♥ ♥ ♥ ♥ ♥ ♥ ♥ ♥ ♥

In a pet shop: **"Don't say 'no' until you look the puppy in the eye."**

At a workshop on dog temperament, the instructor noted that a test for a canine's disposition was for an owner to fall down and act hurt. A dog with poor temperament would try to bite the person, whereas a good dog would lick his owner's face or show concern.

Once, while eating pizza in the living room, I decided to try out this theory on my two dogs. I stood up, clutched my heart, let out a scream and collapsed on the floor.

The dogs looked at me, glanced at each other and raced to the coffee table for my pizza.

—SUSAN MOTTICE

I gave my daughter-in-law a Pekingese puppy from my dog's litter. She tried to find an Oriental-sounding name for the pet, and since my son is an attorney, she thought she had succeeded admirably when she came up with So-Su-Mi.

—JUDY CHARUHAS

As a teacher in an inner-city school, I found that one of my end-of-year activities was to take my class to a park for a day of fun. My 185-pound Great Dane came with us. The children were amazed by what was probably the largest dog they'd ever seen, and they bombarded me with questions: "Does he bite?" "How much did he cost?" One student asked, "What does he eat?"

Before I could answer, a boy shouted, "Man, whatever he wants!"

—BARBARA E. DOYLE

♥ ♥ ♥ ♥ ♥ ♥ ♥ ♥ ♥ ♥ ♥

Our new cairn terrier weighed only three pounds, but he kept trying to run large dogs out of our yard with his tiny growls. We soon hit upon the appropriate name for him— Genghis Cairn.

—ANNE COFFIN YOUNG

My dog is half pit bull, half poodle. It's not much of a watchdog, but it's a vicious gossip.

—CRAIG SHOEMAKER

Ever notice the similarities between man and man's best friend?
- Both take up too much space on the bed.
- Both have irrational fears about vacuuming.
- Neither tells you what's bothering him.
- Neither of them notices when you get your hair cut.
- Neither understands what you see in cats.

—M. D. ROSENBERG/FROM *FUNNY TIMES*

My father and a friend were talking about the doors they had installed so their animals could let themselves in and out of the house. My dad asked his friend, who had two massive Great Danes, "Aren't you afraid that somebody might crawl through the dogs' door and steal something?"

"If you saw an opening that big," said his friend, "would you crawl through it?"

—HORST JENKINS

♥ ♥ ♥ ♥ ♥ ♥ ♥ ♥ ♥ ♥ ♥

The dog owner claimed that his pet, when given money, would go to the newsstand to buy a paper. His friend insisted on a demonstration and handed the dog some money. The dog trotted off, but an hour later he had still not returned with the paper.

"How much did you give him?" asked the owner.

"Five dollars."

"Well, that explains it. When you give him five dollars he goes to the movies."

A woman had a dog who ran away every time he was let out of the house, and no matter how sweetly or how long she called his name, he wouldn't come home until he was good and ready. She sought advice at the pet shop.

"Well," said the salesman, "the best thing would be our new supersonic dog whistle. It's expensive, but well worth it in this case."

"Will my dog like the whistle?" the woman asked.

"Your dog will not only like the whistle," the salesman said, "but because of its design, your dog will be the only living thing to hear it. The only other living thing ever to respond to a whistle of this type was a big, dumb gorilla."

The woman was pleased, purchased the whistle and went home. That evening, as her husband watched TV, she opened the back door after the dog had been gone for ten minutes and blew the whistle as hard as she could.

"Who's blowing a whistle at this time of night?" demanded her husband.

—ALEX THIEN

"Why don't you go outside and chase a real car?"

♥ ♥ ♥ ♥ ♥ ♥ ♥ ♥ ♥ ♥ ♥

After our dog died, my parents had her cremated, and they placed the ashes in a special box on the fireplace mantel. One day the boy next door came over to play and noticed the fancy container. "What's in the box?" he asked.

"That's our dog," my mom replied.

"Oh," the boy simply said.

A minute later he remarked,

"He's awfully quiet, isn't he?"

—JOHN FERENCE

Two tourists notice a funeral procession with hordes of men following a coffin led by a man and a vicious-looking dog.

The tourists stop the man at the front of the procession to ask how the deceased died.

"This vicious dog attacked my mother-in-law," the man replies.

The male tourist says, "May I borrow this dog?"

The man points to the crowd of men behind him and says, "Wait your turn."

—JENNIFER READING

❤ ❤ ❤ ❤ ❤ ❤ ❤ ❤ ❤ ❤ ❤

The designer label craze has us all familiar with names. At a pet store I saw two dog sweaters labeled Pierre Cardog and Goochie Poochie.

—ELIYA OBILLO

The great thing about bumper stickers is they give proud parents a chance to boast about their children. The driver of the pickup in front of me was no different. His bumper sticker crowed "My Australian Cattle Dog Is Smarter Than Your Honor Student."

—STEWART BEUCKER

Each morning at 5:30, I take my Lhasa apso, Maxwell, for a walk. He has the bad habit of picking up bits of paper or other trash along the way. When he does, I command him to drop it, and he usually complies.

One morning, though, he absolutely refused to drop a piece of litter. So I told him to sit and then approached him to see what his treasure was. It was a $10 bill.

—ELSA BOGGS

I always scoffed when my sister insisted that our three dogs are computer literate. Then one day when I was signing on to AOL, I noticed that when the welcome voice came on, the dogs immediately settled down. **Later, when they heard the good-bye sign-off, all three dogs rushed to the door expecting to be walked.**

—MARGUERITE CANTINE

LASSIE 2008

My neighbor's son picked up a stray dog and named it Sam. Sometime later, I was having coffee at their house and inquired about Sam.

"Oh, the dog is fine," my neighbor said. "She had a litter of puppies, and so we fixed the problem. Now we call her Sam Spayed."

—JUDY CHRISTENSEN

> **"Worst dog ever. Free to a good home. Not fixed. Doesn't come when called. Runs away. Kills chickens and has foul smell."**
>
> —LAURA CALENTINE, ATHENS (OHIO) NEWS

My three-year-old granddaughter was staying with me and proudly announced that she had brushed her teeth and then the dog's. The next day I bought her a new toothbrush.

"Why did you buy me this?" she asked.

"Because you brushed the dog's teeth with the old one," I told her.

"No I didn't, Nana," she said. "I used yours."

—BARBARA ROSE

The animal control center in my friend's town decided to conduct a dog census. A census taker called at my friend's home and, upon learning that she did indeed have a dog, asked what kind. "A brown dog," she replied.

"No, no. I mean what breed is the dog?"

"Well, I don't know, she's just a brown dog."

"Perhaps if I could see her," the man said, "I might be able to tell."

My friend brought out the dog and waited patiently while the man studied her pet. In the end, he noted on his form: "one brown dog."

—LEE WEAVER

♥ ♥ ♥ ♥ ♥ ♥ ♥ ♥ ♥ ♥

I needed help training my rambunctious dog.
So I decided to sign him up for some obedience classes.
Flipping through a catalog, I found one class that seemed
perfectly suited for my pup. The description read
"Dog Obedience, Monday; weeks: 8; Instructor: Catt."

—ANN MCKENRICK

George's friend Sam had a dog who could recite the
Gettysburg Address.

"Let me buy him from you," pleaded George after a
demonstration.

"Okay," agreed Sam. "All he knows is that Lincoln speech
anyway."

At his company's Fourth of July picnic, George brought his
new pet and announced that the animal could recite the entire
Gettysburg Address. No one believed him, and they proceeded
to place bets against the dog. George quieted the crowd and said,
"Now we'll begin!" Then he looked at the dog. The dog looked
back. No sound.

"Come on boy, do your stuff."

Nothing. A disappointed George took his dog and went
home.

"Why did you embarrass me like that in front of everybody?"
George yelled at the dog, "Do you realize how much money you
lost me?"

"Don't be silly, George," replied the dog, "think how much
you'll get at the Labor Day picnic if you treat me right."

—JOHN HUEHNERGARTH

❤ ❤ ❤ ❤ ❤ ❤ ❤ ❤ ❤ ❤ ❤

I was leaving the groomer's with my dog when I noticed a pet perfume in a display case. It's a wonder that we don't bowl each other over trying to get it, because the tagline boldly announced, "Strong enough for a man...but made for a chihuahua."

—BECKY KELLEY

Why Dogs Are Better Than Kids

- It doesn't take 45 minutes to get a dog ready to go outside in the winter.
- Dogs cannot lie.
- Dogs never resist nap time.
- You don't need to get extra phone lines for a dog.
- Dogs don't pester you about getting a kid.
- Dogs don't care if the peas have been touched by the mashed potatoes.
- Average cost of sending a dog to school: $42. Average cost of sending your kid: $103,000.
- Dogs are housebroken by the time they are 12 weeks old.
- Your dog is not embarrassed if you sing in public.
- If your dog is a bad seed, your genes cannot be blamed.

—JENNIFER BERMANN, *WHY DOGS ARE BETTER THAN KIDS* (ANDREWS MCMEEL)

 Why did the cowboy buy a dachshund?
Someone told him to get a long little doggy.

♥ ♥ ♥ ♥ ♥ ♥ ♥ ♥ ♥ ♥ ♥

I saw two dogs walk over to a parking meter. One said to the other, **"How do you like that? Pay toilets."**

—DAVE STARR

For years, my family has kept a stray dog as our pet. One day, when my dad's friend came to visit, he asked my sister, "What is that mangy dog doing here?"

Offended, my sister replied, "He's our pet dog and he's like a member of the family."

Surprised, my dad's friend then asked, "Oh! Which one?"

—TAN PEI HONG

I put this question to my dog, a pet who puts on airs: "What, may I ask, makes man's best friend think he owns man's best chair?"

—DICK EMMONS

What Do You Get When You Cross...

...a collie and a Lhasa apso? A collapso, a dog that folds for easy transportation.

...a Pointer and a Setter? A Poinsetter, a traditional Christmas pet.

—ROSE C. WILSON FROM *PETS FOR LIFE*

I had always felt that my friend Neil's English bulldog was not the prettiest dog in the world. My suspicions were confirmed when one day we were taking Blue for a walk. A young boy approached and shyly asked Neil, "Mister, can I pet your pig?

—PAUL SCHNEIDER

♥ ♥ ♥ ♥ ♥ ♥ ♥ ♥ ♥ ♥ ♥

Who Wears the Collar in the Family?

New York City has many dogs, and it's not uncommon to hear people barking commands like, "Sit!" or "No!" or even "Don't sniff that!"

But Chris Atkins was taken aback when, as the light changed and a number of pedestrians started to cross the street, a man said to his dog: "Okay, Max, let's go. And please, let's not forget what almost happened the last time."

—THE NEW YORK TIMES

"When did you start seeing the invisible fence?"

❤ ❤ ❤ ❤ ❤ ❤ ❤ ❤ ❤ ❤

My sister, her husband and their English springer spaniel dog, Sam, stopped at a garage one day when their car horn wouldn't work. Dave slipped out of the driver's seat and the mechanic slid in to check the horn. From the back seat, Sam gently pressed his nose to the man's ear and sniffed. The mechanic screamed and almost fell to the ground in his haste to escape from the car. "I thought your wife was trying to kiss me," he explained later.

—ANNE CROCKER

A man walks into a wine bar with his dog.

"Er, excuse me," says the barman. "No dogs allowed."

"It's okay," the man responds. "This is a super-intelligent, talking dog."

"Oh, yeah?" sneers the barman. "Prove it."

"What grows on trees?" the man asks the animal.

"Bark, bark," replies the dog.

"What do you find on top of a house?"

"Roof, roof," says the mutt.

"What's the opposite of smooth?"

"Rough, rough," growls the hound.

The barman realizes he's being made a fool of and throws the man and his dog out.

"Well, I'm terribly sorry about that, Gavin," says the dog to his owner outside on the pavement. "Just out of interest, which one did I get wrong?"

♥ ♥ ♥ ♥ ♥ ♥ ♥ ♥ ♥ ♥ ♥

Notice in pet shop window: **Five puppies, FREE. Mother a crossbred Labrador. Father a small brown and white dog capable of climbing six-foot fence.**

—MRS. CHRIS SCOTT

During the Friday evening service, a rabbi notices Bernie, a congregation member, walk in with a Rottweiler. Horrified, the rabbi rushes over.

"What are you doing in here with that dog?" he asks Bernie. "It's deeply inappropriate.

"He's here to worship."

"Pull the other one," says the rabbi.

"I'm telling the truth!" protests Bernie and nods to the dog. It produces a yarmulke and tallith and puts them on. Then it opens a prayer book and starts praying in Hebrew.

The rabbi listens rapt for 15 minutes and is deeply impressed by the quality of the praying. "Sorry to have doubted you," he says. "Do you think your dog would consider going to rabbinical school?"

Bernie, throws up his arms in disgust. "You talk to him," he says. "He wants to be a doctor!"

Our much loved elderly dog had to go for a long delayed grooming session and I warned the staff that Sam is now deaf. "To get some response from him and get his attention," I advised them, "make eye contact and use hand signals."

The girl assistant asked, "So what's new? Isn't that what you have to do with all males?" I knew Sam was in safe hands.

—GLORIA O'DONNELL

Cunning
cats

Cats are intended to
teach us that not
everything in nature has
a purpose.

—GARRISON KEILLOR

❤ ❤ ❤ ❤ ❤ ❤ ❤ ❤ ❤ ❤ ❤

"Reward! Lost black male cat (Chucky).
May have gotten into vehicle & driven to other area."

—MARY ANN JOHNSTON

When I hired my part-time housekeeper, I made it clear that her duties did not extend to feeding the cat, since that was the responsibility of my children. Whiskers, however, was not aware of our arrangement.

One day he was being particularly persistent in his demands to be fed. My housekeeper, with her hands on her hips, looked down at him and said sternly, "I don't do cats."

—BARBARA BEAHM

Johnny's mother stops to watch her son read the Bible to their cat. "Isn't that sweet?" she says. But an hour later she hears a terrible racket. Running out the door, she finds Johnny stuffing the cat into a bucket of water.

"Johnny, what are you doing?"

"I'm baptizing Muffin," he replies.

"But cats don't like to be in water."

"Well then, he shouldn't have joined my church."

Every morning my son and daughter-in-law's cat would sit just outside their bedroom patio doors at daybreak demanding to be let in. To break the cat of this annoying habit, one night they put a bucket of water in their room ready for the morning. When the cat started its persistent yowling, my son, half asleep, leaped out of bed, grabbed the bucket and threw the water at the cat. The patio doors were closed.

—THELMA JOHNSON

I was waitressing in a restaurant where the owner's black cat was notorious for sneaking in to enjoy the warmth of the open fire. One night as a couple were dining by candlelight near the fire, I noticed a black object under the woman's chair.

I reached down as discreetly as possible to grab what I thought was our recalcitrant cat when the woman asked indignantly, "What on earth are you doing with my handbag?"

—MARINDA HAWTHORNE

♥ ♥ ♥ ♥ ♥ ♥ ♥ ♥ ♥ ♥ ♥

I worked at a boarding kennel where people leave their dogs and cats while on vacation. One morning I had taken a cat out of his cage, and after playing with him and replenishing his food and water, I put him back in. A few minutes later, I was surprised to see the feline at my feet, since the cage doors lock automatically when they're shut. I couldn't figure out how the cat escaped, until I bent down to pick him up and spied his name tag: Houdini.

—BARBARA ROHRSSEN

When John's cat, Willie, got stuck in a tree, we told John not to worry.

"He'll come down when he gets good and hungry," we said.

Three days later, with Willie still up in the tree, John could stand it no longer and climbed after him. The man was 60 feet up when the cat scampered to the ground.

"It's all right, John, you can come down now," we shouted. Total silence, and then the fearful reply: "I'll come down when I'm good and hungry."

—NINA HARTNETT

While I was waiting my turn at the veterinarian's office, a woman came in holding a large cat.

"Do you really want to have Mitzie de-clawed?" asked the receptionist.

 "Shhhh!" the woman said as she hastily covered her cat's ears, **"I told her she was coming in for a manicure."**

—LUANNE BERGSTROM

After we moved to the country, our cat, Sadie, became a particularly good mouser. I praised her efforts, and she began leaving the mice in conspicuous places so my husband could dispose of them. Along the way, Sadie even developed a good understanding of men. One morning, courtesy of Sadie, my husband found a dead mouse lying on the sofa next to the television remote control.

—BARBARA DIANNIBELLA

Licorice, our cat, usually misses when she tries to pounce on birds. Occasionally, she gets lucky and dashes into the bushes with her prize. If I see this happen, I take my seven-iron and beat the bushes, frightening the cat so the bird can fly to safety. Once, I was whacking the shrubbery with my golf club and shouting, "Get out! Get out of there now!" when a man on the patio next door spoke up.

"Why not just take the two-stroke penalty?"

—KEN KRIVANEK

As a chaplain in a university residence hall, I am supposed to uphold all of the school rules, which include a ban on pets. That changed, however, when a kitten adopted me. The freshmen in my dorm kept my secret. They covered for me by calling my kitten the Book, since I had so many in my room. One morning I was leaving the dorm with the kitten in a carrier. A student stopped me and asked, "Where are you taking the Book?" I explained that I was bringing the kitten to the vet. "She's getting neutered today," I told him. "Hmm," the student responded, "no sequels."

—TOM POWERS

**"I hope you're not allergic to cats—
I'd hate to see you go."**

One woman in our tour group was a strict vegetarian. When she talked about her cat, though, she admitted that she fed her pampered pet expensive canned meats.

"Why is it all right for your cat to eat meat if it isn't for you?" I finally asked her.

"My cat and I don't have the same beliefs," she replied.

—DORA GIGGY

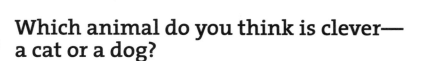

? Which animal do you think is clever—a cat or a dog?

A cat, of course. Have you ever seen cats pulling sleds through snow and ice?

— ANATOLY FROLOV

The first-grade children in a Raleigh, N.C., school were having a wonderful time playing with a stray cat. After a while one little lad asked the teacher if it was a boy cat or a girl cat. Not wishing to get into that particular subject, she said that she didn't believe she could tell.

"I know how we can find out," said the boy.

"All right," said the teacher, resigning herself to the inevitable, "how can we find out?"

"We can vote," said the child.

—SAM RAGAN

Our neighbor asked my granddaughter what she put on her cat to make him smell so good.

"Maybe it's the perfume I use," came the reply. "The cat sleeps with his nose against my neck, so some of the scent must rub off on him."

The next evening our neighbor was in a department store when she noticed a familiar fragrance in the air. She asked the woman who had just walked by what perfume she was wearing. After learning the name, our neighbor said, over the heads of all in the crowded store, "It smells wonderful. My friend's cat wears it."

—T. ELLSWORTH CLARK

❤ ❤ ❤ ❤ ❤ ❤ ❤ ❤ ❤ ❤ ❤

A dog doesn't want much and is happy to get it.
A cat doesn't know what it wants and wants more of it.

—RICHARD HEXEM

A Seattle woman was in the midst of preparations for a dinner for 16 when Penelope, a neighbor's cat, wandered in and kept getting underfoot. Annoyed, the hostess finally burst out, "Oh, go catch a mouse!" and shooed the cat out of the house.

The dinner was a success, and the guests were contentedly sipping their coffee when Penelope appeared in a dining room window, leaped lightly to the table and carefully placed a dead mouse beside the hostess' cup.

As I left the house to go to a luncheon party, one of my husband's students from the hostel house up the street came running toward me.

"Come quickly!" he shouted.

Fearing that one of the boys was in trouble, I took off after him, hanging on desperately to my fancy hat. We dashed into the house and upstairs, and there in the middle of a bed the fraternity cat was having kittens. The boys were all standing around solicitously, and a pre-medical student appeared to have the situation well in hand.

"What do you want me to do, John?" I asked after I caught my breath.

"Why, we don't want you to do anything, ma'am," he said, looking surprised. "We just thought there ought to be a lady present."

—ANONYMOUS

QUOTABLE QUOTES

"The cat could very well be man's best friend but would never stoop to admitting it."

—DOUG LARSON

"You cannot look at a sleeping cat and feel tense."

—JANE PAULEY

"There's no dealing with a cat who knows you're awake."

—BRAD SOLOMON

"The problem with cats is that they get the exact same look on their face whether they see a moth or an axe murderer."

—PAULA POUNDSTONE

"The only mystery about the cat is why it ever decided to become a domestic animal."

—COMPTON MACKENZIE

"Does it ever amaze and delight you that of all the places in the world— cold grassy nests under hedgerows, warm patches of sun on a carpet—the cat chooses to sit on your lap?"

—NEVADA BARR,
SEEKING ENLIGHTENMENT (PUTNAM)

"When I play with my cat, who knows if I am not more of a pastime to her than she is to me?"

—MONTAIGNE

"The interesting thing about being a mother is that everyone wants pets, but no one but me cleans the kitty litter."

—MERYL STREEP IN *VOGUE*

♥ ♥ ♥ ♥ ♥ ♥ ♥ ♥ ♥ ♥ ♥

In the crowded suburban bus, the voice of a six-year-old returning homeward with his mother after a day of shopping, rang out loud and clear, "Is our cat a daddy cat or a mother cat?"

"He's a daddy cat," the mother replied patiently.

"How do we know he's a daddy cat?" the boy asked.

An expectant hush fell over the bus, and the passengers listened attentively to see how the mother would handle this one. She was ready for the challenge.

"He's got whiskers, hasn't he?" she said.

—JOE MCCARTHY

My 18-year-old daughter and I were sitting in the yard one afternoon when our cat sauntered by.

"That cat certainly has a great life," I remarked. "She comes and goes just as she darn well pleases."

"That," my daughter replied dryly, "is because she doesn't live with her mother."

—NANCY SIEGEL

"What would you like?" my wife asked as she prepared the evening meal. "Tuna, salmon, chicken, beef or liver?"

Surprised and pleased by this unusual opportunity to make a selection from such an extensive dinner menu, I replied, "Beef would be nice for a change, thank you."

"Oh," she said, **"I wasn't talking to you. I was asking the cat. We're having soup."**

—C. REDDEN

NO! NO! NO! THAT'S NOT THE WAY WE DO IT, IF YOU WANT TO PET **ME**, YOU'LL HAVE TO COME OVER HERE.
PAT! PAT!
DaveCarpenter

❤ ❤ ❤ ❤ ❤ ❤ ❤ ❤ ❤ ❤ ❤

Notice seen in London:
**Found: Tabby kitten with white paws and bib.
Very affectionate. Answers to the name Go Away.**

While at a friend's house, I told him to keep his small son at least five feet from the color television because radiation from the set might cause sterility.

"Really?" exclaimed my friend, and he plumped the family cat in front of the set.

—B. D. WILDMAN

Delivering a registered letter on my postal round, I rang the doorbell of the address but no one answered. Instead a cat appeared and settled by the door.

I delivered the post to the upstairs flat and then went back down to the front to post the registered letter card.

When I arrived, I found the occupant at his door looking rather distressed. "Am I glad to see you," he said. "I thought our cat had learned how to ring the doorbell."

—DAVID CROSS

Lost, screamed the ad in *The Daily Standard* of Celina, Ohio. Female medium-size gray tiger cat. Answers to Lucy or Here Kitty, Kitty, Kitty.

—RICHARD FLAUGHER

"They say that a black cat brings bad luck. Is that true?"
"Depends on who comes across it: a human, or a mouse."

—CHAYAN

♥ ♥ ♥ ♥ ♥ ♥ ♥ ♥ ♥ ♥ ♥ ♥ ♥

My friend Nancy's babysitter confronted her about the new kitten. "That cat of yours is going to destroy your furniture in no time!" she exclaimed.

A smile grew on Nancy's face. "That's the plan," she said.

—KITTY COCHRANE

Our young daughter had adopted a stray cat. To my distress, he began to use the back of our new sofa as a scratching post.

"Don't worry," my husband reassured me, "I'll have him trained in no time."

I watched for several days as my husband patiently "trained" our new pet. Whenever the cat scratched, my husband deposited him outdoors to teach him a lesson. The cat learned quickly. For the next 16 years, whenever he wanted to go outside, he scratched the back of the sofa.

—LISA GOLDRICK

When our cat had her third litter, we were hard-pressed to find willing owners for the kittens. We decided to leave them in a basket on the front porch of a good-natured friend of ours who was celebrating his birthday.

We put the basket on his doorstep with a note attached: "To Fred on his birthday, many little joyous greetings." Later, our doorbell rang. On our porch was the basket of kittens, with a new note: **"Many happy returns."**

—BETTY L. AERICK

QUOTABLE QUOTES

"Women and cats will do as they please, and men and dogs should relax and get used to the idea."

—ROBERT A. HEINLEIN

"Every dog has his day—but the nights are reserved for the cats."

—UNKNOWN

"Cats names are more for human benefit. They give one a certain degree of confidence that the animal belongs to you. "

—ALAN AYCKBOURN *"TABLE MANNERS*

To a cat, "NO!" means "Not while I'm looking."—UNKNOWN

"Cats are notoriously sore losers. Coming in second best, especially to someone as poorly coordinated as a human being, grates their sensibility."

—STEPHEN BAKER

"No matter how much cats fight, there always seems to be plenty of kittens."

—ABRAHAM LINCOLN

"Thousands of years ago, cats were worshipped as gods. Cats have never forgotten this."

—ANONYMOUS

"Cat: A pygmy lion who loves mice, hates dogs and patronizes human beings."

—OLIVER HERFORD

Our neighbor's cat was run over by a car, and the mother quickly disposed of the remains before her four-year-old son, Billy, found out about it. After a few days, though, Billy finally asked about the cat.

"Billy, the cat died," his mother explained. "But it's all right. He's up in heaven with God."

The boy asked, **"What in the world would God want with a dead cat?"**

—ROSS SAMS, JR.

My friend Kelly's cat, Sam, loved riding in Kelly's car, and it was always a battle if the cat was outside and he wanted to leave it at home. One day Kelly left Sam on the front steps and got into his car. He was on the highway when suddenly he had to slam on the brakes to avoid the car ahead, and a screaming ball of fur slid down the front windshield. Afterward, Sam travelled everywhere with Kelly.

—TERRI-LYNN ROEMER

Every year, we go on vacation to the same place, and our old cat comes with us. The butcher we buy our meat from knows him well now. One day, when I was picking up an order, I asked him, "Would you have any old scraps of meat?"

"Aha," he said, "is it for the old fellow? Isn't he dead yet?"

"He doesn't seem to be," I replied.

I paid and turned around to leave the store only to catch the horrified looks of two customers who were waiting to be served.

—CHRISTIANE MORLET

"Regarding the furniture, I blame the catnip and I'm entering rehab."

❤ ❤ ❤ ❤ ❤ ❤ ❤ ❤ ❤ ❤ ❤

One day I stopped by to visit my friend, the mother of two teenage daughters. Through the screen door I was aghast to hear her say: "I've really had it with you two and your boyfriends! As soon as I get the money, I'm getting you both fixed!"

I was greatly relieved to find out she was talking to her dog, nursing eight puppies, and to her very pregnant cat.

—M. J. MCCOLL

From a neighbor who had gone to Maine for a week's vacation, a woman in Melrose, Mass., received a postcard which bore this message:

"Would you please feed my cat while I'm away?
She will eat anything, but don't put yourself out."

—JOHN J. MCALEER

Living in a household with eight indoor cats requires buying large amounts of kitty litter, which I usually get in 25-pound bags—100 pounds at a time. When I was going to be out of town for a week, I decided to go to the supermarket to stock up.

As my husband and I both pushed shopping carts, each loaded with five large bags of litter, a man looked at our purchases and queried, "Bengal or Siberian?"

—JUDY J. HAGG

♥ ♥ ♥ ♥ ♥ ♥ ♥ ♥ ♥ ♥ ♥

I was waiting in line at my county clerk's office one afternoon and noticed a hand-lettered sign that read: **Any child left unattended will be given a free kitten.**

—JEANNE MAULTSKY

Five Signs Your Cat is Plotting to Kill You
- Seems mighty chummy with the dog all of a sudden.
- Unexplained calls to F. Lee Bailey's 900 number on your bill.
- Ball of yarn tied playfully into a hangman's noose.
- Droppings in litter box spell out "REDRUM."
- You find a piece of paper labeled "My Wil" which reads, "Leev awl kat."

—DAVID BROOME

A gnome is in the garden busily destroying some bushes when a house cat appears. "What are you?" asks the cat.

"A gnome," comes the reply. "I steal food from humans, I kill their plants, I make annoying music at night to drive them crazy, and I love mischief. And what, may I ask, are you?"

The cat replies, "Um, I'm a gnome."

—BLAKE KILTOFF

My brother and his roommate once smuggled two kittens into their college dormitory room. The felines' favorite place to catnap was in the letter trays, so the animals were dubbed **In and Out.**

—SYLVIA L. MAYE

❤ ❤ ❤ ❤ ❤ ❤ ❤ ❤ ❤ ❤ ❤ ❤

The vet prescribed daily tablets for our geriatric cat, Tigger, and after several battles my husband devised a way to give her the medication. It involved wrapping Tigger in a towel, trapping her between his knees, forcing her mouth open and depositing the pill on the back of her tongue.

David was proud of his resourcefulness until one hectic session when he lost control of both cat and medicine. Tigger leaped out of his grasp, paused to inspect the tablet—which had rolled across the floor—and then ate it.

—MADI LEGERE

My marriage brought with it four adult stepchildren (only one of whom I met before the wedding) and a cat. Soon after our honeymoon, my husband and I invited the children to our apartment for a get-to-know-you dinner. I was nervous and wanted to impress the kids with my ability to take care of their father and his cat. The apartment was neat and tidy, and I had cooked a lovely dinner. We greeted the kids with hugs, but they paid as much attention to the cat as to me. Wanting them to know my regard for the cat, I blurted out, "I've never lived with an animal before I married your father."

—JENNIFER GAUCI

Our gas and electric company servicemen are used to finding notes from customers advising them about various pets to be encountered in the house. But a recent one caused our man to do a double take—and this was all he took. The note said: Furnace is in hallway—do service. Dogs are in kitchen—do avoid. Guinea pig in hallway—do not squash. Cats everywhere—do take one home.

♥ ♥ ♥ ♥ ♥ ♥ ♥ ♥ ♥ ♥ ♥

A cat sits on a bench next to a miserable-looking college student. The young man notices that the cat is looking up at him, so he takes the opportunity to unburden himself of his troubles.

"I've spent every dime I had saved, maxed out my credit cards and can't get another student loan.

"I can't pay for school, can't even afford to take a girl out for a drink. What could be worse than being young and broke?"

Says the cat, "Try being young and fixed."

When we moved with our cat to Melfort, Sask., the neighbors soon informed us that they weren't cat people. That was fine: We knew where we stood.

About two months after the move, our neighbor called. "Don't you know your cat has been sitting outside in the cold waiting for you for 20 minutes?" she scolded.

Less than a month later, she called again. "What's wrong with our cat?" she worried. "I bought her steak and she won't eat it."

That's when I realized our cat had two homes and double meals.

—OLGA MCKELLAR

When my daughter and I caught only one perch on our fishing trip—not enough for even a modest lunch—we decided to feed it to her two cats. She put our catch in their dish and watched as the two pampered pets sniffed at the fish but refused to eat it.

Thinking quickly, my daughter then picked up the dish, walked over to the electric can opener, ran it for a few seconds, then put the fish back down. The cats dug right in.

—SUSAN WARD

"Look Whiskers, I think this violates the doctor/patient relationship."

♥ ♥ ♥ ♥ ♥ ♥ ♥ ♥ ♥ ♥ ♥

During the night, strange noises don't usually concern me as my cat, Benny, frequently plays toss and chase with his toy mouse in the middle of the night. This time though, the sound that had woken me was more of a thumping and banging. I lay there listening for a few moments, then I heard the noise right in my bedroom! I bravely reached over and turned on the light and saw Benny with his head stuck in an empty tissue box.

—WILMA HAMER

Husband, as wife shows him cat surrounded by new kittens: "She did all right for a cat that didn't know a soul in the neighborhood three months ago."

—BOB BARNES

The seniors' facility where I work has a resident cat named Frank. At the front door of the building there's a keypad; to exit, you must enter the correct sequence of numbers. One day, a visitor noticed Frank at his feet just as he was about to leave and he turned to a nearby senior and asked, "Is the cat allowed out?"

"Oh yes," she told him smiling. "He just hasn't learned the numbers yet?

—J. FERGUSON

Late one night I heard our cat running back and forth in our bedroom, batting at something on the floor on my husband's side of the bed. I woke my husband and asked him if the cat was playing with a mouse. A half-asleep and confused reply came from his side of the bed, **"You mean on the computer?"**

♥ ♥ ♥ ♥ ♥ ♥ ♥ ♥ ♥ ♥ ♥

My parents were preparing to leave for Nova Scotia for a holiday and I was to take care of their cat, Mittens, while they were away. In order to cut costs, my mom told me that she'd only call me in an emergency.

Two weeks later, I was feeding the cat when the phone rang. The cat ran to the phone, and when the answering machine clicked on, I heard my mother talking to Mittens. As she said goodbye she promised to call again that night.

Curious, I checked the answering machine and saw that

Mom had made 28 calls to Mittens in the two weeks since they'd been gone!

—ROB DUNSWORTH

After house hunting for many months, my husband and I finally found the home we wanted to buy. Our young sons voiced their approval. When I asked what they liked best about it, my four-year-old answered, "The goldfish and the cat."

—JUDY REYNO

"And to think he was so cute and tiny when he was a kitten!"

❤ ❤ ❤ ❤ ❤ ❤ ❤ ❤ ❤ ❤ ❤

Just how much our cat, Judi, is treated like a member of the family became apparent the day we took her to the vet. I was filling out her medical form when my husband, looking over my shoulder, exclaimed, "I didn't know she spelled her name like that!"

—SELINE KUTAN

On a cold winter day, my six-year-old daughter, Elise, was cuddling our Burmese cat in a chair by the fire. As the cat purred contentedly, Elise said, "Look, Mom, he really loves me."

I smiled and said, "He has good taste." There was a brief silence followed by, "You're right, Mom. He does taste good."

—JILL MILNER

One night while I was cat-sitting my daughter's indoor feline, it escaped outside. When it failed to return the following morning, I found the beast clinging to a branch about 30 feet up in a spindly tree. Unable to lure it down, I called the fire department.

"We don't do that anymore," the woman dispatcher said. When I persisted, she was polite but firm. "The cat will come down when it gets hungry enough."

"How do you know that?" I asked.

"Have you ever seen a cat skeleton in a tree?" she said.

Two hours later the cat was back, looking for breakfast.

—TERRY CHRISTIANSEN

What's a cat's favorite dessert?
Chocolate mousse.

— AMITA MANI

♥ ♥ ♥ ♥ ♥ ♥ ♥ ♥ ♥ ♥ ♥

Bartender to customer as they watch a cat eat from a bowl on the bar: **"It's okay, those are kitty treats anyway."**

—WILMA HAMER, VERNON

I was tired and had just reached that almost-asleep moment when my teenage daughter let out a terrifying wail. Our normally placid cat had caught a mouse and both were under her bed. This woke her roommate who added to the din.

Realizing I had to do something before the neighbors complained, I called my son away from his usual position in front of the TV and told him it was his problem: his sister, his girlfriend and his cat. He dealt with it promptly by sending in his dog.

—CHERYL BURNS

My three young children had been asking my husband and me for a pet since they were old enough to talk. Being so busy, the last thing we wanted was more responsibility added to our schedules, so we attempted to fill their pet needs with battery-operated animals. But still they begged for a real pet.

Finally, I gave in and brought home a little orange tabby, then waited for the kids to arrive home from school.

Excited, my five-year-old son, Jesse, examined the kitten for a few minutes, then asked, "Can I call Grandma to tell her about our new cat?"

I agreed and dialed my mother's number. "Grandma, Grandma, we got a cat!" Jesse exclaimed. "A real cat! It doesn't even have any batteries."

—SYLVIE BÉLANGER

♥ ♥ ♥ ♥ ♥ ♥ ♥ ♥ ♥ ♥ ♥

While an old lady is polishing an antique lamp, a genie appears and gives her three wishes. She asks to be young and rich and for her cat to turn into a handsome prince.

Her wishes granted, the prince takes the lady in his arms. As long-forgotten feelings stir, the prince whispers to her,

"Now, I bet you're sorry you took me to the vet for that little operation."

—SUSAN CARR

A man who lived next door to a pub had a favorite tabby cat. Unfortunately the cat was run over by a car and killed. A year later, at about midnight, the pub owner was doing his accounts. Suddenly the ghost of this cat appeared in front of him, holding half his tail in his paw.

"Can you help me, please?" said the cat's ghost. "I expect you remember me when I lived next door. My old master has moved, so I thought I would try you."

"Yes, I do remember you," said the pub owner. "You were a nice cat. What can I do for you?"

"Well," said the cat's ghost. "You see this bit of tail that I'm holding in my hand? It was cut off in my accident and I'm fed up carrying it around with me. Can you mend it for me, please?"

"I'm sorry," said the owner, "but much as I would like to, I can't help you. I'm not allowed to retail spirits after eleven o'clock."

—BRIAN JOHNSTON

❤ ❤ ❤ ❤ ❤ ❤ ❤ ❤ ❤ ❤ ❤

Before I rush out to work, I give my hair a quick going over with a brush I leave on the hall table. One morning I was horrified to see my son grooming the cat with my hairbrush. "What do you think you're doing?" I demanded.

He looked puzzled and said, "But I do this every day."

—BONNIE GAUTHIER

Our curious kitten Bandit tried to open the glass shower doors every time I was behind them. One morning my husband, Chad, lifted Bandit so he could see over the doors while I was showering. "See," I heard Chad say as the kitten peered down at me, "there's nothing exciting in there."

—BETH CANTRELL

I was diagnosed with hypothyroidism some years ago, then we learned that our 12-year-old cat had the same condition. When my 36-year-old daughter thought she might have some of the symptoms, she suggested to her doctor that perhaps she should have a blood test to check it out. He asked if anyone in her family had a thyroid gland disorder. "Yes," she answered, "my father and the cat."

—FRANK J. KENNEDY

Isn't it unfair that women love cats? Cats are independent, they don't listen, they don't come when you call, they like to stay out all night and when they are at home they like to be left alone to sleep.

In other words, every quality that women hate in a man, they love in a cat.

—TERRY SANGSTER

"In retrospect, I could have done more with my lives."

♥ ♥ ♥ ♥ ♥ ♥ ♥ ♥ ♥ ♥ ♥ ♥

Having acquired a stray kitten, we bought him a little collar with his name and telephone number on it. We didn't see much of Sidney. He was always off somewhere getting into mischief. Soon I began to get irate calls from my neighbors.

"Are you Sidney's mother? He's just eaten my goldfish!"

"Your cat's terrorizing my Yorkshire terrier!"

"Have you got a cat named Sidney? He's just knocked a dozen eggs off the table!"

Tired of apologizing, I asked a friend, who was good with cats, what to do. The solution was simple: "Take his collar off."

—ANN CROOKS

When my six-year-old grandson heard that my cat had died, he asked where the cat was now. I told him Grandpa had buried him in the garden. As the son of two avid gardeners, he then asked, "Will another one grow?"

—F. BAKER

My daughter, Lucy, adopted an old abandoned cat that insisted on eating its meals outside the back door, and only at night. Because of his advanced age, Lucy called him Grandpa.

Imagine the horror of her dinner guests one evening when she scraped the leftovers onto a plate and announced,

"These are for Grandpa. He's waiting on the back steps."

—GILLIAN YUNG

❤ ❤ ❤ ❤ ❤ ❤ ❤ ❤ ❤ ❤ ❤

Free: One owner, low-mileage used cat.
Answers to Tabitha or electric can opener.

Niggy, our pampered black cat, was never late for his evening meal, so we were worried when he didn't turn up one wet evening. Our search in the murky darkness ended when we spotted him with its head jammed in the access hole of our garden incinerator lid and some fur lost while trying to free himself.

All efforts by us and neighbors failed to free the cat, and the local veterinarian fared no better. Finally, we turned to the fire department, who used their "jaws of life" to cut through the lid. The instant they freed the cat, it bolted into the darkness.

The next morning, Niggy showed up at our back door, unscathed and blissfully unaware that he had been mistaken for someone else's pet.

—M. PIPER

I was awakened at 4:30 a.m. by a loud, constant chirrup. After a while, annoyed, I slipped on my housecoat, headed to the door and switched on the outside lights. The singing stopped, so I turned off the lights, but seconds later it started again. I peered outside and met a pair of shining eyes glaring at me. The neighbor's cat was stalking our new garden ornament: a motion detector singing robin.

—J. K. RUTLEY

Mother: "Don't pull the cat's tail."
Daughter: "I didn't, Mom. I only held its tail, but it pulled my arm."

—PRINCESS SIRINDHORN

What do you call a cat that joins the Red Cross?

A first-aid kit.

— AMITA MANI

My husband went to the cardiologist after experiencing symptoms of a heart attack.

"I had taken our cat to the vet," he told the nurse, "and while I was there, my chest got tight, and I had trouble breathing. Later, my left arm began aching."

The nurse was clearly concerned. "So," she asked, "how was the cat?"

—GAIL WEBSTER

On their way to town, a five-minute drive on the highway, my husband and three children wondered why other drivers were honking their horns. Upon arriving at a set of traffic lights, a lady in the next lane rolled down her window and yelled, "Your cat's on the roof!"

—PATTY MCKECHNIE

My cat's technicolor coat earned her the name of Fruit Salad. A loving creature, she's also a thief and has been the cause of many complaints. One afternoon I was confronted by a neighbor whose dinner had been stolen from the kitchen table. Wanting to positively identify the culprit, I asked, "Was it Fruit Salad?"

"No," she replied, "It was rump steak."

—MRS. E. LOMBARD

♥ ♥ ♥ ♥ ♥ ♥ ♥ ♥ ♥ ♥ ♥ ♥

When she realized one of her kittens was missing, my friend Toba optimistically posted a few notices around town. Within a week, Toba received a call from a woman with a kitten that matched the description. "You'd better hurry, though," she advised. "My son is getting pretty attached to it."

Wanting to ease the boy's unhappiness at returning the kitten, Toba picked up some fast-food coupons on the way to his house, as well as some cookies and balloons for him and discovered when she got there that the son was 35 years old.

—DARLENE HORN

My seven-year-old son, Josh, was playing in his room. "And our action-figure hero is menaced by a giant monster cat," he yelled, waving his toy in front of our cat, Ghost, who was obligingly playing his part in the drama and batting at the toy. "Then our hero jumps on the monster cat and throws him to the ground!"

Careful not to hurt his pet, Josh began patting the cat gently. Then, with a disgusted voice, he said, "Monsters don't purr!"

—DEANNA BATES

A motorist approached a neighbor one afternoon and said, "I'm awfully sorry, but I think I've just run over your cat. Can I replace it?"

The neighbor looked the motorist up and down and said, **"I doubt if you'd be the mouser she was."**

—ANTHONY GRAHAM

♥ ♥ ♥ ♥ ♥ ♥ ♥ ♥ ♥ ♥ ♥

Overheard: "The best way to get my son out of bed in the morning is to toss the cat on it. He sleeps with the dog."

—MICHELLE BORTEN

Young Rodney was in the garden filling in a hole when his neighbor peered over the fence and asked him what he was doing.

"My goldfish died," replied little Rodney tearfully, "and I've just buried him."

The neighbor was concerned: "That's an awfully large hole for a goldfish, isn't it?"

Young Rodney patted down the heap of earth and answered, "That's because he's inside your horrid cat."

One little girl in my wife's first-grade class appeared to be on the verge of tears. Sherren took her aside and asked what was wrong. "My mommy is allergic to my new kitten," the girl said.

"Oh, that's too bad," sympathized Sherren. "Will you have to give her away?"

"No," the child sobbed. "Daddy says the kitty has to go."

—ALFRED MORRISON

♥ ♥ ♥ ♥ ♥ ♥ ♥ ♥ ♥ ♥ ♥ ♥

My young cousin was playing outside one day when she was bitten by a cat. My aunt scooped her daughter up and raced inside to call the hospital. The nurse listened as she explained what had happened. "Are her shots up to date?" the nurse asked.

"I don't know," my frazzled aunt replied. "It was a stray cat."

—LORI UKRAINETZ

On arriving at my factory one morning, I found it had been burgled for the fourth time in seven months. When the police and chief security officer arrived to investigate, I asked what else I could do to protect the premises, as I already employed a guard. The security officer suggested I get a dog. "But we have a cat," I replied without thinking, worrying about the safety of the animal. "Ah," replied the security officer. "But it cannot bark."

—M. A. TORR

One evening, when our children were already sleeping and my husband was at work, I decided to pamper myself. To create a nice mood, I turned off lights, lit candles, had a bath with fragrant salts, made a cucumber mask for my face, and as I relaxed, I stretched on the couch. As soft music was playing, I sipped wine, filling my mind with soothing thoughts. In such a blissful state, I fell asleep.

Suddenly I woke up, and I saw a pair of green eyes in front me. I screamed. I jumped off the couch and turned on the light. It was my cat. Normally a gentle animal, this time his hair stood up and he was growling. It turned out that my cat, profiting from my sleep, decided to lick off the cucumber mask.

—IRENA KAMINSKA-PLACZEK

♥ ♥ ♥ ♥ ♥ ♥ ♥ ♥ ♥ ♥ ♥

My cat used to go to our neighbor's house and disturb him. One night the neighbor knocked at our door to complain. Being polite, he didn't want to be hasty in his judgment and make unnecessary trouble. In order to be sure he was accusing the right cat, he asked, in a formal tone, "Is your cat at home?"

—MARIA CAROLINA FALLEIROS

It may be said that on behalf of a recently developed robot cat that it needs no food, drink or litter box. Controlled by a microchip, it is capable of purring, crying when spoken to and rolling in various directions at the owner's hand clap. Call that a cat? Unless they can program it to come home with a half-chewed ear, drop a dead mouse at your feet and stalk contemptuously from the room, it's an imposter. If it does anything on human demand, it's no cat.

Our cat, Meowski, is a handsome black cat with white markings. He is also a very determined hunter. We put a bell on his collar to give the local wildlife a chance, only to discover he worked out how to remove it. Meowski doesn't tend to hunt the most endangered species; only sparrows, mice and the odd lizard, but it is still a concern of ours.

We came home one day to find beautiful blue feathers in the hallway. We immediately presumed the worst, suspecting that a rare native parrot had become his latest victim. We followed the trail of feathers to the bedroom, the place where he usually offers up his conquests. There it was under the bed: the remnants of a neighbor's feather duster.

—BRAD WALKER

♥ ♥ ♥ ♥ ♥ ♥ ♥ ♥ ♥ ♥ ♥

"I feel sorry for this soldier," joked my husband as he handed me a flier he'd found in our mailbox. It read:

> Lost Cat
> Black and white
> Answers to Nat
> Belongs to a soldier
> Recently neutered

—SONDRA GILBERTSON

First cat: "How did you get on in the milk-drinking competition?"

Second cat: "Oh, I won by six laps."

—MARY NORMANTON

My friend's daughter, Chelsea, found a baby tooth that her kitten had lost. She and her sister decided that they could put one over on the tooth fairy. That night they placed the tooth under Chelsea's pillow. And it worked. But the tooth fairy left a can of sardines.

—SANDRA E. MARTIN

Tweety birds

A bird doesn't sing because
it has an answer;
it sings because it has a song.

—MAYA ANGELOU

♥ ♥ ♥ ♥ ♥ ♥ ♥ ♥ ♥ ♥ ♥

My wife desperately wanted a parrot. When she found one advertised in the paper, we went to meet it. The owner, however, admitted that the bird had one annoying habit. "He has learned to mimic the ear-piercing sound of the smoke alarm," he said.

"But don't worry. For some reason, he only repeats it when my wife is in the kitchen."

—BARRY G., CLASSIFIEDGUYS.COM

It was my first year teaching tenth-graders geometry, and I was frustrated with the lack of effort in the class. Trying to make the group more interactive, I asked, "Who can define a polygon?"

"A dead parrot," came the reply.

—JOEL ALMEIDA

A lonely woman buys a parrot for companionship. After a week, the parrot hasn't uttered a word, so the woman goes back to the pet store and buys it a mirror. Nothing. The next week, she brings home a little ladder. Polly is still incommunicado, so the week after that, she gives it a swing, which elicits not a peep.

A week later, she finds the parrot on the floor of its cage, dying. Summoning up its last breath, the bird whispers, "Don't they have any food at that pet store?"

—LUCILLE ARNELL

Knowing how much an acquaintance despises his wife's parakeet, I was surprised one day to hear him coaxing it to speak. Upon listening more closely, however, I nearly choked holding back my laughter. Now, along with its constant, annoying jabbering, the bird also calls out a suicidal, "Here kitty, kitty, kitty."

—LISA FRENCH

"Hello, Amnesty International?"

Late one afternoon on the London Underground, I found myself sitting next to a man who held an empty birdcage on his lap. Curiosity prompted me to ask if the bird had escaped.

"Oh, no," the man replied. "You see, my working hours are irregular, and we have no telephone in our home, so my wife never knows when to expect me for dinner. I take my homing pigeon along to work every morning and release it as soon as my job is finished. "Dinner'll be ready when I get home," he concluded.

—OIVIND HOLTAN

❤ ❤ ❤ ❤ ❤ ❤ ❤ ❤ ❤ ❤ ❤

A frenchman with a parrot perched on his shoulder walked into a bar. The bartender said, "Wow, that's really neat. Where did you get him?"

"In France," the parrot replied. **"They've got millions of 'em over there."**

—A PRAIRIE HOME COMPANION,
THE FIFTH ANNUAL JOKE SHOW

A businessman flying first class is sitting next to a parrot. The plane takes off, and the parrot orders a Glenlivet, neat. The businessman asks for a Coke. After a few minutes, the bird yells, "Where's my scotch? Give me my scotch!"

The flight attendant rushes over with their drinks. Later, they order another round. Again, the bird gives the crew grief for being slow, and the businessman joins in: "Yeah, the service stinks!"

Just then, the flight attendant grabs the pair, opens the hatch, and throws them out of the plane. As they hurtle toward the ground, the parrot says to the terrified man, "Wow, that took a lot of guts for a guy with no wings."

It was moving day for a New York company, and one junior executive was seen hurrying into the spanking new office skyscraper carrying a caged canary and a large rock. Asked about this, he explained glumly that the windows in his antiseptic new office wouldn't open.

"If the air conditioning ever stops," he went on, "we'll all suffocate. That's why I have this canary. If he keels over, I'll know we're getting low on air—and then *boom,* my rock's going through that window!"

—ARTURO F. GONZALEZ

♥ ♥ ♥ ♥ ♥ ♥ ♥ ♥ ♥ ♥ ♥

Jim strolls into the paint section of a hardware store and walks up to the assistant.

"I'd like a pint of canary-colored paint," he says.

"Sure," the clerk replies. "Mind if I ask what it's for?"

"My parakeet," says Jim. "See, I want to enter him in a canary contest. He sings so sweet I know he's sure to win."

"Well, you can't do that, man!" the assistant says. "The chemicals in the paint will almost certainly kill the poor thing!"

"No they won't," Jim replies.

"Listen, buddy, I'll bet you ten bucks your parakeet dies if you try to paint him."

"You're on," says Jim.

Two days later he comes back looking very sheepish and lays $10 on the counter.

"So the paint killed him?"

"Indirectly," says Jim. "He seemed to handle the paint okay, but he didn't survive the sanding between coats."

In good weather, my friend Mark always let his yellow-naped Amazon parrot, Nicky, sit on the balcony of his tenth-floor apartment. One morning, Nicky flew away, much to Mark's dismay. He searched and called for the bird, with no luck.

The next day when Mark returned from work, the phone rang. "Is this Mark?" The caller asked. "You're going to think this is crazy, but there's a bird outside on my balcony saying, 'Hello, this is Mark.' Then it recites this phone number and says, 'I can't come to the phone right now, but if you will leave a message at the tone, I will call you back.'"

Nicky's cage had been kept in the same room as Mark's answering machine.

—ANNE R. NEILSON

"Yes, he talks, but he prefers texts or e-mail."

♥ ♥ ♥ ♥ ♥ ♥ ♥ ♥ ♥ ♥ ♥

My parents had a budgie called Joey. He was a talkative bird, although his repertoire was limited to "Hello" and "Who's a pretty boy?"

When my parents went on vacation, a friend and her husband, George, offered to watch Joey. He came home full of life and happy to chat at the end of the week.

However, it was soon obvious that Joey's vocabulary had been extended during his stay. He now squawked in an outraged tone, "Stop it, George!"

—GARTH BUCKLAND

A chinese housewife filed for divorce on the grounds that her husband was having an affair. The woman became suspicious when every time the phone rang, her myna bird spouted things like "Divorce," "I love you" and "Be patient."

—FROM *IDIOTS IN LOVE* BY LELAND GREGORY (ANDREWS MCMEEL)

When my kid sister and my mother bought three exotic birds, they named them This, That and The Other. After a few months, This died, and they buried the bird in the backyard. A few more months later, The Other passed away and they buried it next to This. Then the last bird died. Mom called my sister and tearfully announced, "Well, I guess that's That."

—GLORIA VITULANO

A burglar invaded a home in Los Angeles and tied everyone up. But a pet parakeet quietly opened its cage door, flew to the phone, pushed off the receiver and dialed the police with its beak. The desk sergeant answered and the parakeet chirped desperately: "Pretty baby! Pretty baby!"

—ROBERT J. HERGUTH

Mother to young son:

"Your parrot flew away while you were at school."

"I'm not surprised," sighed the boy. "When I was studying geography yesterday, he sat on my shoulder and closely examined the atlas."

Passing through London, a Frenchman buys a talking parrot. A week later the pet shop receives an outraged letter from the customer: The bird won't utter a word. The conscientious shopkeeper catches a train to Paris and visits the customer. He asks the parrot: "So, Jocko, have you lost your voice?" "No sir, but I don't think anyone should be expected to learn French in a week, replied the bird."

— M. WIDMER

A worried Russian went to the police and reported that his parrot was missing.

"Is it a talking bird?" the police asked.

"Yes, but opinions he expresses are his own, and do not reflect those of the owner."

A woman trained her parrot to give instructions to the tradesmen that called at her house.

One day the coalman came to make a delivery. "Ten sacks please," said the parrot.

"You're a clever bird being able to talk," said the coalman as he finished the delivery.

"Yes," replied the parrot. "And I can count too. Bring the other sack."

—BRIAN JOHNSTON

❤ ❤ ❤ ❤ ❤ ❤ ❤ ❤ ❤ ❤ ❤

Mrs. Van Horn inherited Penrod, a parrot that used dirty words. After several embarrassing experiences, she told her minister about the problem.

"I have a female parrot who is a saint," he said. "She sits on her perch and prays all day. Bring your parrot over, mine will be a good influence."

The woman brought Penrod to the minister's home. When the cages were placed together, Penrod cried, "Hi, baby! How about a little loving?"

"Great!" replied the female parrot, "That's just what I've been praying for."

—LARRY WILDE

Actor Ward Bond liked to tell of the man who went into a pet shop to buy a parrot. The shop owner pointed to a colorful specimen and said, "This is a fine talking bird. For years he was the pet of a famous movie producer, weren't you, Polly?"

"Yes, sir!" screamed the parrot. "Yes, yes, yes, yes, indeed! You are absolutely right. Yes, sir!"

—FRANK GORSHI

Trying to eclipse his brother's gift of a Cadillac, a Hollywood producer paid $10,000 for an amazing mynah bird to give his mother on her birthday. The bird spoke 11 languages and sang grand opera. On the night of her birthday he called her long distance.

"What did you think of the bird, Mama?" he asked.

"Delicious!" she said.

—EARL WILSON

♥ ♥ ♥ ♥ ♥ ♥ ♥ ♥ ♥ ♥ ♥ ♥

A little old lady went into a pet shop and saw a lovely-looking parrot. "I would like to buy that handsome bird, please," she said to the owner.

"Oh, you don't want him," the man replied. "He uses some pretty terrible language. Why don't you get a puppy or a cat?"

"I want that parrot!" the woman insisted, and proceeded to put her money on the counter. The owner shrugged his shoulders and made the sale.

When the woman returned home, she started playing with her new friend. She was petting him and poking at his feathers when all of a sudden he started swearing a blue streak. The woman was so shocked that she grabbed the parrot and stuck him in the refrigerator.

When she took the shivering bird out later, she warned him that every time he used bad language he'd be put back where it was cold. The parrot's behavior was pretty good for a couple days, but then one morning while the cat was putting her paw through his cage, he got really mad and started cursing again.

This time, the woman grabbed the bird and stuck him in the freezer. As he sat there shivering and looking around, he saw a frozen turkey right next to him. "Egad!" squawked the parrot, "What did you say?"

—MARIAN B. WISE

As I was walking through a variety store, I stopped at the pet department to look at some parakeets. In one cage a green bird lay on his back, one foot hooked oddly into the cage wire. I was about to alert the saleswoman to the bird's plight when I noticed a sign taped to the cage: "No, I am not sick. No, I am not dead. No, my leg is not stuck in the cage. I just like to sleep this way."

—JOAN DEZEEUW

QUOTABLE QUOTES

"That's what the cat said to the canary when he swallowed him—'You'll be all right.'"

—ALVAH BESSIE

"She was not quite what you would call refined. She was not quite what you would call unrefined. She was the kind of person that keeps a parrot."

—MARK TWAIN

"Live in such a way that you would not be ashamed to sell your parrot to the town gossip."

—WILL ROGERS

"I know of only one bird—the parrot—that talks; and it can't fly very high."

—WILBUR WRIGHT

"I hope you love birds too. It is economical. It saves going to heaven."

—EMILY DICKINSON

"God loved the birds and invented trees. Man loved the birds and invented cages."

—JACQUES DEVAL,
AFIN DE VIVRE BEL ET BIEN

"Did St. Francis really preach to the birds? Whatever for? If he really liked birds he would have done better to preach to the cats."

—REBECCA WEST

"We can all learn something from the parrot, which is content to repeat what it hears without trying to make a good story out of it."

—MALVINA G. VOGEL, EDITOR

♥ ♥ ♥ ♥ ♥ ♥ ♥ ♥ ♥ ♥ ♥

The pet shop customer couldn't believe his good fortune. The parrot he had just bought could recite Shakespeare's sonnets, imitate opera stars and intone Homer's epic poems in Greek. And he cost only $600.

Once the man got the bird home, however, not another word passed his beak. After three weeks the disconsolate customer returned to the shop and asked for his money back.

"When we had this bird," said the proprietor, "he could recite poetry and sing like an angel. Now you want me to take him back when he's no longer himself? Well, all right. Out of the goodness of my heart I'll give you $100."

Reluctantly the man accepted his loss. Just as the door shut behind him he heard the parrot say to the shop owner, "Don't forget—my share is $250."

—A. A. HENDERSON

"I promise. That bird is so well behaved, you can take it anywhere," the pet-store owner assured the woman. Delighted, she took her parrot to church. Things were great until, halfway through the sermon, the bird blurted, "It's damn cold in here!" Embarrassed, the woman ran out and went to the pet store. "This 'good bird' swore in church today," she told the shop owner.

"I'm sorry. It sometimes does that in new environments," he explained. "Next time, grab its feet and swing it over your head a few times. That should stop it." The next week the woman and her parrot were in church when the bird yelled, "It's damn cold in here!" Quickly, the woman grabbed the bird and swung it above her head six times. Then she put the bird back on her shoulder and sat down.

"Damn," the bird said. "It's windy too."

♥ ♥ ♥ ♥ ♥ ♥ ♥ ♥ ♥ ♥ ♥

Late one night a burglar broke into a house.
He froze when he heard a loud voice say,
"Jesus is watching!" Silence returned to the house, so
the burglar crept forward.

"Jesus is watching!" the voice boomed again. The
robber stopped dead in his tracks and frantically looked
all around. He spotted a parrot in a cage.

"Was that you?" asked the burglar. "Yes," answered the
parrot. The criminal sighed in relief and asked, "What's
your name?"

"Clarence," said the bird.

"That's a dumb name for a parrot," sneered the burglar.
"What idiot named you Clarence?"

"The same idiot who named the
Rottweiler Jesus."

A lady would like to have a parrot to keep her company.
She went to the Sunday market in Bangkok to look for one. At
a pet shop she saw a bird cage. The sign on the cage read: "Pull
the right leg, the bird will greet you. Pull the left leg, the bird
will sing." The lady amazingly asked, "What if I pull both legs?"
While the shop owner was trying to come up with an answer,
the bird replied, "You do that and I will fall off the beam!"

—WUTHICHAI NA-PATALUNG

Eric, a yellow-headed parrot that delighted customers in a shoe store in Houston, Texas, with such phrases as "telephone line one," "rock 'n' roll," and "Polly want a cracker," was stolen. The parrot turned into a stool pigeon when he was found in someone else's apartment. The officers, greeted with "hello Laura" and "hello Eric," checked stolen-parrot reports and turned up the name of Laura, owner of the shoe store. She was summoned to see if the bird was hers. When she arrived, the parrot became very excited, flapping its wings and swinging wildly inside its cage. "Eric just started, screaming "Laura," she said. I didn't have to identify him. He identified me."

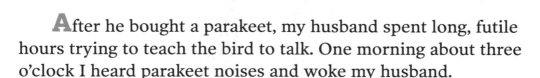

After he bought a parakeet, my husband spent long, futile hours trying to teach the bird to talk. One morning about three o'clock I heard parakeet noises and woke my husband.

"That crazy bird of yours is in the room!" I exclaimed.

We looked everywhere and finally found the bird sleeping peacefully in his cage downstairs. This mystery repeated itself two more nights, and I was a nervous wreck.

The next night I locked the bedroom door. At two o'clock I awoke again to that unnerving chirping. Very quietly I switched on the lights. There lay my husband, sound asleep and chirping his heart out. The bird had taught my husband his language!

—MRS. JACK PENZENSTADLER

Our curiosity was aroused by our neighbors' parakeet, whose raucous warnings, "No handholding! No kissing!" shattered the quiet of their living room. He'd been trained, our friends explained, to chaperone their teenage daughter's parties.

—MAUD NOBRIGA

As a single parent, I know that my ten-year-old daughter has learned to do without many extras. Sometime ago, to make things up to her, I promised to buy her toys as soon as I got a raise. A while later, my boss went on vacation and arranged for me to watch his dog, cats and parrot.

The night before he was due back, we went to feed the animals for the last time. As my daughter busied herself with the parrot, I couldn't believe my ears. She was bombarding the hapless bird with: "Mommy needs a raise! Mommy needs a raise! Mommy needs a raise!"

I got the raise; she got the toys.

—REGINA WIEGAND

♥ ♥ ♥ ♥ ♥ ♥ ♥ ♥ ♥ ♥ ♥

There's a story making the rounds that involves a carpet layer who had worked all day installing wall-to-wall carpeting. When he noticed a lump under the carpet in the middle of the living room, he felt his shirt pocket for his cigarettes—they were gone.

He was not about to take up the carpet, so he went outside for a two-by-four. Tamping down cigarettes with it would be easy. Once the lump was smoothed, the man gathered up his tools and carried them to his truck. Then two things happened simultaneously.

He saw his cigarettes on the seat of the truck, and over his shoulder he heard the voice of the woman to whom the carpet belonged.

"Have you seen anything of my parakeet?" she asked plaintively.

—FRANK RHOADES

A parrot was up for sale at an auction. The bidding proceeded briskly, and soon a winner was announced. When paying, the high bidder asked the auctioneer if the parrot could speak.

"Sure can," replied the auctioneer, "it was the parrot that was bidding against you."

—ANNE H. WINSNES

A pet-shop owner figured out a way to sell his talking parrots. He has a sign over each, reading:

"Suggested for mature audiences only."

—EARL WILSON

♥ ♥ ♥ ♥ ♥ ♥ ♥ ♥ ♥ ♥ ♥

A pet shop owner is asked for a bird that can talk and sing. He shows the customer a scrawny-looking bird with a price tag of $3,000.

"How can it be worth that much?" says the customer.

"That bird can sing the complete works of Elgar," replies the owner. "Or you could try this one." He reveals a second bird, even thinner than the first, with faded plumage. It is priced at $5,000.

"Come on," says the customer. "What's so special about this one?"

"It can reproduce all of Verdi's operas note-perfect," says the owner. "But I have one other that might interest you." The third bird is in a sorry state, bald, rheumy-eyed and weak with age. The customer looks at the price tag.

"$16,000?" he says. "What does this one do?"

The owner shakes his head. "To tell you the truth, we don't know yet. But the other two call him 'Maestro.'"

—MARION CARLSON

My husband and I, newlyweds and animal lovers, bought an Amazon parrot when we moved to our first apartment. Since pets were not allowed, we had to keep Juju a secret. Soon our little friend became an accomplished talker and mimic. His favorite trick was returning parrot kisses after I commanded in a loud voice: "Give me a kiss! Give me a big smooch!"

Within days Juju was repeating those words incessantly, doing his parrot-perfect imitation of me: "Give me a kiss! Give me a big smooch!"

I hadn't realized how thin the walls were until the day I found this note on my door: "Look, lady—I realize you're newlyweds, but give the poor guy a break!"

—BARBARA JANNATPOUR

❤ ❤ ❤ ❤ ❤ ❤ ❤ ❤ ❤ ❤ ❤

The ad on a bulletin board read: For sale: African gray parrot $500. This species is one of the best talkers." Someone had jotted on it in pencil: **"Ask him if he's worth $500."**

—EDWARD J. RAYMOND

A man bought a parrot for $1,000. Sure, it cost plenty, but this bird had talent. Polly not only had a big vocabulary, but could also rattle on in five languages. The pet shop promised to deliver the bird that afternoon.

After work, the proud owner rushed home and asked if it had arrived. It had, his wife told him.

"Where is it?" he asked excitedly.

"In the oven," she replied.

"My god!" said the husband. "In the oven? Why? That bird knows five languages!"

"Well," asked his wife, "why didn't he speak up?"

—JOHN COSTELLO

The kids had been driving me nuts, asking me to buy them a talking bird, until I finally got them a parrot. We named him Wilbur and tried to teach him some words, but all he would say was, "Hello. Hello."

Over and over again my older son tried to get Wilbur to say, "Jeff is the greatest." Nothing. My husband tried with "Give this guy a raise." Nothing. I took a turn with "Clean your room." Still nothing.

Yesterday Wilbur finally started talking. During dinner all we heard was "He did it. No, he did it," and then "Get out of my room!"

—FELICE R. PRAGER

♥ ♥ ♥ ♥ ♥ ♥ ♥ ♥ ♥ ♥ ♥

The canary I bought for my daughter some months before suddenly stopped singing and sat huddled on its perch. Not knowing what was the matter with it, I called the Arnold sisters, who raise canaries and from whom I had bought ours. Miss Agatha, aged 78, answered the telephone. When I described the bird's symptoms, she immediately recommended that we get it a mate. "It's spring," she said, "and the bird is lonely."

I protested that I didn't want two birds, and then launched into a tale about a friend who lost one of a pair of lovebirds and solved the problem by putting a mirror in the cage as company for the other. "Maybe," I added brightly, "that would satisfy the canary."

There was a pause, and then Miss Agatha said softly, "Would that satisfy you, Mrs. Smith?"

—MRS. ROSS W. SMITH

Randy the dishwasher repairman was given specific instructions concerning the woman's two pets.

"The Rottweiler won't hurt you, even though it looks fierce, but whatever you do, don't talk to the parrot." Randy let himself in and set to work, and the dog just lay quietly on the carpet. But the parrot mocked him mercilessly the whole time.

"Wow, you're pretty fat," the bird would say. "Hey, fatso, you couldn't change the batteries in a flashlight, let alone fix a dishwasher."

Before long, Randy had had enough. "You know, bird, you think you're pretty smart for someone with a brain the size of a pea."

The parrot was silent for a moment, and then, with a gleam in its eye, said, "All right. Get him, Spike."

—TERRI BOAS

♥ ♥ ♥ ♥ ♥ ♥ ♥ ♥ ♥ ♥ ♥

In the pet shop of a large department store in
Portland, OR., I stopped in front of the
cage of a mynah bird. The bird cocked its
head and said, "Hello."

I was surprised and didn't say anything.
After a short pause the bird said,

"What's the matter, can't you talk?"

—ELGAR P. BEADERSTADT

When Rich, who graduated last June from West Point, reluctantly agreed to postpone his marriage until he returned from foreign duty, he proceeded to devote considerable time and effort to reducing the calculated risk of the agreement. I saw the result when I attended his girl Ann's graduation exercises at a Massachusetts college.

His present to Ann was a parakeet whose cage bore the inscription: "My ambassador for the duration. Love, Rich."

Ambassador took but a moment to smooth his feathers, then, in a remarkable imitation of Rich's voice, began chanting, "Remember Rich! Remember Rich! Remember Rich!"

—TAY COOK

"How come you're so well informed about your neighbor's doings?

"He went on vacation and I looked after his parrot for two weeks."

—ALBERT W. BROMBACHER

"**F**reddie," read the advertisement I had composed for our local newspaper, "a recently widowed lovebird, desperately seeks a new mate, preferably a gentle young lady who has been hand raised."

I gave the text to the receptionist at the newspaper office and waited while she read it. Surprisingly she glanced up at me disdainfully. "Of course you want this placed in the Personals?"

"Heavens, no!" I hastened to assure her. "The Pet section." Freddie's mate, a lovebird, had escaped from their cage a few months earlier, and he was lonely.

—RAYMOND R. FIELDING

 What do you get when you cross a tiger with a canary?

I don't know. But when it sings, you'd better listen.

— NAVNEET KUMAR

Then there was the old gal who died and left $20,000 to her dog and cat.

"But they're going to have trouble trying to collect," said one chap, "I understand her parakeet is contesting the will."

—CHRIS HOBSON

The devoted couple doted on their peg gray thrushes. One day the female flew out while the cage was being cleaned. The wife was disconsolate, and her husband offered to buy another female thrush on his way home.

"What?" she cried, more disconsolate than ever. "How can you think of remarrying the moment she is gone?"

—CHIK KA KEUNG

As the manager of a bird store, part of my job is to trim the wings and nails of our customers' feathered friends. One day a woman brought in her pet parrot. While working, I lost my grip on the bird and he bit down hard on my finger. I almost let out a yell, but stopped myself before saying something I might regret. Right then our store pet, a very vocal parrot, let out a stream of obscenities. Horrified, I started to make apologies, but the customer held up her hand and said, "I think he just took the words right out of your mouth!"

—LYNN K. CHURCH

♥ ♥ ♥ ♥ ♥ ♥ ♥ ♥ ♥ ♥ ♥

Near the main entrance to Billy Rose's Aquacade at the New York World's Fair was a small exhibit with a sign over the door which read: "Billy Rose's Pet Shop."

Every time Billy went to his great spectacle, he passed this place. He finally decided to get his lawyer to put a stop to the use of his name to peddle bullfrogs and tropical fish. The two marched belligerently into the offending establishment.

"I'm Billy Rose," he announced, "and this is my lawyer."

"Oh, yes, I was expecting you, Mr. Rosenberg," replied the pet-shop proprietor (Rosenberg is Billy's real name).

"Well," Billy went on, "I want you to stop trading on my name to sell your goldfish. Otherwise, we will take action."

The man reached under the counter and brought out his birth certificate, explaining, "I thought you might want to see it."

His square name was Billy Rose. The two callers studied it a minute and then Billy asked, "How much are your canaries?"

"Five dollars each," the man said.

"Let me have two with a cage." Billy walked out with his new pets.

—JOHN WHEELER

There's a magician who works his show on a cruise ship. After a while, the captain's parrot understands how the magician does every trick and starts shouting, "Look, it's not the same hat," "He's hiding the flowers under the table," or "Hey, why are all the cards the ace of spades?" The magician is furious, but can't do anything against the captain's parrot. Then the ship sinks, and the magician and the parrot find themselves on a piece of wood, staring at each other with hatred. This goes on for days. Finally, the parrot can't hold back: "Okay, I give up. Where's the ship?"

—BASIL HENDRICKSON

❤ ❤ ❤ ❤ ❤ ❤ ❤ ❤ ❤ ❤ ❤

As a professional magician, I travel quite a bit. A few years ago, I was flying back home through Pearson airport in Toronto. I checked my baggage and a pet carrier containing several white doves, then mentioned to the young lady behind the counter that I was a magician and that these birds were part of my act.

She looked at me and asked, "Have they flown before?"

"Well," I replied, "they are birds!"

—DALE DOWNING

An elderly man sitting on a park bench was joined by a youth sporting multi-colored spiked hair so bizarre that the man couldn't stop staring at it. "What's the matter, old man?" the youth asked sarcastically. "Never done aything wild in your life?"

"Well, in a moment of alcohol-induced madness, I once made love to a parrot," the man replied. "I'm just wondering if you're my son."

—LISA MCDERMOTT

Tell me, can that parrot talk?
He's just asked the same about you.

—WWW.KULICHKI.RU

A desperate voice calls the police by phone: "Help, come quickly! A cat has just entered my house!"

"A cat? Don't be afraid. There's not need to worry about a cat."

"Please! It's a tragedy!"

"To whom am I speaking?"

"It's the parrot!"

—GILMAR DE OLIVEIRA DORNELAS, JR.

❤ ❤ ❤ ❤ ❤ ❤ ❤ ❤ ❤ ❤ ❤

A man dreamed of owning a parrot. He had never seen one, but had heard that it was a bird that talked. A friend suggested that he visit an aviary of a person he knew, adding that he would telephone to say that he was sending him there. The man went to the aviary, but the owner, who had no parrots at the time, and knew that the man had never seen one, gave him an owl.

Sometime later, the man saw his friend. "How is the parrot?" his friend inquired.

"It's beautiful and I love it!" the man replied.

"So, is it talking yet?"

"To be honest, it doesn't talk. But when I speak to it, it pays close attention to what I say."

—ANTÓNIO DOMINGOS PINHEIRO

That's a pet?

Animals are such agreeable friends— they ask no questions, they pass no criticisms.

—GEORGE ELIOT, *MR. GILFIL'S LOVE STORY*

"While I was watching the dog so he wouldn't eat my homework, the hamster went and shredded it for his nest!"

♥ ♥ ♥ ♥ ♥ ♥ ♥ ♥ ♥ ♥ ♥ ♥ ♥

My little nephew came home from school all excited because a beautiful white rabbit named Snowball, used in his nature-study class, was to be given to the lucky child whose name was pulled out of a hat the next day. To participate in the drawing, each child had to bring a note from home saying his parents would let him keep the animal if he won it. The thought of another pet to cope with unnerved me but, rationalizing that our chances of losing were pretty good with 28 other pupils in the class, I gave him the note. That afternoon, the boy rushed in and announced ecstatically that Snowball was his.

"You mean that, out of the whole class, you won the bunny?" I asked incredulously.

"Well, not exactly," he replied. "I was the only one with a note."

—GERTRUDE H. ANDERSON

The kids had been begging for weeks, so their mom finally gave in and bought them a hamster. But just as she had feared, she was the one who wound up taking care of it. One evening, exasperated, she sat them down and asked, "Why did you even want that darn thing? How many times do you think it would have died if I hadn't been looking after it for you?"

"I don't know," her son said. "Once?"

—ADAM JOSHUA SMARGON

An adorable little girl walked into my pet shop and asked, "Excuse me, do you have any rabbits here?"

"I do," I answered, and leaning down to her eye level I asked, "Did you want a white rabbit or would you rather have a soft, fuzzy black rabbit?"

She shrugged. "I don't think my python really cares."

—CINDY PATTERSON

♥ ♥ ♥ ♥ ♥ ♥ ♥ ♥ ♥ ♥ ♥ ♥

Two campers are hiking in the woods when one is bitten on the rear end by a rattlesnake. "I'll go into town for a doctor," the other says. He runs ten miles to a small town and finds the only doctor delivering a baby.

"I can't leave," the doctor says. "But here's what to do. Take a knife, cut a little X where the bite is, suck out the poison and spit it on the ground."

The guy runs back to his friend, who is in agony. "What did the doctor say?" the victim cries.

"He says you're gonna die."

My friend's husband, Ray, is a state trooper and enjoys sharing the excuses people use when stopped for speeding. One day, however, the tables were turned. Ray maintains an aquarium of exotic fish, and a prized specimen had threatened to turn belly up. The off-duty officer called a pet store, and they advised him to immediately purchase a special additive that would correct the water's pH.

Ray and his wife jumped into the car and rushed to the store. A state trooper signaled them to pull over.

"Go ahead," Ray's wife said. "Tell him you've got a sick fish!"

—DEBRA MCVEY

A Hollywood producer who keeps a goldfish in a bowl on his desk was recently asked why.

"Because," he replied glumly, **"I like to see something around here with its mouth open not asking for a raise."**

—BOB HULL

What's a snake's favorite opera?
Wriggeletto

AROON PURIE

I was helping my daughter scrub her pet pig—250 pounds of squealing indignation—in preparation for an upcoming state fair. The phone in the barn rang and I grabbed it.

"Hello," I screamed above the earsplitting din. No answer. "Hello!" I tried again.

"I can hear you," came the amused reply of Jean, the mother of three active preschool boys, "I just thought I'd never hear anybody whose kids made more noise than mine when their mother got on the phone."

—MARY HAVENS

Poster on a power pole in San Francisco: "Lost: Pet aardvark. Description: Basically your everyday, common aardvark. Long, pinkish snout, one tail, hairy in spots, not overly attractive. Waddles with noticeable limp in right rear leg. Answers to the name Sergio. Last seen on a leisurely stroll down Sacramento Street. Is trailing a three-foot-long leash attached to a rhinestone collar. Your reward: getting rid of it."

—HERB CAEN

A guy walks into a bar with a lizard on his shoulder. "What do you call that?" asks the bartender. "Tiny," says the guy. "Because he's my newt."

♥ ♥ ♥ ♥ ♥ ♥ ♥ ♥ ♥ ♥ ♥

Did you know goldfish don't like to watch television? Yeah, they're afraid they might get hooked.

—JOHN SIERZANT

A friend of mine received a pet ferret as a gift from his girlfriend. This small, weasel-like creature is very tame, but it's small wonder that heads turn when the adorable animal is walked on its leash along the city streets. Its name? Ferret Fawcett, of course!

—TIMOTHY STEWART

A vicious bite from one of his prize-winning show rabbits sent my 15-year-old son to the emergency room. The doctor and attendants who cleaned the wound and bandaged his hand were clearly amused about how he got the injury.

As we were leaving the ER, they handed us a sheaf of papers that included a prescription for antibiotics, a wound-care information sheet and a recipe for rabbit stew.

—JIM LORD

While I was having coffee with a friend, her teenage daughter rushed into the house all excited.

"Mother, could I get a pet rabbit?" she asked.

"Well, you could," said my friend, "but it would cost you about 500 dollars a month to keep it."

The girl looked at her mother in disbelief. "Mom," she said, "the whole rabbit only costs four dollars."

"Yes," said my friend, "but you're not keeping it in my house, so you'd have to rent an apartment."

—M.R. SMITH

"Is it just me...or do you feel like you're in a snow globe?"

♥ ♥ ♥ ♥ ♥ ♥ ♥ ♥ ♥ ♥ ♥ ♥

Steve, a lonely bachelor, decided to get himself a pet. At the pet store, he told the shopkeeper he wanted something unusual. The shopkeeper suggested an exotic centipede he'd just received. Steve readily agreed, bought the centipede and a small box for it to live in, then went home happy.

That evening he decided to go out, so he asked the centipede, "Want to come down to Frank's place for a drink?" There was no answer from the box.

A few minutes later he asked again, still no reply. Finally, he hollered at the box: "Hey! You in there! Do you want to go down to Frank's for a drink with me?"

"I heard you the first time!" said a small, irritated voice.

"I'm putting on my shoes!"

♥ ♥ ♥ ♥ ♥ ♥ ♥ ♥ ♥ ♥ ♥ ♥

My teenage daughter and I were in the yard playing with our new pet nanny goat that was exploring and nibbling everything in sight. We soon noticed that she ignored our lush green lawn and preferred to pick out harmful-looking weeds and other non-nourishing tidbits. "What a strange animal," I commented. "She ignores all the stuff that's good for her and instead eats all the junk food that's lying around."

"Oh, she's not so weird," my daughter replied. "She's no different from any other normal kid!"

—ANNA HOUSTON

The devout cowboy lost his favorite Bible while he was mending fences out on the range.

Three weeks later a cow walked up to him carrying the Bible in its mouth. The cowboy couldn't believe his eyes. He took the book out of the cow's mouth, raised his eyes heavenward and exclaimed, "It's a miracle!"

"Not really," said the cow. "Your name is written inside the cover."

— ROMAN WILBERT

My son's teacher has a miniature pet donkey that accompanied the family on an 800-mile trek along the Appalachian Trail. His name? **Donkey Oatie.**

—CATHIE GLEBA

♥ ♥ ♥ ♥ ♥ ♥ ♥ ♥ ♥ ♥ ♥

A man was admiring the tropical fish in the pet shop where I used to work. When I offered my assistance, he mentioned that his new wife was a fish fancier. After I showed him around, he shouted, "There she is! That's the one I'll take."

As I scooped out a large, sluggish goldfish with a gray splotch at the top of its head, the man exclaimed, "My bride will love this! She's always wanted to know what my first wife looked like!"

—JOAN INGLIS

Just as our neighbor was experiencing a minor household emergency, the telephone rang. She picked up the receiver and hurriedly exclaimed, "I can't talk now, our white mouse is loose in the kitchen and I have to catch him before the cat does!"

She let the receiver dangle from the hook for a good five minutes. When she did get back to the phone, it was only to hear an unfamiliar voice on the other end say, "Excuse me, lady, I knew I had a wrong number, but I just had to find out—who got the mouse?"

—R. FRASER PORTER

A turtle is crossing the road when he's mugged by two snails. When the police show up, they ask him what happened. The shaken turtle replies, "I don't know. It all happened so fast."

—DEBBY CARTER

 What's stranger than seeing a catfish?
Seeing a goldfish bowl.

QUOTABLE QUOTES

"I think there's something great and generic about goldfish. They're everybody's first pet."

—PAUL RUDD

"I don't believe in reincarnation, and I didn't believe in it when I was a hamster."

—SHANE RITCHIE

"My roommate got a pet elephant. Then it got lost. It's in the apartment somewhere."

—STEPHEN WRIGHT

"Dogs look up to you; cats look down on you; pigs treat you as an equal."

—WINSTON CHURCHILL

"Try to be like the turtle—at ease in your own shell."

—BILL COPELAND

"No animal should ever jump up on the dining room furniture unless absolutely certain that he can hold his own in the conversation."

—FRAN LEBOWITZ

"When I was a kid, if a guy got killed in a Western movie I always wondered who got his horse."

—GEORGE CARLIN

"My favorite animal is the turtle. For the turtle to move, it has to stick its neck out."

—RUTH WESTHEIMER

"It's hard to lose weight when I need to stay bigger than anything my pet python can swallow."

♥ ♥ ♥ ♥ ♥ ♥ ♥ ♥ ♥ ♥ ♥ ♥

An old lady was taking a pet tortoise by train from London to Edinburgh and wanted to know whether she ought to buy a dog ticket for it, as one has to do in England when taking a cat by train, because cats officially count as dogs.

"No, mum," said the ticket inspector, "cats is dogs, and dogs is dogs, and squirrels in cages is parrots, but this here turtle is a insect, and we won't charge you nothing."

—ROBERT GRAVES

My young son and I spent much time in pet shops looking for just the right fish for his aquarium and for snails to keep the tank clean. One day he came home from a shopping trip all excited to tell me he had discovered some African frogs that really did a good job cleaning the aquarium.

"Good," I said, "then you won't have to buy any snails."

"Oh, yes," he said, "I have to buy them too. Those frogs don't do windows."

—MRS. ROGER RAYMOND

A computer nerd is crossing the road when he sees a frog who opens its mouth and starts talking.

"If you kiss me," the frog says, "I'll turn into a beautiful princess, stay with you for a week and do anything you want."

The guy smiles and puts the frog in his pocket.

"Did you hear me?" asks the frog. "A beautiful princess? For a week?"

"Look," says the nerd, "I haven't got time for a girlfriend. But a talking frog—now that's cool."

—STUART WIGNALL

❤ ❤ ❤ ❤ ❤ ❤ ❤ ❤ ❤ ❤ ❤

As I strolled through an import shop, I wondered how the proprietors kept customers from sifting through the neatly stacked displays of woven baskets. Then I spotted this sign:

"Please do not rummage through the baskets. We haven't seen our pet cobra in weeks."

—B.V.C.

My brother adopted a snake named Slinky, whose most disagreeable trait was eating live mice. Once I was pressed into going to the pet store to buy Slinky's dinner.

The worst part of this wasn't choosing the juiciest-looking creatures or turning down the clerk who wanted to sell me vitamins to ensure their longevity. The hardest part was carrying the poor things out in a box bearing the words "Thank you for giving me a home."

—JOANNE MITCHELL

A guy finds a sheep wandering in his neighborhood and takes it to the police station. The desk sergeant says, "Why don't you just take it to the zoo?"

The next day, the sergeant spots the same guy walking down the street—with the sheep.

"I thought I told you to take that sheep to the zoo," the sergeant says.

"I know what you told me," the guy responds. "Yesterday I took him to the zoo. Today I'm taking him to the movies."

—TAMARA CUMMINGS

♥ ♥ ♥ ♥ ♥ ♥ ♥ ♥ ♥ ♥ ♥ ♥

My aunt recently had to explain to her four-year-old daughter, Faith, that their pet rabbit had died. Faith thought about this news for a minute, then said, "Well, I guess now I can sing that song from my CD."

"What song is that, honey?" asked my aunt.

With a mournful expression on her face, Faith began to sing, "Bring back, bring back, oh bring back my bunny to me, to me..."

—KATHLEEN SPARKES

On a recent trip to the post office,
I took a few minutes to read the notices posted on the public bulletin board in the lobby. One in particular caught my eye.
It read: "Lost in post-office parking lot, small boa constrictor, family pet, will not attack. Reward."

Below the notice someone had written, in what appeared to be very shaky handwriting:
"Please, would you mind posting another notice when you find your boa? Thank you."

—SUSAN ESBENSEN

♥ ♥ ♥ ♥ ♥ ♥ ♥ ♥ ♥ ♥ ♥

Why did the frog wear a mask to the bank?
He said he wanted to "rob-bit."

Scientists at the University of Pennsylvania School of Medicine announced they have found a cure for baldness in mice. This is great news. Nothing looks more ridiculous than a mouse with a comb-over.

—BEN WALSH

The injury to our piglet wasn't serious, but it did require stitches. So I sent my teenage daughter back into the farmhouse to get needle and thread and bring it to me, while I looked after the squealing animal.

Ten minutes later she still hadn't returned.

"What are you doing?" I called out.

She yelled back, "Looking for the pink thread."

—JUNE HALEY

"What is that sound?" a woman visiting our nature center asked.

"It's the frogs trilling for a mate," Patti, the naturalist, explained. "We have a pair in the science room. But since they've been together for so long, they no longer sing to each other."

The woman nodded sympathetically. "The trill is gone."

—KATHYJO TOWNSON

"Well, the kiss didn't work. How about a cuddle?"

♥ ♥ ♥ ♥ ♥ ♥ ♥ ♥ ♥ ♥ ♥ ♥

FOR SALE:
"Ferret, likes kids, nice pet, but chewed the guinea pig's ear off. Also, partially deaf guinea pig."

—BILL PORTER, FROM THE DANVERS, ILL., *SHOPPER*

When a lonely frog consults a fortune-teller, he's told not to worry.

"You are going to meet a beautiful young girl," she says, "and she will want to know everything about you."

"That's great!" says the excited frog. "When will I meet her?"

"Next semester," says the psychic, "in biology class."

—ZHANG WENYI

"Hey, peanut butter!" the mouse exclaimed, and then climbed on top of the lid and started dancing. A second mouse saw him and asked, "What are you doing?" The first mouse, still shaking his tail, pointed to the lid. "It says, 'Twist to open.'"

—THOM DELUCA

A guy drives into a ditch, but luckily, a farmer is there to help. He hitches his horse, Buddy, up to the car and yells, "Pull, Nellie, pull!" Buddy doesn't move.

"Pull, Buster, pull!" Buddy doesn't budge.

"Pull, Coco, pull!" Nothing.

Then the farmer says, "Pull, Buddy, pull!" And the horse drags the car out of the ditch.

Curious, the motorist asks the farmer why he kept calling his horse by the wrong name.

"Buddy's blind," said the farmer. "And if he thought he was the only one pulling, he wouldn't even try."

—CHARLES LEERHSEN

❤ ❤ ❤ ❤ ❤ ❤ ❤ ❤ ❤ ❤ ❤

A duck walks into a drugstore and asks for a tube of ChapStick. The cashier says to the duck, "That'll be $1.49."

The duck replies, "Put it on my bill!"

The pregnant guppy in the science-room fish tank fascinated my seventh-grade class. We all anxiously awaited the arrival of her babies. But a lesson on human growth and development raised a question for one student.

"Mrs. Townsend," she called out, "how will we know when the fish's water breaks?"

—DANA TOWNSEND

A lonely farm boy returning to an air force recruit training center after his first 48-hour pass carried his pet pig under his arm.

"You can't have a pet in barracks." said the guard at the gate.

"I can keep him under my bunk."

"That's impossible," said the guard. "What about the smell?"

"He'll just have to get used to it like I did."

—DAVE MCINTOSH

There, in the reptiles section of our zoo, a male turtle was on top of a female behaving very, um, affectionately. My daughter was transfixed. She asked, "Mommy?"

Uh-oh, I thought. Here comes The Question. "Yes?" I said.

"Why doesn't he go around?"

—DAWN HOISINGTON

"OK, when I was a kitten I may have lied about where I came from."

♥ ♥ ♥ ♥ ♥ ♥ ♥ ♥ ♥ ♥ ♥

Following the recent mad cow disease scare in our state, one local rancher sought to allay fears by posting this sign: "All our cows have completed anger management classes."

—A. C. BOYETTE

"Can I purchase frogs for my new pond here?" a customer asked at our garden center.

"You don't buy frogs," I explained. "They just sort of choose where they live, then turn up."

"Right..." agreed the gentleman. "And is the same true with fish?"

—SAMANTHA DAVIS

Having lost one of our goldfish, I went to the pet shop to pick a replacement. Among the dozens in the tank, I pointed one out to the shop owner, who stood with net poised.

On seeing the net, the fish darted to the other side of the tank. Pursued by the shop owner, it then darted in the opposite direction. This went on for a while. Due to the frenzy in the tank and the shop owner's stress, I opted instead for any fish, and one was quickly caught.

On revisiting the shop weeks later, I saw a new sign: "Personally chosen fish, 50¢ extra."

—KATHRYN MURRAY

My greatest contribution to humor came when I taught my pet lizard to walk on its hind legs. It was the world's first stand-up chameleon.

—JOHN S. CROSBIE

♥ ♥ ♥ ♥ ♥ ♥ ♥ ♥ ♥ ♥ ♥ ♥

I have the most frustrated pet in the world—
a turtle that chases cars.

—ROBERT ORBEN

One day while we were doing yard work, my nine-year-old daughter found a baby snake, and I encouraged her to catch it and put it in a jar. Later she found a huge bullfrog and got another jar to put it in. After dark I told her she would have to set them free. With the frog in one hand and the snake in the other, she started down the porch steps. Suddenly she screamed wildly, dropped both the snake and the frog, and ran into the house.

"What happened?" I asked, my heart thumping.

"Did you see that?" she replied. "That moth almost got me."

—CASSANDRA DALZELL

Squirrels had overrun three churches in town. After much prayer, the elders of the first church determined that the animals were predestined to be there. Who were they to interfere with God's will, they reasoned. Soon, the squirrels multiplied.

The elders of the second church, deciding that they could not harm any of God's creatures, humanely trapped the squirrels and set them free outside of town. Three days later, the squirrels were back.

It was only the third church that succeeded in keeping the pests away. The elders baptized the squirrels and registered them as members of the church. Now they only see them on Christmas and Easter.

♥ ♥ ♥ ♥ ♥ ♥ ♥ ♥ ♥ ♥ ♥

A mother mouse and her baby were scampering across a polished floor when they heard a noise. They hoped it would be a human being, but it turned out to be the family cat. Upon seeing the mice, the cat gave chase. Mama mouse felt a swipe of paw and claw. She turned in her tracks and called out in her loudest voice, "Bow-wow!" and the cat ran off.

Gathering her baby to her and catching her breath, Mama mouse explained, "Now, my child, you see how important a second language is."

—SANDRA J. HULDEN

It's really humid in the woods, so the two hiking buddies remove their shirts and shoes. But when they spot the sign Beware of Bears, one of them stops to put his shoes back on.

"But what's the point?" the other hiker asks. "You can't outrun a bear."

"Actually," says his friend, "all I have to do is outrun you."

—DON PAQUETTE

My niece bought her five-year-old daughter, Kayleigh, a hamster. One day he escaped from his cage. The family turned the house upside down and finally found him. Several weeks later, while Kayleigh was at school, he escaped from his cage again. My niece searched frantically but never found the critter. Hoping to make the loss less painful for Kayleigh, my niece took the cage out of her room. When Kayleigh came home from school that afternoon, she climbed into her mother's lap.

"We've got a serious problem," she announced. "Not only is my hamster gone again, but this time he took the cage."

—PATSY STRINGER

One February, a 13-year-old boy in Mount Airy, N.C., found a turtle near his home, carved his name and address on the shell and turned the turtle loose.

In September, he received a postcard from Ohio that said: "Dear Jeff, I found a small turtle with your name and address on it heading north on U.S. 35 at Jackson, Ohio. **I turned him around; be on the lookout."**

—JEAN KELLY

Sharing the two bathrooms in his house with a
wife and five daughters has at times
been very trying for a close friend of mine.
However, his sense of humor has carried
him through.

Recently, his two youngest daughters received a
large turtle as a gift. They put the new
pet in the bathtub while they went
looking for more permanent accommodations
for it. I was visiting with the man of the
house in the living room when the oldest
daughter suddenly burst in.

"Daddy!" she screamed, "There's a turtle in the bathtub
and he's trying to get out!"

Without even shifting position in his favorite
chair, my friend calmed her with,

"Just close your eyes, honey, and hand him a towel."

—BILL GRANT

♥ ♦ ♥ ♥ ♥ ♥ ♥ ♥ ♥ ♥ ♥

A sign over goldfish display: "Wet Pets"

—DILYS JONES

Four jack rabbits are strolling in the prairie. Out of nowhere, a gang of coyotes begins to chase them. So the rabbits run under a huge cactus for refuge.

Then the hungry coyotes surround the cactus. One jack rabbit says to another, "Okay, should we make a run for it, or wait till we outnumber them?

—BENITO F. JUAREZ

"Nice dog. What's its name?" I asked my friend's 10-year-old son.

"Bob," he said.

"And your cat?"

"Bob."

"How do you keep them straight?"

"Well, one is Bob Cat and the other is Bob Barker," the boy answered.

"Tell him your rabbit's name," his father suggested.

The kid smiled and said, "Dennis Hopper."

—MIKE HARRELSON

A farmer wonders how many sheep he has in his field, so he asks his sheepdog to count.

"So what's the verdict?" the farmer asks when the dog is done.

"Forty."

"Huh?" the farmer says, puzzled. "I only had thirty-eight."

"I know," the dog says. "But I rounded them up."

"It's for you."

During the first week of school, one of my high school science pupils brought me a hamster. To prevent the confusion that always occurs with the appearance of an animal in the classroom, I placed the hamster safely out of sight in the breast pocket of my blouse, where he promptly fell asleep.

All went well until my third-period class, when the hamster awoke and created a small commotion in the pocket. It was then that one of my more perceptive boys turned to a nearby classmate and commented, "It looks like she's got on one of those living bras."

—ANN W. ABERNATHY

A panda walks into a bar, sits down and orders a sandwich. He eats, pulls out a gun and shoots the waiter dead. As the panda stands up to go, the bartender shouts, "Hey! Where are you going? You just shot my waiter and you didn't pay for the food."

The panda yells back, "Hey, man, I'm a panda. Look it up!"

The bartender opens his dictionary to panda: "A tree-climbing mammal of Asian origin, characterized by distinct black and white coloring. Eats shoots and leaves."

Recently, my colleague took a goldfish into her kindergarten classroom for her students. She asked them to suggest names for their new pet. One little fellow seemed deep in thought, so she asked him for his contribution. He looked intently at the small fish, then announced confidently, **"Bait!"**

 What do you get when you cross a turtle with a porcupine?

A slow poke.

So I went into a pet shop and said, "Can I buy a goldfish?"

"Do you want an aquarium?" said the shopowner.

"I don't care what star sign it is," I said. "Just give me the fish."

—DORIS POOLE

After years of raising donkeys, an old farmer discovered an unusually intelligent one.

He remembered stories of horses learning to add and subtract by stomping their hooves. Thinking his donkey was smarter than any horse, he went a step further and taught him to multiply and divide.

The farmer was sure the public would pay to see his amazing donkey, so he sold his farm and went on the road, renting booths at fairs to show off the animal's mental prowess.

Unfortunately, he could never find customers who wanted to see his donkey perform. It seems he learned the hard way that nobody likes a smart ass.

—JEFF LISZKA

A guy walks into a bar and there's a horse serving drinks. The horse asks, "What are you staring at? Haven't you ever seen a horse tending bar before?"

The guy says, "It's not that. I just never thought the parrot would sell the place."

❤ ❤ ❤ ❤ ❤ ❤ ❤ ❤ ❤ ❤ ❤ ❤

It's a very tony bar in a hotel in Manhattan. A scruffy guy walks in. The bartender's kind of giving him the eye. The guy comes up to the bar and says, "Yeah, I know I look kind of scruffy, but can I at least get a beer if I show you something really cool?" There's no one else in the place, so the bartender says, "Sure. Why not?"

The guy takes out a little ebony box. He opens it up and takes out a little ebony piano, a little ebony piano bench and a little mouse dressed in black pants. Then he takes out a little ivory box. Out comes a beautiful monarch butterfly. And after the mouse warms up on the piano, the monarch starts singing the famous aria "Un Bel Di" from the opera Madama Butterfly. The music fills the room, and it's so moving that there are tears running down the bartender's cheeks. He gives the man a whole bottle of the best stuff on the top shelf and says, "You know, I'm just moved beyond belief. Why don't you go into show business? Go on Letterman, go on Leno. They'll love this. You'll make a fortune."

The guy says, "No, no, I tried that. They won't touch it."

"What do you mean? It moved me to tears, and I don't even like opera."

"It's really not as good as it seems. The butterfly can't sing a note—the mouse is a ventriloquist."

—ROBERT STANLEY

"I think my goldfish has seizures," a man tells the veterinarian.

"He seems fine now," says the vet.

"Now, sure. But wait till I take him out of the bowl."

—NANCY SEND

I took my two children to the county fair, and each of them won a chameleon. But after a few weeks, one of the reptiles died. Thinking it would be a good opportunity to teach them about responsibility, I said to the kids, "You know, it probably died of neglect."

"Don't blame me, Dad," my daughter said quickly. "I never touched them."

—CURTIS HOKE

When our pet tortoise, Torty, discovered our newly built rockery, he took a fancy to a round, flat stone about his own size. Throughout the long, hot days of summer he made amorous advances toward it. When we took it away he became extremely distressed and would race round the garden looking for it until it was returned.

Last week I went into the garden and discovered a very interested tortoise inspecting four large, oval pebbles next to the big stone.

"Well," said my husband when I asked him about them. "the poor chap has worked so hard, I thought he deserved some reward for his efforts."

—BARBARA MCGEE

 A rabbit and a duck went to dinner. Who paid?

The duck—he had the bill.

♥ ♥ ♥ ♥ ♥ ♥ ♥ ♥ ♥ ♥ ♥ ♥

? **What did the turtle lying on its back say?**
"No, I didn't turn turtle. I've always been one!"

— GEORGE N. NETTO

My sister's children finally got their turn to take home the school's incredibly long-lived guinea pig, Peter. After enjoying his company for a few days, my sister was horrified to find Peter dead one morning. She and her husband hid the cage and dashed to the pet store, intent on replacing the guinea pig before anyone was the wiser.

The pet-store owner listened carefully to their description of Peter's markings. "You're looking for the St. Peter's school guinea pig. I think I have another one," he said calmingly. "You're not the first, you know. Guinea pigs don't live very long."

—CAROL ENGELBERTS

While I was raking leaves along the waterfront of our cottage, I unearthed a fairly large turtle. It appeared to be dead but thinking it might be hibernating, I decided to leave it. Three days later, when it still hadn't moved, I took my rake and gingerly flipped it over. Imagine my surprise when I saw made in china on its underside. I had waited three days for one of my lawn ornaments to move!

—J. LOUISE DEMCZYNA

♥ ♥ ♥ ♥ ♥ ♥ ♥ ♥ ♥ ♥ ♥ ♥

Our daughter, a riding instructor, began a lesson with a young girl who was seated on her pony trotting around the school arena.

"How much riding have you done?" she asked the eight-year-old, but there was no answer.

Again, "How much riding have you done?" Still no answer.

In a very loud voice, in case the child was deaf, my daughter bellowed, "How much riding have you done?"

"Oh, sorry," said the girl. "I thought you were talking to my horse."

—LYNN HUGHES

Our two pet bunnies were going to a new home due to the onset of rabbit allergies. Our eight- and five-year-old daughters were sad to see them go. The night after the bunnies went to their new home, my husband told them that he wouldn't be home for lunch the next day because he had to work.

"Oh, great!" said our five-year-old in disgust. **"First the rabbits, now you."**

—JEN KUHL

Not the "vet"

The best doctor in the world
is a veterinarian.
He can't ask his patients
what is the matter—
he's got to just know.

—WILL ROGERS

"Who called me a quack?"

♥ ♥ ♥ ♥ ♥ ♥ ♥ ♥ ♥ ♥ ♥

Most of us long for recognition as individuals in our own right, but all too often we are known, as we go through life, as the Jones kid, then Sally Jones' husband, then Johnny Jones' father. But the biggest blow came recently when I visited the vet to pay a bill for our dog.

"Oh, yes," said the secretary when I gave my name, "King's owner!"

—A. B. CALLAWAY

My father-in-law had prostate surgery. We brought him to the hospital at 7:30 a.m., and he was operated on at 8. We were amazed when the hospital called at noon to tell us he could go home. Two months later our beagle, Bo, also had prostate surgery. When I brought him in, I asked the veterinarian what time I should pick him up. The vet told me Bo would remain overnight.

"Overnight?" I said. "My father-in-law came home the same day."

The vet looked at me and said, "Bo's not on Medicare."

—CLYDE DYAR

Concerned, a man took his Rottweiler to the veterinarian. "My dog's cross-eyed," he said. "Is there anything you can do for him?"

"Let's have a look at him," said the vet, lifting the dog up to examine its eyes. "I'm going to have to put him down," he finally said.

"Just because he's cross-eyed?" exclaimed the alarmed pet owner.

"No," said the vet. "Because he's heavy."

—CAO XIN

Veterinarian examining cat to cat's owner:
**"I'm afraid we'll have to keep him overnight.
Are you going to need a loaner?"**

—M. TWOHY

I hear plenty of unusual pet names in my job as a veterinarian's assistant. One afternoon I noticed that our next patient was a golden retriever named Brazen.

"I got the idea from my brother," the dog's owner explained when I asked him about the unusual moniker. "His dog is named Shameless. Our last name is Hussey."

—KIRSTEN JOHNSON

While waiting at the veterinarian's office, I overheard two women chatting about their dogs.

"What's your dog's name?" asked the first woman.

"We used to call her Pork Chop," answered the second. "But after all the vet bills we've had for her, we now call her Filet Mignon."

—LAURA SANDERS

It was time for my dog's annual checkup. Following the vet's instructions, I collected a stool sample and dropped it in a plastic container before we left for his office. When we arrived, I handed the sample to the receptionist, who immediately cracked a smile.

The container read: **"I Can't Believe It's Not Butter."**

—MITZI BARNES

♥ ♥ ♥ ♥ ♥ ♥ ♥ ♥ ♥ ♥ ♥

My friend Allison adopted a stray cat and took it to the vet to be neutered.

"I'm about ninety percent certain he's been fixed," the vet said.

"How can I be a hundred percent?" Allison asked.

"Wait to see if he does any 'male' things."

"He already lies on the couch all day," she said. "If he starts hogging the remote, I'll bring him in."

—DORIS MUSICK

When my brother Neill and I were sharing a house, I suggested that he get his pet cat, Speedy, neutered. He agreed but asked me to take Speedy to the veterinarian because his work schedule did not permit him to do so. I dutifully dropped the cat off and was told he would be ready to go home at six o'clock.

Neill was home then, so I told him to go get his cat. To my surprise, he refused and asked me to do it. Annoyed, I demanded that he explain.

Sheepishly, he replied, "I don't want Speedy to know I had anything to do with it."

—AMELIA SCOTT

In his younger days our golden retriever, Catcher, often ran away when he had the chance. His veterinarian's office was about a mile down the road, and Catcher would usually end up there. The office staff knew him well and would call me to come pick him up. One day I called the vet to make an appointment for Catcher's yearly vaccine. "Will you be bringing him?" asked the receptionist. "Or will he be coming on his own?"

—LAURA STASZAK

❤ ❤ ❤ ❤ ❤ ❤ ❤ ❤ ❤ ❤ ❤ ❤

A tourist in Maine paid an emergency visit to a veterinarian's office when his dog got the short end of a brawl with a porcupine. After the dog was de-quilled, the man went to pay, but was shocked when the receptionist handed him a bill for $450.

"Four hundred and fifty dollars!" he shouted indignantly. "What do you Mainers do in the wintertime when all the tourists are gone?"

"Raise porcupines," said the receptionist, as she took his check.

—BEATRICE MATHIEU

When our client's dog lapped up anti-freeze, the veterinarian I work for ordered a unique treatment: an IV drip mixing fluids with vodka. "Go buy the cheapest bottle you can find," he told me.

At the liquor store, I was uneasy buying cheap booze so early in the day, and I felt compelled to explain things to the clerk.

"Believe it or not," I said, "this is for a sick dog."

As I was leaving, the next customer plunked down two bottles of muscatel and announced, "These are for my cats."

—DOROTHY SCHOENER

"So...what are you in for?"

❤ ❤ ❤ ❤ ❤ ❤ ❤ ❤ ❤ ❤ ❤

Walking past my father's veterinary clinic, a woman noticed a small boy and his dog waiting outside. "Are you here to see Dr. Meyer?" she asked. "Yes," the boy said. "I'm having my dog put in neutral."

—SALLY MEYER-SHIELDS

Polly the parrot didn't look well, and the vet confirmed it. "I'm sorry," he told the owner, "I'm afraid your bird doesn't have long to live."

"Oh, no," wailed the owner. "Are you sure?"

The vet left the room and returned with a big black Labrador, who sniffed the bird from top to bottom, then shook his head. Next the vet brought in a cat. He too sniffed the parrot and shook his head.

"Your bird is definitely terminal," said the vet, handing the owner a bill.

"Wait—$500! Just to tell me my bird is dying?"

The vet shrugged. "If you'd taken my word for it, the bill would only have been $20, but with the Lab Report and the Cat Scan..."

—DUSTIN GODSEY

Our short-haired collie mix, Toby, was being examined for a cut paw by the veterinarian. "Give me a paw," said the vet. Toby ignored him. "Can he give a paw?" asked the surprised surgeon.

My wife leaned forward and mysteriously replied, "You need to know the right words when there are teenagers in the family."

Then, bending down, she said, "Gimme five, dude," and Toby eagerly held out the wounded paw.

—JIM CLARK

My mother-in-law's dog was overweight, so the vet gave her some diet pills for the dog. On the return visit the dog's weight was unchanged. The vet asked if she was having trouble getting the dog to take the pills. "Oh no," my mother-in-law answered.

"I hide them in her ice cream!"

—BRENDA SHIPLEY

A man brought in a homing pigeon to a friend of mine who is a veterinarian at an animal hospital. The bird was suffering from an eye infection, and my friend assured the man that treatment would be completed by the next day and the pigeon could be taken home then.

"I'm afraid I'll be out of town tomorrow," the owner replied. "Why not bill me now and let him fly out the window when he's okay?"

—BRUCE LANDESMAN

I was relaxing on the sofa late one evening when I heard my dog crunching something under the table. I lifted the tablecloth, and instead of ruining my favorite shoes, she was devouring my one-month birth-control pill supply.

Worried about the side effects the drug might have on my cherished pet, I phoned the veterinary hot line. With some embarrassment, I explained the situation to the veterinarian on duty, and asked if this "self-medication" could possibly harm my dog.

"Madame, there's absolutely no danger for her," he replied. "But I wouldn't say as much for you!"

—EVELYNE JARRY

❤ ❤ ❤ ❤ ❤ ❤ ❤ ❤ ❤ ❤ ❤

Sign in an animal hospital in Grayslake, Ill.:
"Please do not put pets on counter.
Receptionist bites."

—JEROME BEATTY

Sitting in the vet's waiting room with my dog on my lap, I realized that his tail was slapping the man sitting next to me.

"I'm sorry," I apologized. "There must be a bit of a greyhound in him." Just then the waiting room door opened and a person with a rabbit came in.

"Looks like we're about to find out for sure," commented the man.

—ELIZABETH SIMPSON

"What should I do?" yelled a panicked client to the receptionist at our veterinarian's office. "My dog just ate two bags of unpopped popcorn!" Clearly not as alarmed as the worried pet owner, the receptionist responded coolly, "Well, the first thing I would do is keep him out of the sun."

—BRENDA SHIPLEY

A friend of mine is a deputy with the sheriff's department canine division. One evening, the deputy was dispatched to the scene of a possible burglary, where he discovered the back door of a building ajar. He let the dog out of his patrol car and commanded it to enter and seek. Jumping from the back seat, the dog headed for the building. After lunging through the doorway, the dog froze and backed out. My friend was puzzled until he investigated further. Then he noticed the sign on the building: "Veterinarian's office."

—ELIZABETH BENNETT

QUOTABLE QUOTES

"First I wanted to be a veterinarian. And then I realized you had to give them shots to put them to sleep, so I decided I'd just buy a bunch of animals and have them in my house instead."

—PARIS HILTON

"Of all the things I miss from veterinary practice, puppy breath is one of the most fond memories!"

—DR. TOM CAT

"We can judge the heart of a man by his treatment of animals."

—IMMANUEL KANT

"I had planned to retire when I was 13...I had wanted to be a veterinarian."

—LINDA BLAIR

"Everything I know I learned from my cat: When you're hungry, eat. When you're tired, nap in a sunbeam. When you go to the vet's, pee on your owner."

—GARY SMITH

"A man who carries a cat by the tail learns something he can learn in no other way."

—MARK TWAIN

"A piece of grass a day keeps the vet away."

—UNKNOWN DOG

"Outside of a dog, a book is man's best friend. Inside a dog, it's too dark to read."

—GROUCHO MARX

♥ ♥ ♥ ♥ ♥ ♥ ♥ ♥ ♥ ♥ ♥ ♥

One day at the veterinarian's office where I take my cat, a man and the receptionist were verbally sparring. After a few moments a technician came to her coworker's defense. "Sir," she interjected, "do you know what happens to aggressive males in this office?"

—VIVIANE HUESTIS

Like most puppies, mine is not finicky about what he puts in his mouth; he eats anything. But the day he swallowed a quarter, I panicked and called the vet. "What should I do?" I pleaded over the phone.

My extremely laid-back vet answered calmly, "Swallowing a quarter is nothing to worry about. But if he does it again and a can of Pepsi shoots out of his rear, give me a call."

—SUSAN GORBY

A client recently brought her two cats to my husband's veterinary clinic for their annual checkup. One was a small-framed, round tiger-striped tabby, while the other was a long, sleek black cat.

She watched closely as I put each on the scale. "They weigh about the same," I told her.

"That proves it!" she exclaimed. "Black does make you look slimmer. And stripes make you look fat."

—SUSAN DANIEL

 Why did the snail take off his shell?
He was feeling a little sluggish.

—— KEITH JOHNS

"Well, I'd say it's from too many years of being patted on the head."

I heard the dog barking before he and his owner actually barreled into our vet practice. Spotting a training video we sell, the owner wisely decided to buy one.

"How does this work?" she asked, handing me a check. **"Do I just have him watch this?"**

—BRANDI CHYTKA

When she got back to her rural home after participating in an animal rights march in Washington, D.C., my friend Joan let her pet cat out into the yard. Twenty minutes later she was shocked to find the cat returning with a baby rabbit in its mouth. Removing the rabbit, Joan placed it in a box, grabbed her car keys, and headed for the animal shelter. On the way, she accidentally hit a squirrel. She stopped the car, put the squirrel in the box and went on to the shelter. There, a wildlife worker told Joan that he could do nothing for the animals.

"But I'm glad you brought them in," he said, "now we can feed the owl."

—FRANK MALANDRA

Our grandson has a pet rabbit named Wabbit. One day David came home from school and found that Wabbit had injured a front foot and couldn't walk. He was rushed to the veterinary clinic. After examining Wabbit, the vet returned him to the front desk. Entered on his medical chart was this diagnosis: "Wabbit Gilbert. Wist not bwoken, onwy spwained. Spwint not necessawy."

—ESTHER GILBERT

♥ ♥ ♥ ♥ ♥ ♥ ♥ ♥ ♥ ♥ ♥ ♥

There was no way we were giving up the stray kitten who adopted us. We called her Princess. When we took her to the animal hospital to get her checked out, the vet had news: She was actually a he. "So what's the new name going to be?" he asked. "The Cat Formerly Known as Princess?"

—JEANETTE ANDERSON

My five-year-old daughter, Rahne, and I had been discussing what people eat and how some people choose to be vegetarian. About a week later, Rahne was talking about what she wanted to be when she grew up. "It would be great to be a veterinarian," she said, "but I wouldn't want to stop eating bacon."

—ANGELA TEMPLETON

As a veterinarian, I was called at home in the middle of the night by a woman in distress. She had swallowed her dog's heart-worm pill by mistake. I knew it wouldn't harm her, but by law, I'm forbidden to give medical advice.

"If your dog had swallowed your pill, then you'd call me," I explained. "In this case, you really should consult with your own physician."

"But it's one in the morning!" she exclaimed,

"I can't wake my doctor."

—CHERYL SACKLER

"Please stick out your tongue again, only much, much, much slower."

♥ ♥ ♥ ♥ ♥ ♥ ♥ ♥ ♥ ♥ ♥

Veterinarian to cat owner:
"Give him one of these pills every four hours.
 Then use this to stop your bleeding."

—GEORGE WOLFE

Our veterinarian gave us the following instructions for our cat, Friday, who was scheduled for surgery: "Don't give Friday any food after 8 p.m. on Wednesday. Bring Friday in first thing Thursday morning. You can pick him up Thursday evening. But if you want, Friday can also stay until Friday."

—MARY MALLOY

A woman walked into my aunt's animal shelter wanting to have her cat and six kittens spayed and neutered.

"Is the mother friendly?" my aunt asked.

"Very," said the woman, casting an eye on all the pet carriers.

"That's how we got into this mess in the first place."

—SARAH MITCHELL

A new client brought his poodle to my office. As I approached the dog, it growled. "How is he with veterinarians?" I asked.

"Oh, fine!" The owner responded jovially, "He hasn't bitten one yet!"

Reassured by this, I began my examination. Suddenly, before I could react, the dog turned and bit my hand. "I thought you said he'd never bitten a veterinarian!" I exclaimed.

"He hadn't," the owner replied. "until now they've all been fast enough."

—R. SNOPEK

♥ ♥ ♥ ♥ ♥ ♥ ♥ ♥ ♥ ♥ ♥

A woman telephoned a veterinarian and asked him to come examine her cat.

"I don't know what's wrong with her," the woman told him. "She looks as if she's going to have kittens, but that's impossible. She's never been out of the house except when I had her on a leash."

The vet examined the cat and said there was no doubt of her pregnancy.

"But she can't be," protested her mistress. "It's impossible."

At that point a large tom cat emerged from under the sofa.

"How about him?" the vet asked.

"Don't be silly," said the woman. "That's her brother!"

—R.K. CLIFTON

Higgins, our dog, was sick throughout the weekend, so first thing Monday my wife, Hildy, took him to the vet. The doctor prescribed antibiotics and suggested Higgins be given just small amounts of food. Soon after, Hildy called me at the office before she left for work to explain when to give the antibiotics and what to feed him. "I'm cooking rice and hamburger meat for the dog now," she told me.

"How nice," I said. "What about me?"

"Don't worry," she replied. "You can have some, too."

—PAT BATTISTA

On a visit to the veterinarian with our schnauzer, my mother saw a post card on the bulletin board: "Dear Buffy, we are having a wonderful vacation. Hope you are enjoying your stay with Dr. McAfee and being a good dog. Next year you can come with us, and the kids will stay with Dr. McAfee."

—DENNA C. GLEASON

In my house we always treated our pets as if they were members of the family. Our dog, Lord, occupies a privileged position. One Saturday morning the telephone rang and, when I answered it, I heard a female voice on the other end.

"Good morning! Is this the Lord Gonçalves house?"

It was the veterinarian calling to change the time of Lord's appointment to have his coat clipped.

—MARIA FERNANDA GONÇALVES

In the waiting room of our local vet's surgery, an elderly woman sitting opposite me patted my pup and asked what kind of dog it was.

"He's a border terrier," I said proudly. "Oh, so is mine," she replied.

"Is it?" I said with surprise, looking at the ancient mongrel at her feet.

"Yes," she continued. "He's on the borders of a terrier, a Labrador and a sheepdog."

—ELIZABETH ANN CROPPER

My son, Isaac, had had a number of operations by the time he was 4 years old and had become quite matter-of-fact about them.

One day when we were at the veterinarian's office for our new kitten's checkup, Isaac suddenly looked up from the toys he was playing with and seemed to notice his surroundings for the first time. **"Mom," he asked in a room full of people holding their pets, "am I here to be fixed?"**

—CAROLE NICHOLSON

Seen in the Pets section of the yellow pages:
"Spading and Neutering. We treat your pets like family."

—TIRZAH CARROLL

My husband, an accountant, is allergic to cats, so when he was on an assignment at a veterinarian's office, he made sure there'd be no cats in residence that day. However, he soon started to sneeze and his eyes began to water. The receptionist, who was sitting in the same office, assured Ian that there were no cats present.

A miserable half hour later, he couldn't stand it any longer and decided to finish the work at his own office. As he was packing up to leave, he remarked how odd it was for him to be having a reaction. The receptionist then reached under her desk and pulled out a box. "Well," she said, "we don't have any cats here today, but we do have this litter of kittens."

—R. J. HUTCHINSON

One of our clients brought in his massive pinscher to be spayed. As a veterinary assistant, I escort the patient into the doctor's office. But before taking this dog's leash, I glimpsed those large teeth of hers and asked the owner, "Is she friendly?" "Friendly?" said the man. "She's had five litters!"

—JUNE GOUVAS

As part of a ranching family, our daughters are constantly around animals. This explained the conversation at dinner one night when our six-year-old announced, "I never want to have children."

"Then you'll have to go to the vet," our four-year-old declared.

—KATHARINE HELLER

"I hope your temperature is normal too—
like Spots was."

♥ ♥ ♥ ♥ ♥ ♥ ♥ ♥ ♥ ♥ ♥ ♥

A stockman fell off his horse and broke his leg out in the bush. The horse grabbed the stockman's belt in his teeth, dragged him to shelter, then went to fetch the doctor. Discussing the incident a few weeks later, a friend praised the horse's intelligence. "He's not that smart," replied the stockman. "He came back with the vet!"

—J. WHALLEY

I got my strangest job from a man who was taking care of a puppy for a journalist friend on assignment overseas. He came to me with the dog in one hand and a tape recorder in the other. He told me that the usually docile puppy cried, soiled the carpets, chewed furniture and tore pillows to shreds in its new home, and he had been at a loss to understand why. That is, until he talked to a veterinarian. The doctor explained that the puppy was upset because it missed the constant clatter of the journalist's typewriter. I was hired to tape-record two hours of continuous typing, to be played for the puppy whenever it got restless. It worked.

—JILL K. NEMIROW

A man walked into the vet's office and asked to have his dog's tail removed. Having expressed his reluctance to perform the operation unless it was completely necessary, asked the dog-owner why he wanted this service performed.

"Well," replied the man, **"my mother-in-law is coming to stay, and I don't want her to see any sign of a welcome."**

—DAVID MACRAE

❤ ❤ ❤ ❤ ❤ ❤ ❤ ❤ ❤ ❤ ❤ ❤

Feeling horrible, an alligator goes to the veterinarian.

"What seems to be the problem?" the vet asks.

"I just don't have the drive I used to, doc," the gator says. "Used to be, I could swim underwater for miles and catch any animal I wanted. Now all I can do is let them swim by." Concerned, the vet gives him a thorough examination and hands him a few pills.

"What are these?" the gator asks.

"It's a pill very similar to Viagra," the vet answers.

"Hold on, I don't have that kind of problem," the alligator protests. "What exactly is wrong with me?"

"Well," the vet said, "you have a reptile disfunction."

—MICHAEL SULLIVAN

A veterinarian who works in the same building as I do told me about a young man who had stopped by his clinic earlier that day. "Doc," the man said, "I've got a problem. My buddy gave me a Rottweiler as a present." The man paused.

"Yes," my friend prompted, "but that wouldn't seem to me to be much of a problem."

"You wouldn't say that," the man said, "if it was you who couldn't get back into his own house!"

—BOB JOHNSON

One day at the animal hospital where I worked, an owner brought an African grey parrot in to have its beak and wings trimmed. The owner warned that the parrot disliked these procedures and was apt to bite. I donned thick gloves and cautiously opened the cage. The parrot stepped out and, looking up at me, said, "Don't worry, I won't hurt you."

—MICHELE SERVIDEO

"With this type of condition, it doesn't hurt to be extra careful."

♥ ♥ ♥ ♥ ♥ ♥ ♥ ♥ ♥ ♥ ♥

One day, my daughter came home from school with a kitten in her arms. The poor creature had a limp, but we couldn't keep it, so we decided to take it to the vet's to have it seen to. The diagnostic was disappointment; the leg was broken, and the vet suggested putting the animal down. When I told my daughter what that meant, her reaction was overwhelming: It's all very well for you grown-ups. But what difference does it make to have a painless death once you're dead? And she burst into tears. That night, the kitten slept in her room.

—L. P.

Our vet was called out of his bed at 2:30 a.m. by a taxi driver who had run over a cat. The vet said there was no hope for it and, in consultation with the taxi driver, decided to put it to sleep for good.

"How much do I owe you?" asked the taxi driver.

"Nothing." said the vet. "You came to me even though you really hadn't the time. I just did my duty. That cat must be in heaven by now, so I'll send the bill to our Lord."

Late that morning a box of chocolates was delivered to the vet. In unpracticed writing stood: "With my thanks for the return of my black cat. Yours respectfully, O. Lord."

—H. O.

Caitlyn, our four-year-old niece, lived on a farm and was watching her dad and the vet work with some cattle. When the vet's hat fell off, she jumped down and picked it up but continued searching for something.

Finally, she handed the bald vet his hat saying, "Here's your hat, but I couldn't find your hair."

—BONI SCHILTROTH

♥ ♥ ♥ ♥ ♥ ♥ ♥ ♥ ♥ ♥ ♥ ♥

On a busy morning a veterinarian received a call from a woman who said she was starting a poultry farm and wanted to know how long she should leave the rooster with the hens.

"Just a minute," replied the vet as his other phone rang.

"Thank you very much," said the woman, and hung up.

My cat always struggles as if possessed whenever we have to hold her—even if it's only to trim her claws. Naturally, we were apprehensive when the time came to bring her to the veterinarian. During the examination, I commented, "I sure would hate to be the vet who's going to give her an injection."

"I'd hate even more to be the owner who's going to hold her," the vet replied swiftly.

—CARMEN LANDRY

I told my 11-year-old daughter to telephone the pet store when the hamster we had bought there an hour earlier started chewing feverishly on its leg. She was told the hamster should be taken to a veterinarian right away. I was outraged, knowing the bill for the vet would be greater than the cost of the hamster, so I asked Ali to call the pet store again and hand the phone to me.

"Were you just speaking to my daughter about her sick hamster?" I asked.

"Yes," came the reply.

"Have you any idea how expensive a visit to the vet will be?" I ranted. "You had better either replace the hamster or pay the vet bill!" I demanded.

"Gee, ma'am," came the meek reply, "we're just a television repair store."

—BARBARA RODEN

♥ ♥ ♥ ♥ ♥ ♥ ♥ ♥ ♥ ♥ ♥ ♥

My sister's dog was ill and in need of a veterinarian when we arrived at her house for a visit. After being told by her aunt that a vet was a dog doctor, my four-year-old daughter wanted to accompany them to his office. When the doctor was introduced to her, she looked accusingly at her aunt and declared, **"He's not a dog!"**

—MARGARET ROOT

Working for a veterinarian on a hectic Saturday morning, I picked up the ringing phone and was asked, "How much does it cost to get a dog fixed?"

Not knowing if the pet was male or female, I inquired, "Do you mean neutered or spayed?"

To which she answered, "Whichever is cheapest."

—JEAN KERN

A man had a horse that some days trotted friskily and other days limped. Concerned, he decided to take it to the vet.

"Doctor, I have a horse that sometimes walks well and sometimes limps," he said. "What should I do?"

The vet replied with hesitation: "Well, sell it on a day when it walks well, and you've got yourself a good deal!"

—LUIS FERNANDO ORDOÑEZ

A small town's sheriff was also its lone veterinarian. One night, the phone rang and his wife answered. "Let me speak to your husband!" a voice demanded. "Do you require his services as a sheriff or a vet?" the wife asked. "Both," cried the caller. "We can't get our dog's mouth open and there's a burglar in it."

Dumb and dumber

I gave my cat a bath the other day...he loved it. He sat there, he enjoyed it, it was fun for me. The fur would stick to my tongue, but other than that...

—STEVE MARTIN

"So, we'll give him a bone and whichever end eats it is the front."

❤ ❤ ❤ ❤ ❤ ❤ ❤ ❤ ❤ ❤ ❤

"**H**ow do you spell toad?" one of my first-grade students asked.

"We just read a story about a toad," I said, then helped him spell it out: "T-O-A-D."

Satisfied, he finished writing the story he'd begun, then read it aloud: "I toad my mama I wanted a dog for my birthday."

—JOANNA POTTER

It was our cat's first winter. When a raging blizzard came up suddenly, we tried frantically to find Ginger, calling him repeatedly and poking into snowdrifts around the stoop where he liked to hide. Finally I called the police station to inquire if a "found" cat had been reported. The sergeant listened politely to my concerns and assured me that cats had been known to live through terrible storms.

"Ginger," I added, on a hopeful note, "is exceptionally intelligent. In fact, he almost talks."

"In that case, lady," replied the officer, "hang up. He's probably trying to call you now."

—FLORENCE MCGILTON

I work for an insurance brokerage firm that places unusual risks many underwriters will not assume. One day I had two such requests, so I called Lloyd's of London. Would they insure a show cat for an airplane trip, and would they insure a parrot against any physical harm?

There was a pause, and then a woman responded in a clipped British accent, "Yes, we can insure a bird, or we can insure a cat, but certainly not the both together."

—TOMMY GREIG

♥ ♥ ♥ ♥ ♥ ♥ ♥ ♥ ♥ ♥

When my husband wanted me to accompany him on a business trip of several months, I couldn't bear the thought of putting our old dog in a kennel for so long.

"We'll take him with us," said my husband. "There must be at least one hotel in every city that will take pets."

But in one Texas city our directory did not list a single hotel that accepted dogs.

"I'll write for reservations anyhow," said my husband.

A few days later we received a reply saying that our party would be most welcome.

"What did you say to get such an answer?" I exclaimed. He handed me a carbon of his letter. It was a routine request for reservations, except for this closing sentence: "And would you mind if we bring along an elderly refined old gentleman, who happens to be a dog?"

—VIRGINIA O'FARRELL

A customer at the pet-food store where I work went to the bulk flavor-treat bin and picked out all the green and red bone-shaped biscuits. There weren't enough, so I opened another box and asked if her dog liked only those flavors.

"Oh, no," she replied. "I'm making him a Christmas wreath."

—NICOLA NEWTON

Here's a tip: Make sure your wife knows you're talking to a cat under her chair begging for food before you say,

"You know you're already twice as fat as you should be."

—ROBERT ESPOSITO

❤ ❤ ❤ ❤ ❤ ❤ ❤ ❤ ❤ ❤ ❤

We visited our newly married daughter, who was preparing her first Thanksgiving dinner. I noticed the turkey thawing in the kitchen sink with a dish drainer inverted over the bird. I asked why a drainer covered the turkey. Our daughter turned to my wife and said, "Mom, you always did it that way."

"Yes," my wife replied, "but you don't have a cat!"

—A. C. STOKE, JR.

Several neighbors had gathered for dinner, and the conversation turned to pets. Our hostess commented that she had the dumbest dog ever. "Any dog that digs up the same rose bush twenty times has to be pretty dumb," she said.

Everyone seemed to agree, until the 75-year-old grandmother of the neighborhood remarked, "I'm not too surprised at the dog, but I am a little concerned about the person who planted the rose bush that many times"

—RUTH MADDOX

Department stores were holding "white sales," and I decided to go shopping with my children, telling them they could choose one item that had been reduced. I expected them to head immediately for the bargain table at the toy store. The children ran off. A few minutes later they returned and excitedly dragged me past the toy store and toward a pet shop whose owner was holding a small black dog with a large white spot under its chin. The sign in the pet store window read: "'White sale.' All animals with white on them will be marked down 15%."

The children got their dog.

—CARREN STROCK

♥ ♥ ♥ ♥ ♥ ♥ ♥ ♥ ♥ ♥ ♥

Printed on the back of a bottle of dog shampoo: **"Cruelty free—not tested on animals."**

—WALT BAZELLA

A couple had just moved into a new home. As they were preparing for bed one night, their cat, Mister, started begging to go out. The couple hesitated because they wondered if the cat had become familiar with the new surroundings yet. But the cat kept insisting, and the couple finally decided to let him go.

When the wife awoke at daybreak, she remembered that Mister was still out, so she crept out of bed and tiptoed to the front door.

"Mister, Mister," she called softly. No cat. She stepped outside and called louder, "Mister! Mister! Don't you want to come in?" That time the cat heard her—and so did a jogger running in front of her house. The cat streaked inside and the jogger called back, "No, thank you, ma'am—not this morning."

—GEORGE DOLAN

I work for an allergist, and one frequent patient is a mailman who will often regale me with his on-the-job stories. A homeowner on his new route has a Doberman pinscher that is left outside in the fenced-in front yard, where the mailbox is located. In an excited voice, the mailman told me that he barely made it through the gate when the large dog lunged at him.

"I've decided that I won't make any more deliveries to that house until they put the mailbox outside the fence," he declared.

"How will you notify them about that?" I asked.

"Oh," he answered without thinking. "That's easy. We'll just send them a letter."

—KATE WARNER

♥ ♥ ♥ ♥ ♥ ♥ ♥ ♥ ♥ ♥ ♥

John disliked the family cat, and decided
to get rid of him. He drove the feline 20 blocks
from home and left him. But when he pulled
into his driveway, there was the cat.
The next day he left the kitty 40 blocks away,
but again, the cat beat him home.

So he took the cat on a long drive, arbitrarily
turning left, then right, making U-turns, anything to
throw off the tabby's keen sense of direction before
abandoning him in a park across town.

Hours later John called his wife: "Jen, is the cat there?"

"Yes," she replied. "Why?"

"Put him on the phone.
I'm lost and need directions
home."

❤ ❤ ❤ ❤ ❤ ❤ ❤ ❤ ❤ ❤ ❤

My aunt's neighbor in New York had a beautiful black cat, Villiam, who spent his days outside and came indoors at night. One cool October evening, he disappeared. The neighbor searched for him in vain.

The following spring, however, Villiam reappeared, looking healthy and clean. She figured he'd been sowing his wild oats. Everything was back to normal, until that autumn, when Villiam disappeared again. The next spring, he returned. Perplexed, my aunt's friend began asking neighbors for clues.

Finally she rang the bell of an older couple. "A black cat?" the woman said. "Oh, yes. My husband and I hated to see him out in the cold, so we bought a cat carrier. We take him to Florida every winter."

—NORMA TREADWELL

A dog walks into a telegram office, takes out a blank form and writes, "Woof. Woof. Woof. Woof. Woof. Woof. Woof. Woof. Woof."

"There are only nine words here," says the clerk. "You could send another 'woof' for the same price."

The dog looks at him, confused. "But that wouldn't make any sense."

A customer called our florist shop to order a bouquet. "Make it bright and festive looking," she said. **"I want it to cheer up a friend. She just lost her Seeing Eye dog."**

—KATHY BRENING

♥ ♥ ♥ ♥ ♥ ♥ ♥ ♥ ♥ ♥ ♥

After new neighbors moved in, our garbage was knocked over in the mornings by their big black dog. I'd often try to shoo him away, but he'd only snarl at me. In exasperation, I went to my neighbors to complain.

"Thank you for telling me," said the woman who opened the door. "We noticed he had bad breath, but we didn't know where he was getting it."

—JEANNE WATKO

Veterinarian Louis J. Camuti used to tell of one of his more unusual house calls: My client, Mrs. Rouben Mamoulian, wife of the stage-and-screen director, lived a life of luxury. Her cat, however, was an ordinary gray tabby named Dinah. Or so I thought. Actually, I found out that Dinah was the cat's meow when Mrs. Mamoulian one day asked, "Would you like to see her wardrobe?"

She led the way to a room dominated by a large French armoire. Holding up several tiny outfits, she asked, "Aren't they fine?"

"But your cat wasn't wearing anything when I saw her just now."

Mrs. Mamoulian looked at me as if I were a fool and said, "Of course not. The cat isn't going anywhere."

She kept pulling out more and more cat-size garments: gowns, petticoats, a cape.

"It's incredible," I exclaimed, "these clothes look tailor-made."

"Well, of course they are," she replied, giving me a scorching look. "How else could we get a decent fit?"

—MARILYN AND HASKEL FRANKEL

QUOTABLE QUOTES

"My new horse was sold to me as a real gentleman to ride. He is. When we have to go over a fence, he insists on 'ladies first.'"

—ANONYMOUS

"We've begun to long for the pitter-patter of little feet— so we bought a dog. Well, it's cheaper, and you get more feet."

—RITA RUDNER

"I've got a new invention. It's a revolving bowl for tired goldfish."

—LEFTY GOMEZ

"A dog teaches a boy fidelity, perseverance, and to turn around three times before lying down."

—ROBERT BENCHLEY

"Man is rated the highest animal, at least among all animals who returned the questionnaire."

—ROBERT BRAULT

"To ride or not to ride—this is a stupid question."

—BRANDY MICHELLE

"Be the person your dog thinks you are."

—UNKNOWN

"Relax. I just had a cappuccino."

❤ ❤ ❤ ❤ ❤ ❤ ❤ ❤ ❤ ❤ ❤

Two brothers, Herbert and James, lived with their mother and a cat named Edgar. James was particularly attached to the cat, and when he had to leave town for several days, he left Herbert meticulous instructions about the pet's care. At the end of his first day away, James telephoned his brother. "How is Edgar?" he asked.

"Edgar is dead," Herbert answered. There was a pause. Then James said, "Herbert, you're insensitive. You know how close I was to Edgar—you should have broken the news to me slowly. When I asked about Edgar tonight, you should have said, 'Edgar's on the roof, but I've called the fire department to get him down.' And tomorrow when I called, you could have said the firemen were having trouble getting Edgar down, but you were hopeful they would succeed. Then when I called the third time, you could have told me that the firemen had done their best, but unfortunately Edgar had fallen off the roof and was at the veterinarian's. Then when I called the last time, you could have said that although everything possible had been done for Edgar, he had died. That's the way a sensitive man would have told me about Edgar. And, oh, before I forget," James added, "how is mother?"

"Uh," Herbert said, pausing for a moment, "she's on the roof."

—SAMUEL F. PICKERING

 What did the airhead name her pet zebra?
Spot

I had an inauspicious start as a dog groomer when one of my first clients bit me. Noticing my pain, my boss voiced her concern. **"Whatever you do,"** she said, **"don't bleed on the white dogs."**

—JAN VIRGO

A fellow salesperson, an animal lover, was suddenly overcome by allergies at one of our company meetings. Coughing, sniffling, watery eyes...she was a mess.

"If you have such terrible allergies, why do you keep so many pets?" asked a friend.

"Because"—sneeze, cough, hack—"if I'm going to be sick, I might as well have company."

—JOHN CALDWELL

Two friends run into each other while walking their dogs. One suggests lunch. The other says, "They won't let us in a restaurant with pets." Undeterred, the first guy and his German shepherd head into the restaurant. The maitre d' stops them, saying, "Sir, you can't bring your dog in here."

"But I'm blind," the man replies, "and this is my guide dog." The maitre d', apologizing profusely, shows both man and dog to a table. His friend waits five minutes, then tries the same routine.

"You have a chihuahua for a guide dog?" the skeptical maitre d' says.

"A chihuahua?" the man says. "Is that what they gave me?"

—MORT SHEINMAN

❤ ❤ ❤ ❤ ❤ ❤ ❤ ❤ ❤ ❤ ❤

On the beach, a poacher was stopped by a game warden who said he'd be fined for taking lobsters without a permit.

"What do you mean?" the man said, "I didn't break the law. These two lobsters are my pets. I'm just going for a walk with them."

"Nonsense," the game warden replied.

"It's true," said the man. "They go into the surf for a swim, and when I whistle they come back to me."

"This I've got to see," the game warden said.

So the man tossed both of the lobsters out into the waves and the game warden said, "Okay. Now let's hear you whistle for your pet lobsters to swim back to you."

"Lobsters?" asked the poacher. "What lobsters?"

—THE JOKESMITH

My sight-impaired friend was in a grocery store with her guide dog when the manager asked, "Is that a blind dog?"

My friend said, "I hope not, or we're both in trouble."

—SUE YOUNG

Each year, the pet shop where I work participates in a parade with other stores located in the same strip mall. The pet-shop owner "volunteers" a friend to march in costume as Blue Kitty and then to walk through the mall greeting shoppers and their children.

After one parade, Blue Kitty came racing through the store and disappeared into the back room. I followed, somewhat perplexed. When I reached Blue Kitty, he was frantically trying to remove the costume.

"Boy, is this a problem," he said, "I have to use the litter box."

—M. C. WEIMAN

♥ ♥ ♥ ♥ ♥ ♥ ♥ ♥ ♥ ♥ ♥

My sister adopted a scraggly black puppy just before she was to catch a flight from Kansas to Florida. She immediately made special arrangements with the airline to take her new pet on the plane. At the Kansas City airport my sister prepared to board, puppy in a carrying case tucked under her arm. To the amusement of fellow travelers, she was wearing a t-shirt that read: "Dear Auntie Em, hate the farm, hate Kansas, taking the dog.—Dorothy."

—CINDY VOIGT

I was given a kitten by a coworker, and we went to a snack bar to find a box for the trip home. One labeled "chocolate raisins" seemed perfect. I put my new pet in it, loosely fastened the top and headed for the building elevator.

A young marine in full dress uniform—obviously about to go on duty at the nearby White House complex—entered the elevator with me. To my embarrassment, the kitten began trying to get out of its box, scratching and mewing furiously. The Marine stood ramrod straight, looking neither to the right nor left.

"Ma'am," he stated with finality, "your raisins are trying to escape."

—VANNA J. SHIELDS

Police officers in Brockton, Massachusetts, received a call regarding an injured animal lying on a street corner. When they arrived at the scene, they found a dog that had been hit by a car. But according to the *Brockton Enterprise,* the police report stated that the dog was okay and "refused medical treatment."

—ELEANOR CLAFF

"Let me show you what you're doing wrong."

♥ ♥ ♥ ♥ ♥ ♥ ♥ ♥ ♥ ♥ ♥

Spotted outside a veterinary hospital in Clinton, Utah: **"Happy Father's Day! Neutering Special."**

—SHARON NAUTA STEELE

Our local newspaper, *The DeSoto Appeal,* runs a popular column called "10 Questions" that spotlights people who live in our community. In addition to the usual inquiries about occupation and age, people are asked the questions that give a snapshot of their personalities. Recently, one woman was asked, "What's the strangest thing you ever bought?" She answered, "Dog toothpaste." Next question: "What is the most common thing people say to you?" Answer: "Where did you get your white teeth?"

—JACKIE HANNAMAN

Parking on a hill near a supermarket, a woman got out of her car, locked the door and gave a parting command to her dog, who was lying low on the rear seat.

"Stay!" she said loudly.

Unable to see the dog, a bystander watched with amused interest. "Hey," he called out. "Why don't you try putting on the emergency brake?"

—J. M. STEWART

I went looking for a restroom and found two doors with pictures of dogs on them. I was completely baffled, so I searched out the manager and admitted I couldn't tell the difference between the male dog and the female dog. The manager smiled and said, "That's not the idea. One dog is a pointer, the other a setter."

—EDWARD D. GRIMES

♥ ♥ ♥ ♥ ♥ ♥ ♥ ♥ ♥ ♥ ♥

As I drove into a parking lot, I noticed that a pickup truck with a dog sitting behind the wheel was rolling toward a female pedestrian. She seemed oblivious, so I hit my horn to get her attention. She looked up just in time to jump out of the truck's path, and the vehicle bumped harmlessly into the curb and stopped.

I rushed to the woman's side to see if she was all right. "Thanks, I'm fine," she assured me, "but if that dog hadn't honked..."

—PEGGY GREENWOOD

My uncle lives alone with a menagerie of animals—dogs, cats, rabbits and goats. One day, I was visiting and found a note stuck to the door, which read, "The dogs ate Boo Boo."

Knowing how my uncle felt about his pets, I frantically searched the yard for Boo Boo's remains, but found nothing. "Sorry to hear about Boo Boo," I said to my uncle later, as I showed him the note. "Which one was he?"

My uncle read the note, and then grinned. "Boo Boo's my neighbor. He means he fed the dogs."

—MARTHA CARROLL

After yet another toilet-bowl funeral for a pet goldfish, my three-year-old granddaughter, Harper, was telling her mom how sad it was to have all her pets die. My daughter agreed, and added, "At least they're in heaven."

"Heaven's in the toilet?" Harper asked.

—PAM YEMEN

"I guess I won't wear the bonnet."

♥ ♥ ♥ ♥ ♥ ♥ ♥ ♥ ♥ ♥ ♥

A guy spots a sign outside a house that reads "Talking Dog for Sale." Intrigued, he walks in.

"So what have you done with your life?" he asks the dog.

"I've led a very full life," says the dog. "I lived in the Alps rescuing avalanche victims. Then I served my country in Iraq. And now I spend my days reading to the residents of a retirement home."

The guy is flabbergasted. He asks the dog's owner, "Why on earth would you want to get rid of an incredible dog like that?"

The owner says, "Because he's a liar! He never did any of that!"

—HARRY NELSON

A man and his dog go to a movie. During the funny scenes, the dog laughs. When there's a sad part, the dog cries. This goes on for the entire film: laughing and crying in all the right places. After the show, a man who was sitting in the row behind them comes up and says, "That was truly amazing!"

"It sure was," the dog owner replies. "He hated the book."

—DONALD GEISER

Entering a friend's home for his weekly poker game, Slick is amazed to see a dog sitting at the table. He's even more surprised when the dog wins the first hand with a full house, and takes the second with a royal flush.

"This is unreal," Slick says after the dog wins the next two hands "He's got to be the only dog in the world that can play like that."

"Aw, he's not so great," says the host. "There's a dog in Vegas who doesn't wag his tail every time he gets a good hand."

❤ ❤ ❤ ❤ ❤ ❤ ❤ ❤ ❤ ❤ ❤

At first it was funny. Whenever our mother played the piano, our poodle would sing along—enthusiastically, in an earsplitting howl. We would all laugh, but after a while, my dad couldn't take it any longer. "For Pete's sake," he begged, "play something the dog doesn't know."

—TEMPLE LYMBERIS

The week we got our puppy, I caught a stomach bug and stayed home from work one day. That afternoon, my wife called to check up on me.

"I'm okay," I said. "But guess who pooped in the dining room."

My wife's response: "Who?"

—RUSSELL MOORE

One afternoon I was walking on a trail with my newborn daughter, chatting to her about the scenery. When a man and his dog approached, I leaned into the baby carriage and said, "See the doggy?"

Suddenly I felt a little silly talking to my baby as if she understood me. But just as the man passed, I noticed he reached down, patted his dog and said, "See the baby?"

—CATHERINE REARDON

A woman at my friend's pet shop pointed to a Labrador puppy. "I want that one," she said.

"But I don't want the floor model."

—CINTHIA GAGNON

 Where do you find a dog with no legs?
Exactly where you left it.

—— KEITH JOHNS

One morning while a locksmith had come to change the locks in my house, I realized I had to run a few errands. I turned to him, a sweet older man, and said I was heading out. As I got to the front door, I noticed my sad-faced dog staring at me from the living room.

"I love you, sweet boy," I said. "Now you be good. Okay?"

From the other room I heard a voice answer, "Okay."

—ANGELA MILLER

When my friend spotted a blind man and his guide dog at a crosswalk, she stopped her car and waved them on.

"Uh, Cynthia," I said, "he can't see you."

"I know that," she said indignantly. "I'm waving the dog on."

—CAREN FORREST

Enclosed with the heartworm pills my friend received from a veterinarian was a sheet of red heart stickers to place on a calendar as a reminder to give her pet the medication. She attached these stickers to her kitchen calendar, marking the first Saturday of every month. When her husband noticed the hearts, he grinned from ear to ear, turned to his wife and asked, "Do you have something special in mind for these days?"

—MARY LOUISE RUSSO

♥ ♥ ♥ ♥ ♥ ♥ ♥ ♥ ♥ ♥ ♥ ♥

In an upscale pet-supply store, a customer wanted to buy a red sweater for her dog. The clerk suggested that she bring her dog in for a proper fit.

"I can't do that!" she said. "The sweater is going to be a surprise!"

—HAROLD M. JOHNSEN

After buying our new home, we landscaped it. Since this was my husband's first attempt at planting a lawn, he was careful to do the job right. He prepared the soil, put in a sprinkler system and waited. Finally, after work on a day when the weather was exactly right, he seeded the lawn, rolled it and watered it—finishing by artificial light because it got so late.

For the next three weeks he watered the lawn daily, often rushing home at noon to run the sprinklers for an hour. He fussed over it, shooed away birds and our cat, and looked for the first blade of grass to peek through. Except for a few weeds, nothing happened. Then one Saturday morning my husband came in and announced sheepishly, "I just found the sack of grass seed in the garage."

"What in the world did you plant?" I asked.

With a sigh he replied, "Kitty litter."

—RUTH N. KOHL

While in San Antonio, Texas, my wife and I decided to visit the zoo, and I called ahead to ask if it would be all right to bring our pet. The woman I spoke to answered sternly, "We don't allow animals in the zoo."

—JOHN DEFRONZO

"You're really quite mad."

♥ ♥ ♥ ♥ ♥ ♥ ♥ ♥ ♥ ♥ ♥

Doctor holding cat above his patient's head:
"I'm just going to give you a cat scan."

In a hurry to deliver her cupcakes to the school bake sale, my sister JoAnn went to her storage area and quickly grabbed the lid to an old cardboard gift box to carry the goodies. At the end of the sale, she was dismayed that almost everything else had been sold, except her cupcakes. Puzzled and a bit hurt, JoAnn returned home, transferred the cupcakes to a plate, and was on her way to return the cardboard lid to the shelf when she noticed neatly printed on the side of it in her own clearly legible handwriting: "Kitty's Litter Box."

—CLETE BRUMMEL

Whack! A woman hits her husband right on the head with a rolled-up magazine! "What was that for?" he shouts.

"That," she says, "was for the piece of paper I found, with the name Laurie Sue on it."

"But, dear," he says, "that was just the name of a horse I bet on when I went to the track."

"Okay," she replies. "I'll let it go, this time."

Two weeks later, *whack!*

"Now what?" he wails.

"Your horse called."

—L. ROHLENA

Item in the Cazenovia, N.Y., *Hi, Neighbor* weekly: "A resident of Fenner Street complained of a barking dog. Police investigated and found the dog to be home alone. The dog was told to keep the barking to a minimum."

—ANGELINA HARRIS

♥ ♥ ♥ ♥ ♥ ♥ ♥ ♥ ♥ ♥ ♥

The first thing I noticed about the pickup truck passing by the grocery store was the goofy-looking pooch sitting in the passenger seat wearing goggles. The second thing was the rear bumper sticker, which read:

"Dog is my copilot."

—ANNA COOPER

How many dogs does it take to change a light bulb?

- Golden retriever: "The sun is out, the day is young and you're worrying about a stupid light bulb?"
- Border collie: "Just one. And then I'll replace any wiring that's not up to code."
- Lab: "Oh, me! Me! Please let me change the bulb! Can I? Can I?"
- Rottweiler: "Make me."
- Old English sheepdog: "Light bulb? I don't see a light bulb."
- Cat: "Dogs do not change light bulbs. People change light bulbs. So the question is, how long will it be before I can expect light?"

—RICHARD WRIGHT

My local coffee shop knows how to make sure that children are well behaved. A sign advises parents: "All unattended children will be given two shots of espresso and a free puppy."

—STEPHANIE JENSEN

"Her bridge game running late again?"

♥ ♥ ♥ ♥ ♥ ♥ ♥ ♥ ♥ ♥ ♥

I once had a Saturday job in a pet shop. A young lad who'd never worked with animals before joined the staff. At closing time on his first day, I was busy tidying, so I asked him if he wouldn't mind shutting the rabbits up for me.

He emerged a while later saying he'd tried, but they weren't making that much noise anyway.

He'd been standing by the hutches saying, "Shhhhh!"

—EMMA PALMER

Traveling through New York State on a bus, I heard two men discussing their pets. One man was complaining about the powerful attraction that his female dog exercised. He claimed that on one day he counted 25 suitors in his yard. The other man remarked that they must have come from all over town.

"All over town?" exploded the dog owner, "There were two with California licenses.

—ARLENE DERETO

I am a postman. One day a colleague was delivering a package to a house, but no one was in so he pushed it through an open window. As the parcel dropped, it knocked over a goldfish bowl, which spilled onto the carpet. While wondering what to do, he saw a cat on the doorstep. He dropped the pet through the same window, hoping it would be blamed for the mess he had made.

Back at the office, my colleague found there had been a phone call to the manager. An irate neighbor wanted to know why her cat had just been pushed through her neighbor's window.

—DERRICK ROBINSON

♥ ♥ ♥ ♥ ♥ ♥ ♥ ♥ ♥ ♥ ♥

In Seattle, where a kennel license is required if you house four or more pets, a woman with two dogs and a cat called the pet-license office for information. She explained that she was considering marriage to a man with two cats and a dog.

"We both love our animals dearly and don't want to give any up," the woman said. "But if we get married, could we somehow continue to have the dogs and cats—under separate ownerships, as it were—so we wouldn't have to take out a pet-kennel license?"

The official explained that since the three dogs and three cats would be housed on the same premises, a kennel license would be required. There was a moment's silence at the other end of the line. Then, the woman said, "I think you have just stopped a wonderful marriage," and hung up abruptly.

In our neighborhood pet shop, I overheard a conversation between a mother and her young son regarding the purchase of a poodle puppy. When the mother learned that the price was $150, she gasped, grabbed her son by the hand and started out the door.

"Come on, George," she said, "you're sticking to fish."

—DELORES A. DEWHURST

One day after a nasty streak of bad weather, I asked my teenage son to take our dog out for a long walk after school. When I came home from work, I found my son stretched out on the recliner. **He had leash in hand, while the dog trotted happily away on the treadmill!**

—KAREN KELLY

I was admiring a picture on my design client's wall when she came up from behind and mentioned, "That's my mother and her dog."

"She's very attractive," I said.

"She was more like a friend, really. I miss her."

"She's no longer alive?" I asked.

"No. But my mother is."

—SANDRA BOLETCHEK

An old farmer is inconsolable after his dog goes missing. His wife suggests he take out an ad in the newspaper, which he does. But two weeks later, there's still no sign of the mutt.

"What did you write in the ad?" his wife asks.

"Here, boy," he replies.

—DENISE STEWART

John Bird and Bill Parrot worked in sales and marketing. One day as I was passing through their department, I heard Bill answering John's phone and wondered what the caller may have thought when he heard Bill's greeting: "Bird's line. Parrot speaking."

—ROGER D. FAY

Somewhat hard of hearing, my mother is forced to turn up the volume of her television. When I visit her, I immediately reach for the remote-control unit to turn down the racket. One day, however, our conversation was being drowned out by incessant loud singing from her pet canary, Picolo. Frustrated, mother grabbed the remote control aimed at his cage and "zapped" him.

—DENISE BROCHU

❤ ❤ ❤ ❤ ❤ ❤ ❤ ❤ ❤ ❤ ❤

At a garage sale I sampled a dab of perfume on my wrist. I loved the scent and took two bottles, but was slightly insulted by the label, which read "Dignity Dog." I brought my items to the fellow in charge, who asked me what kind of dog I had.

"I don't have a dog. Why do you ask?" I replied.

"Then why are you buying this dog-grooming formula?"

Through my embarrassment, I confessed I thought it was women's perfume, and the sale went to the dogs.

—DONNA THOMPSON

As coordinators of a school for working youths and adults in our city, we sometimes get notes from our students with excuses for their absence. One night, we were sitting in our office when one of our middle-school students asked if he could come in to explain why he'd been absent for the previous days.

"I'm getting a medical statement that justifies my absence," he began, "The reason I didn't bring it right away is because the vet didn't show up to work."

—RITA DE CÁSSIA LOPES SOARES

My wife and I were quarrelling because she thought I watched too many horror films. "Think of the effect it could be having on your mind," she complained.

"Don't be ridiculous," I scoffed and she stormed out.

She hadn't returned after several hours and, as we had guests that night, I started preparing the meal. Unfortunately, as I was chopping vegetables, the cat knocked over the pan containing my tomato sauce. I picked up the poor red-stained moggie with one hand, while holding my knife in the other. At that moment my wife walked in.

—VINCENT IWUOHA

♥ ♥ ♥ ♥ ♥ ♥ ♥ ♥ ♥ ♥ ♥

For my stepdaughter's 14th birthday, I had picked up a birthday card to be from the dog, in which I wrote numerous woofs and enclosed $50. I placed it by the front door knowing Jessica would see it before leaving for school.

In the morning my fiancée, Denine, was driving Jessica and her younger sister, Olivia, to school when Jessica opened the card and read it out loud.

"Fifty dollars!" Olivia exclaimed. "I didn't think the dog even liked you that much!"

—DAREN WESTMAN

One afternoon my six-year-old daughter showed me a picture of a fat cat she had drawn. I asked her what kind it was and she told me it was a cat that was going to have kittens. See, I'll show you, she said. Carefully she outlined in pencil four very small kittens inside the cat's body. I then asked, do you know how they got there? Looking at me seriously, she said, of course I know. I drew them.

—LINDA CLARK

On our family farm in my early teens, I had a lovely pet pig called Lizzie. Every morning Lizzie would follow me down to the paddock where I would turn on the tap. As the running water was forming a nice puddle, Lizzie would hop in and wallow and splash to her heart's content. One day I was late going to the pigpen. When I got there, Lizzie was nowhere to be found but the gate to the pen was in a mess. Lizzie had put her nose under the door, pushed it up and escaped. She was already down in the paddock. She had managed to rub against the tap, which was still running, and was busy enjoying her daily wallow in the mud and water.

—JENNY DAVIES

♥ ♥ ♥ ♥ ♥ ♥ ♥ ♥ ♥ ♥ ♥

My neighbor's dog could hardly hear, so she took him to the vet. The problem was hair in the dog's ears; once the vet removed it, the dog could hear fine. The vet then told the lady that if she wanted to keep this from reoccurring, she should buy some hair-remover lotion and rub it in her dog's ears once a month.

At the store, the druggist offered this advice: "If you're going to use the lotion under your arms, don't use deodorant for a few days."

"I'm not using it under my arms," my neighbor replied.

"Okay," the druggist said, "if you're using it on your legs, don't shave for a couple of days."

"I'm not using it on my legs, either," the lady said. "If you must know, I'm using it on my schnauzer."

"Stay off your bicycle for a week," the druggist replied.

—DARRYL MACDONALD

"I feel like a dog, Doc."
"How long has this been going on?"
"Since I was a puppy."

Our four-year-old son came home one day with a sudden interest in goldfish. After the usual lecture on caring for them, I gave in. The next time we were in the city, I took him to a pet store, and he picked out three fish. While paying for the fish, a bowl and some other necessities, I asked the salesman how long a small can of fish food would last. He looked past me at my son, who was happily shaking the fish in a plastic bag. "Probably longer than the fish," he replied.

—CLIFF WARREN

❤ ❤ ❤ ❤ ❤ ❤ ❤ ❤ ❤ ❤ ❤

After stopping at the pet store to pick up supplies for Whiskey, their dog, my sister-in-law, Kay, and her young daughter, Sheila, went to the supermarket. At the checkout, Kay couldn't figure out why she didn't have enough money to pay for the groceries. "Don't you remember, Mom?" Sheila reminded her in a loud voice. **"You spent all your money on Whiskey."**

—GERRY MCCALLUM

On Halloween, I opened the door to a child no more than four years old. As I held out the candy dish, our dog Samy came up to her, barking joyously.

"You have a dog?" said the little girl, surprised.

I told her that Samy likes children and would not hurt her. Still, she stepped back.

"Yes," she said, not reassured, "but I'm dressed as a cat!"

—MARTINE L. GONTHIER

Obviously distressed, a woman rushed up to a fellow volunteer coast guard on our local beach.

"There's a dead dog over there with its legs cut off," she said.

My colleague strode toward the spot where the body was located. He stopped short, unable to believe what he saw.

Returning to the woman, he told her, "Madam, we really do appreciate your report of the dead dog with no legs. But around here we call them seals. The little chap has just woken up and gone back into the sea."

—MIKE NEWBOLD

America's Funniest Jokes, Quotes, and Cartoons from Reader's Digest

Laughter, the Best Medicine

More than 600 jokes, gags, and laugh lines drawn from one of the most popular features of *Reader's Digest* magazine. This lighthearted collection of jokes, one-liners, and slices of life is just what the doctor ordered.

ISBN 978-0-89577-977-9 • $9.95 paperback

Laughter Really Is the Best Medicine

Guaranteed to put laughter in your day, this sidesplitting compilation of jokes and lighthearted glimpses of life is drawn from *Reader's Digest* magazine's most popular humor column. Poking fun at the facts and foibles of daily routines, this little volume is sure to tickle your funny bone.

ISBN 978-1-60652-204-2 • $9.95 paperback

Humor in Uniform

This laugh-out-loud collection includes 400 of the funniest jokes, quotes, and cartoons from the well-known column in *Reader's Digest* magazine. Enjoy these anecdotes, all supplied by those in the U.S. military and their families.

ISBN 978-0-7621-0929-6 • $9.99 paperback

Quotable Quotes

A collection of wisdom, wry witticisms, provocative opinions, and inspiring reflections—from Benjamin Franklin to Colin Powell, Abraham Lincoln to Mother Teresa, Margaret Mead to Garrison Keillor—from one of the most popular features of *Reader's Digest* magazine.

ISBN 978-0-89577-925-0 • $9.99 paperback

For more information, visit us at RDTradePublishing.com
E-book editions are also available.

Reader's Digest books can be purchased through retail and online bookstores.
In the United States books are distributed by Penguin Group (USA) Inc.
For more information or to order books, call 1-800-788-6262.